D1603372

Doing Justice, Preventing Crime

Recent Titles in STUDIES IN CRIME AND PUBLIC POLICY
Michael Tonry, General Editor

The Partisan Politics of Law and Order
Georg Wenzelburger

Of One-eyed and Toothless Miscreants
Making the Punishment Fit the Crime?
Michael Tonry

Sentencing Fragments
Penal Reform in America, 1975–2025
Michael Tonry

Unwanted
Muslim Immigrants, Dignity, and Drug Dealing
Sandra M. Bucerius

Living in Infamy
Felon Disfranchisement and the History of American Citizenship
Pippa Holloway

Children of the Prison Boom
Mass Incarceration and the Future of American Inequality
Sara Wakefield and Christopher Wildeman

The City That Became Safe
New York's Lessons for Urban Crime and its Control
Franklin E. Zimring

The Toughest Beat
Politics, Punishment, and the Prison Officers Union in California
Joshua Page

Punishing Race
A Continuing American Dilemma
Michael Tonry

Policing Problem Places
Crime Hot Spots and Effective Prevention
Anthony A. Braga and David Weisburd

The Policing Web
Jean-Paul Brodeur

Doing Justice, Preventing Crime

MICHAEL TONRY

OXFORD
UNIVERSITY PRESS

OXFORD
UNIVERSITY PRESS

Oxford University Press is a department of the University of Oxford. It furthers
the University's objective of excellence in research, scholarship, and education
by publishing worldwide. Oxford is a registered trade mark of Oxford University
Press in the UK and certain other countries.

Published in the United States of America by Oxford University Press
198 Madison Avenue, New York, NY 10016, United States of America.

© Oxford University Press 2020

All rights reserved. No part of this publication may be reproduced, stored in
a retrieval system, or transmitted, in any form or by any means, without the
prior permission in writing of Oxford University Press, or as expressly permitted
by law, by license, or under terms agreed with the appropriate reproduction
rights organization. Inquiries concerning reproduction outside the scope of the
above should be sent to the Rights Department, Oxford University Press, at the
address above.

You must not circulate this work in any other form
and you must impose this same condition on any acquirer.

Library of Congress Cataloging-in-Publication Data
Names: Tonry, Michael author.
Title: Doing justice, preventing crime / Michael Tonry.
Description: New York : Oxford University Press, 2020. |
Series: Studies in crime and public policy |
Includes bibliographical references and index. |
Contents: Philosophy and Policy : Doing Justice—Human Dignity—
Proportionality—Social Disadvantage—Multiple Offenses—
Preventing Crime—Deterrence—Prediction and Incapacitation :
Moving Forward—Doing Justice Better
Identifiers: LCCN 2020003945 (print) | LCCN 2020003946 (ebook) |
ISBN 9780195320503 (hardback) | ISBN 9780199910649 (updf)|
ISBN 9780199717668 (epub) | ISBN 9780197523094 (online)
Subjects: LCSH: Criminal justice, Administration of—United States. |
Sentences (Criminal procedure)—United States. |
Law reform—United States.
Classification: LCC KF9223 . T66 2020 (print) |
LCC KF9223 (ebook) | DDC 364.60973—dc23
LC record available at https://lccn.loc.gov/2020003945
LC ebook record available at https://lccn.loc.gov/2020003946

1 3 5 7 9 8 6 4 2
Printed by Sheridan Books, Inc., United States of America

Contents

Preface   vii

1. Philosophy and Policy   I

PART I: *Doing Justice*

2. Human Dignity   15
3. Proportionality   43
4. Deep Disadvantage   73
5. Multiple Convictions   95

PART II: *Preventing Crime*

6. Deterrence   127
7. Prediction and Incapacitation   147

PART III: *Moving Forward*

8. Doing Justice Better   189

References   195

Index   219

Preface

NEARLY A HALF-CENTURY ago, when long-established ways of thinking about crime and punishment were beginning to change, I met University of Chicago law professor Norval Morris and Andreas von Hirsch, then executive director of the Committee for the Study of Incarceration. Both became life-long friends. Morris was at the front edge of what became a widespread, widely shared, and fundamental reconsideration of the purposes and morality of the criminal law and punishment. Von Hirsch's committee sought to declare for its time the principles of justice that should govern decisions about punishment of convicted offenders. Its landmark 1976 report, *Doing Justice— The Choice of Punishments*, insisted that an offender's "Just Deserts" provide the only morally justifiable basis for determining punishments for crime.

Morris and von Hirsch disagreed about many things, often vigorously. Each in his own way was prescient. Their ideas influenced generations of practitioners, policymakers, and professors and continue to reverberate in our time. Their proposals influenced policy changes in the United States and elsewhere. Members of the Minnesota Sentencing Commission, for example, debated whether its governing philosophy should be "just deserts" or "modified just deserts." An English White Paper in 1990, the basis of the *Criminal Justice Act 1991*, declared that offenders' just deserts should be the primary determinant of punishment. An English commission report, the basis of the *Criminal Justice Act 2003*, declared that Morris's "limiting retributivism" provided the conceptual framework for its sentencing proposals. The American Law Institute's *2017 Model Penal Code—Sentencing* contains a similar declaration.

The beginnings of a paradigm shift were underway when Morris's and von Hirsch's most influential works were written. Indeterminate sentencing, premised on the ideas that rehabilitation is the primary aim of punishment and that judges and corrections officials need wide discretion to individualize their decisions, had existed throughout the United States for a half-century. Decisions about punishment were supposed to focus on offenders, not offenses. Cracks in the foundations of indeterminate sentencing, however, were appearing in the 1970s —sentencing disparities, racial injustices, procedural unfairness, absence of official accountability. The solution to all those problems appeared to be to shift the focus from offenders to offenses. Morris, von Hirsch, and many others sought to show and explain what a system of justice would like that aimed to assure that people convicted of the same or comparable crimes received the same or comparable punishments. Put differently, prevailing ways of thinking were shifting from consequentialism to retributivism.

The shift occurred remarkably quickly. Indeterminate sentencing, rehabilitation, and consequentialism fell from favor. Determinate sentencing, equal treatment, and retributivism replaced them. The rest is history. Retributivist ideas soon predominated in philosophy departments and law schools, and still do. In the corridors of power, however, the new way of thinking remained influential only for a decade. Law reform initiatives in the 1970s and early 1980s, such as determinate sentencing laws, sentencing and parole guidelines, and parole abolition, sought to make punishment fairer and more consistent. That ended within a decade. In the 1980s through the mid-1990s, law and order became a focal partisan political issue. Doing justice ceased to be a primary aim. Politicians competed to show who was tougher on crime. Laws of historically unprecedented severity were enacted. The results include mandatory minimum sentencing laws in 50 states, life without parole laws in 49, and three-strikes and truth in sentencing laws in more than 25.

In the 2020s, no informed person disagrees that punishment policies and practices in the United States are unprincipled, chaotic, and much too often unjust. The financial costs are enormous. The moral cost is greater: countless individual injustices; mass incarceration; the world's highest imprisonment rate; extreme disparities, especially affecting members of racial and ethnic minority groups; high rates of wrongful conviction; assembly-line case processing; and a general absence of respectful consideration of offenders' interests, circumstances, and needs.

Prevailing ways of thinking are changing. Among philosophers and other theorists, a shift away from retributivism is underway. Among policymakers and practitioners, the shift is from certainty, rigidity, and toughness toward fairness and reintegration. In other words, as in the 1970s, almost everyone agrees that current ways of doing business aren't good enough.

My aim in *Doing Justice, Preventing Crime* is to lay normative and empirical foundations for building new, more just, and more effective systems of sentencing and punishment in the twenty-first century. The overriding goals are to treat people convicted of crimes justly, fairly, and even-handedly, to take sympathetic account of the circumstances of peoples' lives, and to punish no one more severely than he or she deserves. Along the way I discuss work by philosophers and others on punishment theory, survey what is known about the deterrent, incapacitative, and rehabilitative effects of punishment, and explain what needs to be done to move from an ignoble present to a better future.

Anyone trying to develop new ideas on so complex a subject necessarily stands on the shoulders of others. For me the giants are Jeremy Bentham, Immanuel Kant, Georg Wilhelm Friedrich Hegel, and Emile Durkheim. We can learn more from them about solving contemporary problems than is widely recognized. Along the way, I have learned much from modern writers including Antony Duff, Norval Morris, Andreas von Hirsch, and many others who followed in their footsteps. I owe special thanks to friends who read and criticized drafts, taught me things I didn't know, led me to sources I would not have found, or tried to save me from error. They include Andrew J. Ashworth, Richard Berk, Sir Anthony Bottoms, Francis T. Cullen, Anthony Doob, Arie Freiberg, Jan de Keijser, Seena Fazel, David P. Farrington, Richard S. Frase, Douglas Husak, Tapio Lappi-Seppälä, Richard L. Lippke, John T. Monahan, Daniel S. Nagin, Joan Petersilia, Alex Piquero, Kevin Reitz, Julian V. Roberts, Andrew Simester, Jennifer Skeem, Carol Steiker, and Robert Weisberg. Su Love, as she has done many times before, provided invaluable editorial assistance. Scott Dewey and David Zopfi-Jordan of the University of Minnesota Law School Library tracked down obscure and fugitive materials and provided bibliographical support of a quality and extent of which, I suspect, less lucky writers can only dream.

Michael Tonry, Isola d'Elba, March 2020

I

Philosophy and Policy

PUNISHMENT THEORIES AND policies have marched in different directions in the United States for nearly 50 years. Philosophers and others who try to understand what justice requires, policymakers who create the rules for dispensing it, and practitioners who try to achieve it don't communicate with each other very well, or at all. They lack a common vocabulary. More importantly, they lack a shared understanding of what punishment is and does, and what it should aspire to be and to do. This is unusual. Shared understandings exist in most countries and did in the United States through the 1960s.

The costs have been high. They include mass imprisonment, extraordinary injustice, assembly-line case processing, and moral impoverishment. Here are two concrete examples. California's three-strikes law required minimum 25-year prison sentences for many trifling property crimes. Notorious cases involved thefts of three pizza slices, three golf clubs, and a handful of videotapes. The golf clubs and videotapes made it to the US Supreme Court. Many states' laws authorized, sometimes mandated, life sentences without parole for young teenagers, some convicted of homicide but many convicted of lesser crimes. Those laws would have been unimaginable in the United States before the 1980s and they are unimaginable today in other Western countries. That is because of widely shared agreements in most times and places that fierce punishments for minor crimes are unjust and that troubled young people should be dealt with sympathetically.

Philosophers and others who write about punishment theory condemn decades-long prison sentences for minor property crimes and life without parole for children, and can explain why they are unjust. Policymakers in the 1980s and 1990s, however, happily enacted those and many comparable laws, and prosecutors enthusiastically applied them.

There is wide agreement in 2020 that mass imprisonment was a mistake of historic proportions, that many sentencing laws are deeply unjust, and that things have to change. Movements are afoot in most states and the federal system to make sentencing and correctional policies more rational and more humane. So far, however, only small, tentative changes have been made. Fundamental changes are unlikely unless and until widely shared understandings about punishment and justice re-emerge.

Most people who write about punishment theory and philosophy are retributivists of one sort or another who believe offenders should be treated justly and, with the Mikado, that the punishment should fit the crime. Policymakers in recent decades, to the contrary, have not much cared whether individual offenders are treated fairly or punished justly. Thence came mandatory minimum sentence laws in 50 states, three-strikes laws in 26, truth in sentencing in an overlapping 26, and life without parole in 49. They apply to all adults and to children whose cases are tried in adult courts. All exist in the federal system.

Those laws threaten such fearsome punishments that innocent defendants are sorely tempted to plead guilty rather than risk a wrongful conviction. Guilty defendants usually feel they have no choice. The late Harvard Law School professor William Stuntz observed in 2011 that "outside the plea bargaining process" prosecutors' threats to file any of those charges "would be deemed extortionate." Extortion works. Trials are much rarer than they were 30 or 50 years ago, punishments are incomparably harsher, unprecedented numbers of people are locked up, and wrongful convictions are sadly common. The most sophisticated analysis of the prevalence of wrongful convictions, by Charles Loeffler of the University of Pennsylvania and colleagues in 2019, estimated that, in Pennsylvania, wrongful convictions occur in 6 percent of convictions that result in imprisonment.

The discordance between theory and policy was not always thus. Before 1975, they dovetailed for nearly a century. Most theorists were consequentialists who believed that offenders should be rehabilitated and retributive impulses be resisted. Most practitioners and policymakers believed that sentencing and parole decisions should be individualized to take account of offenders' circumstances, characteristics, and needs. Policy and theory came together in the American Law Institute's *Model Penal Code* (1962). It contains detailed proposals for individualized, indeterminate sentencing; judges, probation officers, parole board members, and prison officials are told to focus primarily on how best to rehabilitate most offenders and to incapacitate the dangerous and incorrigible few.

Herbert Wechsler, the *Code*'s primary draftsman, in 1961 made its premise clear: "The rehabilitation of an individual who has incurred the moral condemnation of the law is in itself a social value of importance, a value, it is well to note, that is and ought to be the prime goal." Contemporaneous national commissions agreed, including the President's Commission on Law Enforcement and Administration of Justice in 1967, the National Commission on Reform of Federal Criminal Laws in 1971, and the National Advisory Commission on Criminal Justice Standards and Goals in 1973.

As those reports were being written, however, the winds of crime and punishment were changing direction. Crime rates had begun a seemingly inexorable rise in the early 1960s. Conservatives accused indeterminate sentencing of paying too much attention to rehabilitating offenders and too little to preventing crime. Civil rights groups, prisoners' rights groups, and proponents of procedural fairness accused it of inconsistency, racial bias, unfairness, and opaqueness.

The criticisms bit. Indeterminate sentencing, in place in every state and the federal system since the 1930s, imploded. Maine in 1975 abolished parole release. California in 1976 enacted its Uniform Determinate Sentencing Law. Reform was in the air. Every state changed its laws and policies in the 1970s and 1980s, most repeatedly. Almost no one, and that included philosophers and other theorists, defended indeterminate sentencing or its rehabilitative premises. University of Chicago law professor Albert Alschuler in 1978, for example, bewilderedly observed: "That I and many other academics adhered in large part to this reformative viewpoint only a decade or so ago seems almost incredible to most of us today." Scholarly books and journals abounded with "determinate" sentencing proposals and elaboration of retributive theories.

For a time it looked as if prevailing ways of thinking had shifted from consequentialism to retributivism. Most sentencing reform initiatives, including sentencing guidelines, appellate sentence review, and laws like California's, sought to structure decision-making, reduce disparities, and lessen the influence of racial bias and officials' idiosyncrasies. Philosophers and other theorists followed suit. Retributive theorizing blossomed, and conformed comfortably to the new policy emphases: do the crime, suffer the deserved time. Policy and theory appeared to be in sync. That soon ended.

Policymakers in the mid-1980s lost interest in procedural unfairness, sentencing disparities, and racial injustice. Instead, they enacted rigid, severe laws that promoted personal, political, and ideological agendas. The new laws ostensibly sought to prevent crime by means of deterrence and incapacitation. "Ostensibly" because the empirical evidence did not show then, and does not show now, that deterrence and incapacitation have significant effects on crime rates or patterns.

The toughest laws, enacted mostly between 1984 and 1996, are incompatible with retributive theories of punishment. Retributive theories vary in details but all insist on proportionality, on scaling the severity of punishments to the seriousness of crimes. Horizontally, this requires that comparably serious crimes be punished comparably severely and, vertically, that more serious crimes be punished more severely than lesser ones, and vice versa.

Mandatory minimum sentence, three-strikes, and life without parole laws by contrast require starkly disproportionate punishments. The federal 100-to-1 law for cocaine sentencing required vastly longer prison sentences for small sales of crack than for sales of the same amount of pharmacologically indistinguishable powder, and a longer sentence for sale of a sixth of an ounce of crack than for robbery, child abuse, or major white-collar crimes. California's three-strikes law until recently required minimum 25-year prison terms, and sometimes life, for many minor property and drug offenses even though robberies, rapes, and serious assaults are often punished much less severely. Many life without parole laws apply to offenses other than homicide and some even to property crimes, implying that murders, rapes, robberies, and property crimes are equally serious, something no one believes. How severely people are punished often depends less on what they have done than on the charges prosecutors choose to file, and the plea bargains they are willing to offer.

Theorists in the 1980s and 1990s continued to assert that proportionality is a fundamental requirement of justice. Policymakers, and practitioners who applied the new laws, behaved as if they disagreed. Many in their hearts probably agreed, but because of political considerations, personal self-interest, or ideological commitments, pretended they didn't.

There are signs, however, that the winds are again beginning to change direction. Crime rates peaked in 1991 and have since fallen continuously. Violent crime has fallen by two-thirds. Few harsh sentencing laws have been enacted since the mid-1990s. Almost none have been repealed, but many have been slightly moderated. The imprisonment rate, which rose continuously, quintupling, beginning in 1973, peaked in 2007 and has since declined by 10 percent. That is small change. The rate remains near 650 per 100,000 population, by far the world's highest and 4 to 10 times higher than in other Western countries. Conservative and liberal law reformers, including the ACLU and George Soros on the left and Right on Crime and the Koch brothers on the right, often join forces to try to reduce the use of imprisonment, change sentencing laws, and help offenders live law-abiding lives.

The theory class has not kept up. Retributivism remains intellectually predominant, and nonretributivists remain largely silent, but signs of rethinking are beginning to appear. In this book, I survey the current state of punishment theory, current knowledge about the effectiveness of criminal sanctions, and emerging ideas about creation of just sentencing systems. Americans may once again want to have morally coherent criminal justice systems in which offenders are punished as they deserve to be and crime is effectively prevented. I show how they can be built.

The rudiments of just punishment systems are clear. If political posturing and cynicism, passions provoked by notorious crimes, and irrational fears and anger could be set aside, there is wide agreement about what a just system should look like. The best way to think about this is to ask yourself how you would want the system to work if someone you love was ensnared in it. Here are my answers. Most people would offer similar ones.

I would want them to be treated fairly and respectfully.

I would want the officials involved to be objective, unbiased, and fair-minded.

I would want them to be treated as others in their sad situation are. That doesn't mean that everyone should be treated mechanistically, in exactly the same way, but that everyone's circumstances and interests should be considered sympathetically, with equal respect and concern.

I would want them to be punished no more severely than they deserve or, if there were good reasons to justify it, less severely.

If the wrongdoing resulted partly from mental illness, drug or alcohol dependence, lack of fundamental skills and capacities, or comparable disabilities and handicaps, I would want them helped to address those challenges.

If you doubt that most people in their hearts support those propositions, think about what happens when prominent people, or their children or others they care about, are charged with crimes. Even politicians who support harsh sentencing laws, rail against "technical" procedural protections, and decry "lenient" sentencing want to benefit from all available protections. They want to be treated fairly and sympathetically, and want judges to take account of the circumstances, pressures, and challenges that influenced their wrongdoing. What I would want for myself and my children, and what prominent people want for themselves and their children, should be provided to everyone's children.

Decades of research on public opinions, attitudes, and beliefs show that none of those propositions is likely—in the abstract, without politics, ideology, or emotion taking over—to be controversial. Almost everyone has opinions and intuitions about why crimes are committed and what should happen to people who commit them. Most people say they believe that offenders should be punished as much as they deserve, but not more, and all else being equal that more serious crimes deserve harsher punishments than lesser ones. Most people understand that many crimes result in part from offenders' disadvantaged backgrounds, drug, alcohol, and mental health problems, and similar calamities, and believe that appropriate treatment and services should be provided to them—for their sake and everyone else's. Reconciling support for deserved punishment with recognition of human frailty is, of course, not easy, but it can be done. Good judges do it all the time, when applicable laws allow. Judges in western and northern European countries, where laws are less rigid and severe, justice systems are better insulated from political influence and public emotion, and social welfare systems are more extensive, do it more often than American judges.

The five propositions that encapsulate what I would want to happen if people I love were caught up in the criminal system can be, and usually are, presented more abstractly. In that language, here are the concepts and principles that characterize just punishment systems.

- *Justice as Proportionality*: Offenders should never be punished more severely than can be justified by their blameworthiness in relation to the severity of punishments justly imposed on others for the same and different offenses.
- *Justice as Fairness*: Processes for responding to crimes should be publicly known, implemented in good faith, and applied even-handedly.
- *Justice as Equal Treatment*: Defendants and offenders should be treated as equals; their circumstances and interests should be accorded equal respect and concern when decisions affecting them are made.
- *Justice as Parsimony*: Offenders should never be punished more severely than can be justified by appropriate, valid, normative purposes.

Until recently most punishment theories were classified as being retributive or utilitarian. That isn't exactly right semantically. Retributive theories, often said to derive from the writings of the German idealist philosophers Immanuel Kant and Georg Wilhelm Friedrich Hegel, assert that punishment is a Good Thing and should be proportionate in severity to the seriousness of the crime for which it is inflicted. Utilitarian theories, most famously associated with the British polymath Jeremy Bentham, assert that punishment is a Bad Thing, an "evil," he said, because it inflicts suffering, and can be justified only if through its deterrent effects it averts greater suffering by others.

Retributivism thus centers on imposition of deserved punishment and utilitarianism on crime prevention through deterrence. Indeterminate sentencing, by contrast, focused on both rehabilitation and incapacitation. Although it and its epitome, the *Model Penal Code*, were often referred to as utilitarian, they were not utilitarian in Bentham's narrower deterrent sense. As a result, in our time many people contrast retributive with "consequentialist" or "instrumental" theories that justify punishment in terms of all its crime-preventive effects.

Positive Retributivism. Just systems of punishment incorporate elements from classical retributivism and classical utilitarianism. From retributivism comes the idea that people should never be punished more than they deserve. This takes two forms. "Positive" retributivists say that offenders may and must be punished precisely as much as they deserve. Positive retributivism is, however, humanly impossible to achieve. God may know what any offender absolutely deserves but human beings have only intuitions and opinions to draw on, and these vary widely. God may know everything there is to know about an offender's life, characteristics, virtues, vulnerabilities, accomplishments, and misdeeds, but humans do not and lack processes and methods reliably to learn about them. Oxford philosopher H. L. A. Hart, the twentieth century's most influential writer about punishment philosophy, observed in 1968 that punishment systems cannot achieve "any precise assessment of an individual's wickedness in committing a crime (who can?)."

Negative Retributivism. "Negative" retributivists say that offenders may be punished as much as they deserve, but need not be. This is much more achievable than positive retributivism because precisely deserved punishments need not somehow be determined. A simple system of proportionate upper limits for all crimes based on widely shared intuitions will assure that comparably serious crimes are potentially subject to comparably severe punishments and more and less serious crimes to more and less severe ones. This fits with the widely held ideas that offenders should be punished no more severely than they deserve and, because much crime derives in part from offenders' disadvantaged backgrounds and drug, alcohol, mental health, and comparable problems, often less.

Negative retributivism can be reconciled with tailoring punishments to offenders' characteristics, disabilities, and needs, and when a credible base of reliable evidence exists to justify it, to crime prevention considerations. Negative retributivism, however, by itself faces a fundamental problem: How can the values underlying Proportionality, Fairness, Equal Treatment, and Parsimony be made manifest? Classical utilitarianism provides the answer.

Utilitarianism. Bentham offered a sizable number of detailed rules for calculating the optimal deterrent punishment for any offense and offender, but subject to one overriding constraint: no punishment is justifiable that imposes more suffering on the offender than the suffering to be avoided or that imposes more suffering than is needed to accomplish its aims. He referred to this as the principle of "frugality." In our time, following the usage of the Australian-American legal scholar Norval Morris, the term "parsimony" is more often used. The term was new, but not the idea. The drafters of the *Model Sentencing Act*, among many others in the indeterminate sentencing era, called for use of the "least restrictive alternative."

Parsimony provides the mechanism to address the looseness of negative retributivism. If offenders may justly be punished by a certain amount, but need not be, how much should they be punished? Jargon of our electronic times provides the answer. The default should always be the least severe punishment that the seriousness of the crime allows. In our time when the coin of punishment is imprisonment, the default for most crimes should instead normally be a community punishment though sometimes with a variety of controlling and rehabilitating conditions. For the most serious crimes, the default should normally be a specific term of confinement or something roughly equivalent.

Rebutting Presumptions. Negative retributivism sets limits on punishment severity, and parsimony creates a presumption that the least severe appropriate punishment should normally be imposed. An important question remains unanswered: What kind of evidence adequately rebuts the default parsimony presumption? In earlier times, this was impossible to answer because there were no systematic bodies of reliable knowledge about the deterrent, incapacitative, and rehabilitative effectives of punishment. Judges had only idiosyncratic intuitions and conventional wisdom to draw on. In our time, massive literatures have accumulated on the crime-preventive effects of criminal sanctions and treatment programs. There will seldom be adequate evidence-based reasons to overcome the default parsimony presumption though, sometimes, aggravating characteristics of the crime may.

Many individuals and organizations have recently surveyed the pertinent bodies of knowledge. The most exhaustive and authoritative analysis, by the National Academy of Sciences Committee on the Causes and Consequences of High Rates of Incarceration, concluded in 2014 that deterrent and incapacitative effects of punishment are, if any, modest at best and that imprisonment is on balance criminogenic, making ex-prisoners more, not less, likely to reoffend.

Another exhaustive National Academy of Sciences survey, this time by the Committee on Community Supervision and Desistance from Crime, concluded in 2007 that the evidence on rehabilitation is more positive. Well-designed, targeted, managed, and funded programs can reduce reoffending. Assignment to diagnostically appropriate treatment programs does not, however, require that people be imprisoned, or held longer than they otherwise would be. Treatment programs are more effective in the community. Taken as a whole, evidence-based knowledge about the effects of punishment will seldom overcome the default parsimony presumption and will often provide justification for diverting people from imprisonment.

Skeptics or crime control enthusiasts might take umbrage at the proposition that deterrence and incapacitation have no or only modest roles to play in punishing offenders. Their umbrage would be misplaced. Any system of punishment necessarily has deterrent and incapacitative dimensions. Even Kant and Hegel, positive retributivists who insisted that blameworthiness is the only morally relevant consideration to be taken into account in determining punishments, observed that imposition of deserved punishments necessarily sends deterrent messages and restrains offenders. C. S. Lewis long ago wrote that retributive punishment, "as the saying goes, kill[s] two birds with one stone; in the process of giving him what he deserved, you set an example for others." Imposition of punishments inexorably conveys the message to citizens that wrongful acts have painful consequences. Scaling punishments to the seriousness of crime communicates that some crimes are more serious than others. Confining people and subjecting them to controls on their movements and actions incapacitates them.

The critical policy question is whether increasing punishments beyond levels that a retributive/parsimonious system would allow has significant additional preventive effects. The evidence is clear that it would not. To the extent that punishment has deterrent and incapacitative effects, they are important but incidental consequences of treating people justly.

No doubt there will be exceptional cases that require exceptional handling. Dealing responsibly with some mentally disturbed or pathologically dangerous people may justify more extended or intrusive measures than would normally be deployed. Those individuals are, however, better dealt with by mental health professionals who have special knowledge, resources, and skills than by criminal justice professionals who don't.

Emile Durkheim, the pioneering French sociologist, a century ago observed that the criminal justice system has only a marginal but a nonetheless crucial role to play in shaping behavior. Deterrent effects, he wrote, if any, are likely to be minor but are in any case not especially important. Whether individuals do or do not commit crimes, he said, is not because they calculate risks of punishment, but because they have or have not been socialized into good values. That heavy lifting is done by primary institutions—families, churches, schools, neighborhoods, workplaces. The criminal justice system comes much too late in peoples' lives to play a major role. However, he said, it is important that the legal system reinforces important norms and values and does not undermine them. Significant wrongdoing should have consequences, and the consequences should be scaled to the degree of wrongdoing. Otherwise, prevailing norms will be undermined if, for example, minor property crimes are punished more severely than sexual assault, as long happened in the United States when auto theft was taken seriously but domestic violence was not. Prevailing norms are systematically undermined in our time when minor drug and property offenders receive harsher punishments than many violent and white-collar offenders.

Not all prevailing norms deserve respect, of course. Think only of widespread beliefs in earlier generations about racial inferiority, sexual preferences, and women's roles and capacities. To the extent such beliefs exist, they should be repudiated both in the larger society and in the law. Most of the norms Durkheim was concerned about are not like that. They involve basic standards of right and wrong and mutual respect for one another's well-being and interests.

Americans could easily establish punishment systems that are both retributive and parsimonious. The tools exist and are in use, though they are crude and need to be adapted. Some states operate presumptive sentencing guidelines systems that rank crimes in relation to their seriousness and for each ranking establish upper and lower limits of punishments that should normally be imposed. For many crimes, both limits involve confinement. For others the upper limit is a term of confinement and the lower a community punishment or a fine. Occasionally only community punishments are specified.

Existing guidelines systems are typically much too severe in general and too often require confinement. They are fundamentally undermined in most states by mandatory minimum sentencing and similar laws that trump the otherwise applicable standards and require disproportionately severe punishments. Setting that problem aside, and it is a big one and implies that all such laws should be repealed, presumptive guidelines could be adapted to be consistent with a punishment philosophy premised on negative retributivism and utilitarian parsimony. Most sentences would normally be set at the established minimum, though could be reduced when the judge believed that necessary in the interest of justice, and could be increased up to the established maximum when good evidence-based reasons or aggravating characteristics of the offense justified doing so. In a system governed by the rule of law, decisions to impose sentences below or above the minimum would require judicial explanations and be subject to appeals to higher courts.

The rest of this book provides the evidence and analyses on which this introduction and its claims and proposals are based. The first part discusses punishment philosophies and theories. The second, framed by normative theory, examines the evidence on the deterrent and incapacitative effects of punishment. The third explains what needs to be done to build systems of sentencing and punishment that do justice and prevent crime.

PART I

Doing Justice

2

Human Dignity

THERE IS NO commonly accepted normative framework in the United States for thinking or talking about punishment. This is unique among Western European and English-speaking countries. In Scandinavian countries, almost all philosophers, lawyers, and judges, and most policymakers, agree that the severity of punishments should be proportioned to the seriousness of crimes, that comparable offenders should be treated as equally as is humanly possible, and that offenders should not be avoidably damaged by what happens to them. In German-speaking, Benelux, and southern European countries, proportionality is widely agreed to be the primary consideration but counterbalanced by reluctance to harm people by imprisoning them and by aspirations to help offenders achieve productive, law-abiding lives. In other English-speaking countries, proportionality and equality receive relatively less emphasis but considerably more than in the United States. Consequentialist considerations of deterrence, incapacitation, and moral education are constrained by widely shared concerns that offenders be treated fairly and not be punished unduly severely.[1]

Please don't misunderstand. The preceding paragraph is not meant to suggest that other Western countries' systems deliver perfect justice. Human institutions never work like that no matter how hard people try. The descriptions nonetheless accurately depict common aspirations to treat offenders justly and sympathetically, to honor the biblical injunction to do unto others as you would have them do unto you.

In all of those other countries, legal institutions, processes, and rules aim to assure that offenders are treated justly, consistently, and humanely or, as the

---

1. Sources for the uncontroversial assertions about other countries' legal systems in this paragraph and the next few can be found in Tonry (2012, 2016*a*).

late American philosopher Ronald Dworkin put it in 1977, as equals and with respect and concern.[2] Punishment decisions are insulated from influence by politicians, public opinion, and the media: judges and prosecutors are career civil servants. There are tight, modest limits on maximum sentences. When, rarely, laws specify particular or minimum punishments for specific crimes, judges have discretion to impose lesser ones in the interest of justice.

The United States is an outlier in all these matters. Except for a handful of Swiss cantons, only in America are judges and prosecutors elected and in no other Western country are public opinion, media attention, or political considerations widely believed to be germane to their work. Only in the United States has the sentencing authority of judges, who are ethically required to do justice in individual cases, been subordinated to powers of prosecutors and legislators to whom respect and concern for offenders' interests are seldom centrally important. Often—as when mandatory minimum sentence, truth in sentencing, three-strikes, and life without parole laws apply—they are entirely absent. Only in the United States are prison sentences often measured in decades and lifetimes. Only in the United States is meaningful appellate review of sentences in individual cases largely unavailable. The US Supreme Court has since the 1970s emasculated constitutional standards for review of unjustly severe punishments.[3]

Those stark contrasts are recent. They date from the 1970s, 1980s, and 1990s. Before that, the American approach was different from those elsewhere, but principled and coherent in its own way. Every jurisdiction had an indeterminate sentencing system in which treatment of offenders was to be individualized in every case and at every stage. There was wide support for rehabilitation as the primary goal; for judges, parole boards, and prison officials to take account of individuals' circumstances and interests in making decisions about them; and for imposition of the least restrictive appropriate sentence. Retribution per se was not a goal. Harvard Law School professor Sheldon

---

2. "Equal concern and respect" was Dworkin's phrasing. I prefer the reversed order because I believe respect for human dignity should underlie all state actions. Concern for individuals' well-being and interests is a component of that respect.

3. In *Harmelin v. Michigan*, 501 U. S. 957, 1001 (1991), in which the defendant, a first offender convicted of cocaine possession, was sentenced to life without parole, Justice Kennedy observed, "The Eighth Amendment does not require strict proportionality between crime and sentence. Rather, it forbids only extreme sentences that are 'grossly disproportionate' to the crime." Earlier in *Rummel v. Estelle*, 445 U. S. 263, 274 (1980), upholding a life sentence for theft of $120.75, the court observed that the proportionality principle "would . . . come into play in the extreme example . . . [for example,] if a legislature made overtime parking a felony punishable by life imprisonment."

Glueck in 1928 expressed a widely shared belief that endured through the 1960s: "The old argument was that punishment was necessary as a 'just retribution' or requital of wickedness. No thoughtful person today seriously holds this theory of sublimated social vengeance." Jerome Michael and Herbert Wechsler, two of the twentieth century's most influential criminal lawyers, observed in 1940 that retribution is "the unstudied belief of most men," but, like any other ignoble intuition, should be ignored. "No legal provision can be justified merely because it calls for the punishment of the morally guilty by penalties proportioned to their guilt," they continued, "or criticized merely because it fails to do so."[4]

Wechsler was later the primary draftsman of the 1962 *Model Penal Code*; rehabilitation was its goal, to be sought by tailoring sentencing decisions to offenders' distinctive needs and circumstances. Under the *Code*, judges could in every case impose any lawful sentence from unsupervised probation to the maximum authorized by law. There were no mandatory minimums and no probation ineligibility laws. Parole boards could release prisoners any time after they became eligible; often that happened after serving the minimum 1 year required by most state prison systems. The *Code* created presumptions against the use of imprisonment in every case, including homicides, and in favor of parole release. Prison officials could grant time off for good behavior.

The *Model Penal Code* embodied widely shared mainstream views. It was not merely an academic exercise. Two-thirds of the states revised their criminal codes to incorporate some of its provisions and, in New York, New Jersey, and Oregon, many. The *Code* was commissioned and approved by the American Law Institute, an elite law reform organization then composed mostly of lawyers in large law firms, state and federal judges, and law professors in leading universities. The drafting committee contained more judges, prosecutors, defense lawyers, and corrections officials than professors.

Politicians and public officials supported the *Code*'s rehabilitative premise and its ambition to modernize and rationalize American criminal law. This can be seen in a series of contemporaneous initiatives. In 1963, the Advisory

---

4. In "A Rationale of the Law of Homicide," a landmark 1937 article in the *Columbia Law Review*, Michael and Wechsler (p. 1262) explained that there are "two competing normative hypotheses which merit serious attention" concerning punishment. In our time, they would be retributivism and consequentialism. In their time, they were "(1) the so-called classical [utilitarian] hypothesis . . . that the dominant purpose of treatment should be the deterrence of potential offenders; (2) the positivist hypothesis which dominates contemporary criminological thought, that incapacitation and reformation should be the dominant treatment ends." Retributivism was relegated to a footnote.

Committee of Judges of the National Council on Crime and Delinquency proposed the *Model Sentencing Act*. In 1967, the President's Commission on Law Enforcement and Administration of Justice led by US Attorney General Nicholas Katzenbach issued its report, *The Challenge of Crime in a Free Society*. In 1971, the National Commission on Reform of Federal Criminal Laws chaired by California Governor Edmund Brown released a Proposed Federal Criminal Code. In 1973, the National Advisory Commission on Criminal Justice Standards and Goals, appointed by President Richard M. Nixon and chaired by Republican Delaware Governor Russell Peterson, issued its report. All, like the *Model Penal Code*, supported indeterminate sentencing and rehabilitation and sought to improve them.

That consensus soon collapsed. In the cultural climate of the 1970s, when the prisoners' rights, civil rights, and due process movements were strongest, individualized decision-making was widely believed to be unfair, to result in unjust disparities, and to produce inconsistent, capricious, and racially biased results. Emphases on individual rights, exemplified by the writings of philosophers John Rawls (1971), Robert Nozick (1977), and Ronald Dworkin (1977), helped shape an intellectual climate that emphasized fairness, consistency, and equal treatment.

All of those developments fit more comfortably with retributive than with consequentialist values.[5] Marvin Frankel, a prominent federal judge, in *Criminal Sentencing: Law without Order* (1973), described American sentencing as "lawless" and offered then-radical proposals to improve it. Influential books by Norval Morris in 1974, Andreas von Hirsch in 1976, and Alan Dershowitz in 1976 promoted theories and policies calling for "limiting retributivism," "just deserts," and "fair and certain punishment." All rejected indeterminate sentencing and called for the fairness, even-handedness, and consistency it was said to lack.

A large and sophisticated theoretical literature on retribution began to emerge, exemplified by writings in the late 1960s and early 1970s by philosophers Joel Feinberg (1965), Herbert Morris (1966), John Kleinig (1973), and Jeffrie Murphy (1973), but quickly became entirely disconnected from punishment policies and practices. Although it appeared possible in the

---

5. None of the statements made on this and following pages concerning the collapse of support for indeterminate sentencing, the policy developments that followed, and contemporaneous changes in prevailing ways of thought are controversial. Principal, well-known, sources can be found in the bibliography and in Blumstein et al. (1983), Tonry (1996, 2016*b*), and Travis, Western, and Redburn (2014).

1970s that fairer, more just sentencing systems would be widely adopted to replace indeterminate sentencing, that happened only in a few places, and in most of those only for a few years.

Criminal justice policy instead became highly politicized, legislatures enacted laws of historically unprecedented severity, and imprisonment rates rose to levels never before seen in a democratic country. Few policymakers seemed much to care about the new laws' effects on individual offenders. It is impossible to develop principled retributive justifications for lengthy prison terms for sellers of a few grams of drugs, minimum 25-year or life sentences for routine property crimes, or life without parole for almost anything or anyone. Proportionality between offense seriousness and punishment severity is an element of all retributive theories of justice. Minor drug sales, thefts, and assaults are in everyone's minds less serious than rapes and serious violence, but often were and still are sometimes punished more severely.

As things now stand, there is no generally accepted American jurisprudence of punishment. Mandatory minimum sentence, three-strikes, and life without parole laws, indefensible by any imaginable retributive or consequentialist theory, coexist with a few state sentencing guidelines systems loosely based on retributive premises and remnants in many states of indeterminate sentencing. A plethora of drug and other problem-solving courts, restorative justice initiatives, prisoner re-entry programs, and reinvigorated treatment programs fit comfortably within the consequentialist values of indeterminate sentencing.

The lack of a widely agreed jurisprudence is not merely untidy, a matter that should be of concern mostly to ivory tower intellectuals. It has huge and morally troubling consequences. Punishments are often determined not by what an offender did but by how his or her case is processed. Defendants charged with drug or violent offenses subject to lengthy mandatory minimum prison sentences, for example, almost always serve those sentences in full if they are convicted. However, if prosecutors or judges choose to divert them or comparable defendants to drug courts, mental health programs, or elsewhere, they may avoid conviction, imprisonment, or both. If prosecutors can but do not choose to file charges subject to mandatory minimums, or agree to dismiss charges in exchange for a guilty plea to a lesser one, punishments are very different.

For cases not subject to mandatory minimum sentences, most sentencing judges possess unfettered discretion. This is because meaningful appellate sentence review is seldom available in most states, because the US Supreme Court in *Bordenkircher v. Hayes*, 434 U.S. 357 (1978), held that discretionary decisions by prosecutors are almost never reviewable by courts,[6] and because many of the 95 to 99 percent of defendants who plead guilty are required to waive their rights to appeal as a condition of plea bargains. The luck of the draw, not normative ideas about justice, determines whether people wind up in prison for decades, or less, or in community treatment programs, or are diverted altogether.

Retributive theories remain in vogue in law schools and philosophy departments but do not provide adequate guidance for thinking about justice in the real world. Theorists focus mostly on blameworthiness and moral communication, and incidentally on crime prevention, even though punishment implicates a far wider range of important values and interests. Difficult problems, the English political theorist Isaiah Berlin wrote in 1959, almost always encompass competing normative principles: "The world that we encounter in ordinary experience is one in which we are faced with choices between ends equally ultimate, and claims equally absolute, the realization of some of which must inevitably involve the sacrifice of others."

Abortion is one example. Some people believe embryos and fetuses are human beings, human life is sacred, and abortion is morally wrong. Others believe women are entitled to control their bodies, pregnancy is quintessentially a private matter, and state interference is morally wrong. Public policy must favor one set of beliefs over the other or compromise both.

Child protection offers a less polarized example. Most people believe in family autonomy: parents should be allowed to decide what kinds of lives they and their children live. This implies a strong presumption against state interference. Minimization of harm to children implies a presumption in favor of state action whenever risks exist. Probably everyone believes both that family autonomy should be respected and that children should be protected. Both goals cannot simultaneously be fully realized. Any imaginable policy choice involves trade-offs. Greater parental autonomy means heightened risks for children. Reduced risk means less autonomy.

---

6. Paul Lewis Hayes was charged with forgery, an offense subject to a 2- to 10-year prison sentence. The prosecutor offered to propose a 5-year sentence if Hayes pled guilty and threatened that, if he did not, a new indictment would be sought under the Kentucky Habitual Crime Act. If convicted, Hayes would then be imprisoned for life. Hayes did not plead guilty, the prosecutor obtained the new indictment, and Hayes was convicted and sentenced to life. The Federal Court of Appeals in *Hayes v. Cowan,* 547 F.2d 42, 44 (6th Cir. 1976), overturned the sentence because it offended settled law that "protect[ed] defendants from the vindictive exercise of a prosecutor's discretion." The Supreme Court to the contrary, extolling the benefits of plea bargaining, approved the prosecutor's behavior and upheld the sentence.

The way forward concerning punishment becomes clearer when we acknowledge that it implicates multiple, competing values, including not only deserved punishment and crime prevention, but also fairness and equal treatment. A comprehensive jurisprudence of just punishment would thus incorporate four propositions:

- *Justice as Proportionality*: Offenders should never be punished more severely than can be justified by their blameworthiness in relation to the severity of punishments justly imposed on others for the same and different offenses.
- *Justice as Fairness*: Processes for responding to crimes should be publicly known, implemented in good faith, and applied even-handedly.
- *Justice as Equal Treatment*: Defendants and offenders should be treated as equals; their circumstances and interests should be accorded equal respect and concern when decisions affecting them are made.
- *Justice as Parsimony*: Offenders should never be punished more severely than can be justified by appropriate, valid, normative purposes.

Those four propositions describe what people accused or convicted of crimes would want for themselves or their loved ones. They describe minimum, interacting requirements of a just system of punishment. Together they provide answers to problems that traditional punishment theories, whether retributive or consequentialist, by themselves cannot resolve. Respect for human dignity does not appear as a separate proposition. It encompasses all four propositions.

Human dignity is often dismissed as a nebulous, primarily rhetorical concept. Partly this is because, as Harvard Law School professor Carol Steiker showed in 2014, neither the term nor the concept play an independent, substantive role in American law. Partly it is because, as Columbia Law School philosopher Jeremy Waldron observed in 2014, the term appears prominently in the preambles to international human rights documents such as the 1948 UN Universal Declaration of Human Rights, but in their texts is given no concrete work to do.

These critiques have merit when the term "human dignity" is used rhetorically, but not when it is used concretely, as I show in section II of this chapter, in relation to sentencing and other decisions affecting individuals. Torture denies human dignity to its victims. So does solitary confinement in a supermaximum security prison. So does requiring people to live in squalid, inhuman conditions. So does denial to individuals of the possibility ever to live a satisfying life. None of those practices is necessary or morally justifiable. Conceptual and procedural tools exist to acknowledge human dignity in relation to punishment and sentencing. The preceding four propositions about justice in punishment encapsulate them.

Recognition that punishment implicates values and interests other than moral blameworthiness and crime prevention is not new. Immanuel Kant and Jeremy Bentham, the pioneers of retributive and utilitarian punishment theories, recognized two centuries ago that extrinsic considerations sometimes limit or forbid punishments that could otherwise be justified.[7] Kant observed that sometimes a sovereign who "does not want to dull the people's feeling . . . must also have it in his power, in this case of necessity (*causa necessitatis*), to assume the role of judge (to represent him) and pronounce a judgment that decrees for the criminals a sentence" other than the uniquely deserved one (p. 117). Bentham wrote that otherwise appropriate punishments should not be imposed "when too many people would have to be punished, making the aggregate punishment too great"; when "the effect of the punishment would be to deprive the community of the benefit . . . of the extraordinary value of the services of some one delinquent"; and when "an indefinite number of the members of the same community . . . conceive that the offence or the offender ought not to be punished at all, or at least ought not to be punished in the way in question" (pp. 163–64). I don't necessarily endorse those statements but quote them to illustrate that even those most single-minded of men recognized that punishment implicates values besides retribution and crime prevention.

In this chapter, I explain why retributive theories that dominate contemporary scholarly writing cannot adequately elucidate what a just punishment system should look like. Section I provides a brief overview of punishment theories, ideas, and concepts. I then canvass a series of fundamental dilemmas courts face on which retributive theories cast little light. These include how to assess blameworthiness, practical problems in administration of the criminal law, and the paradox that—in practice—punishments per offense usually increase when they are sentenced successively but decrease when they are sentenced simultaneously.

In the second section, I elaborate on the normative framework set out above. Proportionality, a retributive touchstone, is a core component. It

---

7. Passages from Immanuel Kant can be found at pages indicated in Kant ([1797] 2017) unless otherwise indicated; from Jeremy Bentham in Bentham ([1789] 1970); from Georg Wilhelm Friedrich Hegel in Hegel ([1821] 1991). Page numbers are shown in the text.

provides tools for comparing punishments for different offenses and different offenders. It and Benthamite parsimony set intelligible limits on punishments that may justly be imposed. So, independently, do fairness and equal treatment.

I. *The Limited Reach of Retributivism*

Few would disagree that authoritative expression of censure for wrongdoing is the, or a, core function of criminal convictions and punishments imposed by judges. Big disagreements emerge, however, when the focus shifts to details. To decide how much censure one offender deserves relative to others, convincing ways to assess relative blameworthiness and determine just punishments are needed. Conceptual dilemmas and practical impediments stand in the way.

A. Punishment Theories

Three main strands of punishment theory—retributivism, utilitarianism, and positivism—emerged over the last two centuries. Retributive theories, first developed in some detail in Germany by Immanuel Kant and Georg Wilhelm Friedrich Hegel, called for imposition of punishments apportioned to the seriousness of crimes. Kant famously observed: "But what kind and what amount of punishment is it that public justice makes its principle and measure? None other than the principle of equality.... Accordingly, whatever undeserved evil you inflict upon another within the people, that you [deserve].... But only the *law of retribution* (*jus talionis*) ... can specify definitely the quality and the quantity of punishment" (p. 115; emphasis in original). Hegel expressed a similar view: "The universal feeling of peoples and individuals towards crime is, and always has been, that it *deserves* to be punished, and that *what the criminal has done should also happen to him*" (p. 127; emphasis in original). The Italian historian Michele Pifferi in 2016 showed that retributive ideas, less rigid than Kant's, have been continuously influential in continental Europe since the 1920s. In the United States they gained support in the 1960s and 1970s and remain influential today. There are many different kinds of retributive theory but they share the view that moral blameworthiness is a fundamental consideration in determining just punishments.[8]

Utilitarian punishment theory is usually dated from the publication in 1764 of Cesare Beccaria's *Dei delitti e delle pene* (*On Crimes and Punishments*).

---

8. Many efforts have been made to describe and taxonomize varieties of retributivism. Classic ones include Hart (1968, postscript), Cottingham (1979), Mackie (1982), and Walker (1991).

He urged that punishments be scaled to the seriousness of crimes and used to deter offenders and others from wrongdoing. Jeremy Bentham, the archetypal utilitarian, developed deterrent ideas in far greater detail. His proposals were based on ideas he shared with Beccaria, combined with a model of rational human beings who engage in calculation of pains and pleasures. The pains of punishment should always exceed crime's anticipated pleasures.

The object of the criminal law for Bentham was to "augment the total happiness of the community" and "to exclude as far as may be, everything that tends to subtract from that happiness: in other words, to exclude mischief." Crime is a form of mischief. To prevent crime through deterrence, Bentham offered detailed prescriptions. Punishments should be severer for more serious crimes to encourage offenders to commit lesser ones, should be increased if the likelihood of apprehension is low so the deterrent message will not be diluted, should be incrementally scaled to each detail of a contemplated offense so offenders have incentives to desist partway, and should be lower for attempted than for completed offenses to provide incentive to stop. Critically, however, everyone's happiness—including that of offenders—counts: "But all punishment is mischief: all punishment in itself is evil. Upon the principle of utility, if it ought at all to be admitted, it ought only to be admitted in as far as it promises to exclude some greater evil" (p. 158). Bentham's ideas, broadened to include rehabilitation and incapacitation as goals, shaped prevailing ways of thinking in English-speaking countries and provided the premises for indeterminate sentencing as it emerged and endured in the United States. They suffuse the *Model Penal Code*.

In earlier times, many American intellectuals who wrote about punishment were positivists. Harvard Law School professor Sheldon Glueck, in a 1928 article, "Principles of a Rational Penal Code," set out the most fully developed analysis. Positivism was most famously associated with the Italian criminal lawyer Enrico Ferri who, like many others of his time, believed that crime resulted primarily from social, economic, and psychological forces' effects on individuals. The only valid purpose of the criminal law, he and Glueck separately wrote, is the prevention of crime: the likelihood of reoffending should be the primary consideration. Prison sentences should be indeterminate, potentially for life, including for people convicted of minor offenses. Convicted offenders should be imprisoned only if they are dangerous. Prisoners should be released when they cease to be dangerous but held indefinitely if their dangerousness does not abate. Reverberations of positivism echoed through the mid-twentieth century, most influentially in the writings of Baroness Barbara Wootton (1959, 1963) in England and Wales, Judge Marc Ancel (1965) in

France, and psychiatrist Karl Menninger (1968) in the United States, but have largely disappeared.

Utilitarianism and retributivism have long been described as the principal competing paradigms for thinking about punishment. In our time, "consequentialism" is often substituted for utilitarianism. Consequentialism, a broad category of ethical theory traceable to pre-Socratic Greece, embodies the view that normative judgments should depend only on anticipated consequences. Bentham's classical utilitarianism, focused primarily on deterrence, and Enrico Ferri's positivism, focused primarily on incapacitation, are consequentialist theories. In relation to punishment, consequentialism is usually synonymous with a broad conception of utilitarianism that encompasses deterrent, incapacitative, rehabilitative, moral educative, and other preventive effects.[9]

That broad conception, exemplified by the 1962 *Model Penal Code*, is by far the most influential consequentialist theory of punishment. Restorative justice theories are also consequentialist, focusing on restoration of frayed or broken relations among victims, offenders, and communities, but are seldom discussed in relation to punishment generally.[10]

Benthamite utilitarianism, however, whether narrowly or broadly conceived, is out of intellectual fashion. Only retributivist theories are much discussed in our time or, for that reason, in the rest of this chapter. Their details vary; the implications vary less. Retributivist ideas began to revive in the 1950s in writings by Norval Morris (1953) in Australia, John Rawls (1955) in the United States, and H. L. A. Hart (1959) in England. All argued, though in different ways, that sensible theories of punishment should combine preventive goals with retributive considerations.

---

9. The substitution of consequentialism for utilitarianism in relation to punishment partly rests on a misconception. Bentham emphasized deterrence but he also wrote about rehabilitation, incapacitation, and moral education ([1789] 1970, p. 158, note a). So did earlier proto-utilitarians. William Blackstone, in his *Commentaries on the Laws of England*, for example, asserted that the end of punishment is not "atonement or expiation" but "a precaution against future offenses of the same kind. This is effected three ways: either by the amendment of the offender himself; . . . or by deterring others . . .; or, lastly, by depriving the party injuring of the power to do future mischief [by execution, permanent confinement, slavery, or exile]" (Blackstone [1769] 1979, p. 13).

10. John Braithwaite and Philip Pettit's "republican theory" (1990, 2001) is the only well-developed nonutilitarian punishment theory in our time that falls under the consequentialist heading. It seeks to maximize not happiness or, synonymously, utility, but "dominion," the human capacity to live an unconstrained life of one's choosing, limited by the obligation to respect others' rights to dominion over their own lives. Crimes violate victims' dominion. The theory has been discussed mostly in relation to restorative justice.

Many kinds of primarily retributive theories emerged. In the first generation, Herbert Morris (1966), Jeffrie Murphy (1973), and Andreas von Hirsch
(1976) argued that people in a democratic society benefit from public order
and security, including others' law-abidingness, are reciprocally obligated to
accept the burdens and responsibilities of citizenship, and should be punished
if they do not. The next generation, exemplified by Joel Feinberg (1965),
Herbert Morris (1981), Jean Hampton (1984), and Antony Duff (1986) in
different ways emphasized moral communication about the wrongfulness
of crime, directed variously at offenders, victims, and the larger community.
Related censure theories offered by Duff (2001) and von Hirsch (1993) focused more narrowly on authoritative denunciation of wrongdoing. A third
strand, harking back to Kant and Hegel, in our time associated with Michael
Moore (1993), portrayed punishment as a morally necessary consequence of
culpable wrongdoing.

The lines that separate different kinds of retributive theory blur. Some, especially communicative theories, are difficult to distinguish from consequentialist ones. Most deal only with how state punishment can be justified, and
do not address questions pertinent to punishment of individual offenders.
A 2010 writing by the law professors Dan Markel and Chad Flanders is
illustrative:

> One question is: What might justify the state's creation of legal
> institutions of punishment? This is what we call the "justification"
> question. The second question is: Once the state has determined
> someone's liability for a crime, how much and what kind of punish-
> ment should the state mete out in response? This is the "sentencing"
> question. That a retributivist theorist gives a retributive . . . answer to
> the justification question does not require her to offer a precise answer
> for each sentencing question. . . . *A retributive conception of proportion-
> ality need not have much in the way of precision to say about the partic-
> ular details of punishment's implementation.* (emphasis added)

Discussions of whether the state may justly punish offenders, and why, are intellectually interesting but not especially helpful to policymakers, prosecutors,
judges, and corrections officials.

Retributivists of every stripe believe that offenders' blameworthiness is
fundamental in some way to justification of punishment. They differ on what
way. Because basic retributivist concepts and distinctions recur in subsequent
parts of this chapter and book, I highlight several.

1. *Positive and Negative Retributivism.* Positive retributivism is a sword that cuts deservedly deeply and precisely. Negative retributivism is a shield that protects against undeservedly severe punishments.

Positive retributivists believe that deserved punishments must be imposed. Kant and Hegel are positive retributivists. Remember the "principle of equality" and the *jus talionis* in the passage from Kant I quoted a few pages back? Modern writers, including Andreas von Hirsch, Paul Robinson, and Michael Moore offer similar arguments.

Negative retributivists, to the contrary, believe that offenders' blame-worthiness in relation to particular crimes sets upper limits on deserved punishments that may but need not be imposed. If good reasons exist for a lesser punishment, or no punishment at all, that is what should be done.

"Limiting retributivism," a form of negative retributivism associated with Norval Morris, warrants separate mention primarily because it has been particularly influential. The American Law Institute's 2017 *Model Penal Code: Sentencing*, for example, explicitly adopts it as a normative premise.

2. *Mixed Theories.* "Mixed theories" encompass combinations of retributive and consequentialist ideas about preventive effects of sanctions, the significance of contextual considerations, and special circumstances of individual cases. All negative retributivist theories, including limiting retributivism, are mixed theories.[11]

Use of the term mixed theory dates from H. L. A. Hart's *Punishment and Responsibility* (1968), a seminal work, in which he summarized his primarily consequentialist personal beliefs but acknowledged that widely held views about deserved punishment need also to be taken into account. Hart and Norval Morris believed that widely shared intuitions about equality and proportionality in punishment are important and should generally be respected. They feared that the criminal law would lose legitimacy in citizens' eyes, and thus its effectiveness, if it departed too much from prevailing community sentiments. Few people today espouse unqualified retributive views like Kant's and Hegel's or thoroughgoing utilitarian views like Bentham's. Nearly all modern writers offer mixed theories.

3. *Censure and Hard Treatment.* Punishment is commonly said to have two components: the blaming or censure inherent in conviction and

---

11. Braithwaite and Pettit's republican theory (1990, 2001) is better thought of as a form of negative retributivism than as a consequentialist theory. They are adamant that the offender's moral culpability sets an absolute, proportionate upper limit on punishment severity and equally adamant that retributive considerations are otherwise irrelevant (e.g., Braithwaite 2018).

imposition of punishment, and "hard treatment" consisting of punishment's pains and burdens. Most punishments for crime involve painful, intrusive, burdensome, and otherwise unpleasant elements. Many influential contemporary retributivists, including Herbert Morris, Anthony Duff, and Andreas von Hirsch, regard punishment as primarily a form of moral communication. They generally feel obliged, however, to explain why communication of censure by itself—"You have sinned; go forth and sin no more"—is not the end of the matter. Some offer nonretributive embellishments to their retributive theories. Von Hirsch's justification, for example, is that humankind are not angels and need "prudential reasons to obey the law" (seems like deterrence, doesn't it?). Other justifications are unconvincing. Duff and Herbert Morris argue that offenders, wanting closure, would themselves want to experience hard treatment or should at least be provided the opportunity for closure that hard treatment ostensibly provides. Many or most offenders would happily accept censure alone.

4. *Ordinal and Cardinal Desert.* This distinction, first proposed by von Hirsch, addresses the problem of knowing what specific punishment a particular offender deserves. There are no obvious answers. Human beings have widely different intuitions. The solution, von Hirsch proposed, is to distinguish between punishment that is in some sense absolutely deserved, which he called cardinal desert, and punishment that is deserved for particular crimes relative to those deserved for other crimes. This he called ordinal desert. Ordinal desert can be coherently calculated by creating scales of offense seriousness and specifying appropriate punishments for the most and least serious. Once that's done, a punishment scale can be created that parallels the offense seriousness scale. The absolutely deserved punishment for robbery may be unknowable, but everyone would agree that the relatively deserved punishment for simple robbery, all else being equal, should normally be less than for aggravated robbery and more than for theft.

B. Conceptual Impediments

Retributive and mixed theories cannot by themselves resolve two inescapable problems: the multiple offense paradox and assessment of blameworthiness. I discuss them in some detail in chapters 3, 4, and 5. Here I sketch their contours.

1. *The Multiple Offense Paradox.* Most people writing about punishment philosophy, beginning with Kant and Bentham, discuss punishment of individuals convicted of a single offense. At least in our time, only a minority

of defendants are first-timers charged with a single offense. A significant majority face multiple charges, have been convicted before, or both. The most recent available data from the US Bureau of Justice Statistics on felony charges in state courts show that 55 percent of felony defendants in 2009 faced multiple charges, including 63 percent of those charged with violent crimes. Sixty percent of all felony defendants had prior convictions, as did 53 percent of those charged with violent crimes. Detailed data are presented in chapter 5 in Tables 5.1 and 5.2.

Most punishment theorizing does not have much to say about cases involving multiple offenses. That is beginning to change. The emerging but scant literature has exposed a paradox. Punishments of people convicted of more than one crime are usually discounted if imposed at the same time (a "bulk discount") but augmented if imposed at different times (a "recidivist premium"). These different practices are irreconcilable with retributive theories. If the deserved punishment for one burglary is a 1-year prison term, a retributivist should say that three burglaries deserve 3 years, not fewer. If a 1-year sentence was deservedly imposed for a single previous burglary, a retributivist should say that each of two subsequent burglary convictions warrants an additional 1-year sentence, nothing more.

The multiple offense paradox makes a big difference. Bulk discounts can be substantial, five burglaries punished a bit more severely than one would have been, and recidivist premiums are often enormous. Rhys Hester and his colleagues showed in 2017 that punishments prescribed for recidivists in American sentencing guidelines systems are four to 15 times greater than for first offenders.

a. *The Recidivist Premium.* Almost everyone who has assessed efforts to justify the recidivist premium concludes that they are unpersuasive. Most apologists argue either that recidivists' bad characters justify harsher punishments or that recidivists have special obligations to observe the law. Reoffending, it is said, demonstrates disrespect or defiance and that justifies the additional punishment. Neither claim is convincing. In free societies, citizens are entitled to be defiant, disrespectful, and eccentric, even to manifest what others see as bad character. All citizens, however, have the same obligation to comply with the criminal law. I am not alone in this view. Indiana University philosopher Richard Lippke, one of many skeptics, surveyed the arguments in 2016 and concluded, "Like others, I find the arguments given on behalf of recidivist premiums unconvincing."

b. *The Bulk Discount.* Almost everyone approves of the bulk discount as a policy matter, but no one has figured out how to justify it in retributive terms.

The same Richard Lippke in 2011 offered the most extensive analysis to date of what a retributive jurisprudence of bulk discounts, taken seriously, might look like. He showed that it would be immensely complex and not generally justifiable in retributive terms.

Policy rationales have been offered. One is that no punishment should be so "crushing" that it deprives a person of a large fraction of his or her remaining life or of a large fraction of the prime years of life. A second is that bulk discounts can be justified as extensions of mercy based on judges' holistic assessments of offenders' lives and blameworthiness. These propositions recur regularly in judicial opinions. They are, however, ad hoc, unimbedded in broader general theories, and ungeneralizable.

Convincing empirical evidence, much of it developed by Oxford criminologist Julian Roberts, shows that majorities of the public, judges, and offenders approve of both the bulk discount and the recidivist premium. Those broadly shared intuitions, he argues, justify the paradox because democratic values require deference to widely shared beliefs. Failure to do so could undermine the legitimacy of law and the legal process in citizens' minds. Common intuitions, however, by themselves cannot offer a principled justification for anything. Think about the damage done not so many years ago by widely shared intuitions or beliefs about race, gender, and sexual preference.

The first-time defendant with a clean record is not rare but also not the norm. The multiple offender paradox exposes the incompleteness of traditional retributive punishment theories. Theories of punishment that cannot coherently explain how half to two-thirds of people convicted of crime should be punished are fundamentally incomplete.

2. *Blameworthiness*. Most retributive theories assume that assessments of blameworthiness can be made more or less objectively, on the basis of the offense of conviction sometimes modified by evidence of circumstances such as weapon use, gratuitous violence, or a victim's special vulnerability that seem inextricably related to moral assessment of the seriousness of the crime. Credible arguments have been made, however, that decisions about punishment should incorporate subjective assessments of the offender's blameworthiness and of the foreseeable effects of contemplated punishments on him or her as a unique individual.

Assessments of blameworthiness are difficult and contested. Nothing inherent in any retributive theory entails a particular approach. Assessments might be based, objectively, solely on the seriousness of the crimes of which individuals are convicted or, subjectively, on crimes' distinctive features and the social, psychological, economic, and situational circumstances causally related to their commission. Criminal law in English-speaking countries takes no account of offenders' motives, caring only about the classic mens rea categories of intention, knowledge, recklessness, and negligence. It allows only limited space for defenses of duress, necessity, immaturity, emotional distress, and mental disability and usually none at all concerning harms resulting from imperfect self-defense and other honest but unreasonable mistakes.[12] If the substantive criminal law does not take explicit account of these and other complexities of human lives, judges in their sentencing decisions can and, when sentencing laws allow, often do.

A similar question can be asked about the effects of punishments on individuals. Law professor Adam Kolber in 2009 proposed that judges making sentencing decisions take account of punishment's foreseeable subjective effects on individuals. Most retributivists disagree. Kolber's view has an illustrious pedigree. Jeremy Bentham was adamant that punishments must be adjusted to offenders' "sensibilities," by which he meant those of their characteristics that would make a punishment more or less painful to them. Immanuel Kant called for attention to be paid to adjusting punishments to the "special sensibilities" of the upper classes so that the privileged will be punished equivalently to the poor.[13]

The suffering caused by seemingly generic punishments can be radically different. Mentally ill people are often affected by close confinement substantially differently than others are. Imprisonment in the same place for the same period means very different things to a young gang leader, a claustrophobe, an employed middle-aged parent, an elderly person, and someone who is seriously or terminally ill. To ignore such things in relation to comparably

---

12. In common-law countries but typically not in continental European civil law countries, affirmative defenses such as self-defense are often not available to defendants who honestly but unreasonably believe their actions to be justifiable. Imperfect self-defense cases, for example, involve defendants who genuinely believe themselves to be threatened by serious bodily harm or death when they were not and when a reasonable person would have realized they were not. Such defendants are simultaneously morally innocent and legally guilty.

13. As a passage quoted in chapter 3, note 8 makes clear, Kant's aim was not to reduce punishments for privileged people but to augment them so they would be subjectively equivalent to those imposed on the less privileged.

culpable people, however culpability is measured, is to accept huge differences in the pains imposed upon them.

C. Practical Impediments

The practical impediments to achievement of just punishment systems are little less confounding. Many different kinds of blameworthy acts are hidden behind the names of the offenses of which people are convicted. This problem is most acute in the United States where 95 to 99 percent of convictions result from guilty pleas, most emerging from diverse forms of bargaining. Practices vary widely. In many charge bargains, some among multiple charges of similar offenses are dismissed. Even with bulk discounts, this reduces sentences. Other times defendants plead guilty to less serious charges (e.g., theft or sexual assault); more serious ones (e.g., robbery or rape) are dismissed. Still other times, defendants are required to plead guilty to the offense or offenses charged on the understanding that the prosecutor will propose a reduced sentence. Conviction numbers and labels thus become fundamentally misleading: defendants appropriately charged with commission of three robberies may be convicted of all three, or only one, or some number of thefts. If punishments are based on offenses of conviction, determination of proportionate deserved punishments is easier said than done.

Retributive theories cannot in their own terms provide much guidance for thinking about imposition of deserved punishments in particular cases. Blameworthiness, the core concept, is difficult to define in theory and harder to characterize in practice. That does not, of course, make blameworthiness unimportant, but it can provide at best a partial account of how a principled system of punishment should operate. Like the shadows flickering on the walls of Plato's cave, it provides impressions of what a just system might look like, but no more than that.

The problems with real-world application of retributive punishment theories are fundamental. They are also ironic; the retributivist revival was a reaction to real-world problems. It occurred neither in a vacuum nor from turbulence in university philosophy departments but in response to widely shared perceptions of stark injustices in American sentencing and punishment. By emphasizing blameworthiness as a primary consideration, and seeking to limit the discretions of officials, it aimed to right wrongs. What is needed is a conceptual account of punishment that can address real-world problems in principled ways.

II. Just Punishment

Questions about justice in punishment cannot be answered by invocation only of retributive and consequentialist theories. They are "monist," which implies, asserted Isaiah Berlin, the false view that moral questions have single correct answers and that all those answers dovetail within a single, coherent moral system. In the introduction to this chapter, I quoted and illustrated Berlin's famous assertion about value pluralism and the inevitability of conflicts between implications of equally important first principles.

Punishment is a realm in which value pluralism is unavoidable. Since the times of Bentham and Kant, conflict between the implications of preventive consequentialist and blame-imputing retributive premises have been evident, leading to the emergence of mixed theories and zero-sum-game arguments about retributivism as sublimated vengeance and utilitarian indifference to punishment of the innocent. Values other than those associated with retributivism and consequentialism also need to be taken into account. Before making that case, two preliminary matters.

First, choosing between polar approaches is not an option. No one in our time subscribes to unconstrained consequentialism, whether conceptualized narrowly as utilitarian deterrence or broadly as optimal crime prevention. Almost no one subscribes to positive retributivism, the view that punishments must be perfectly proportioned to the seriousness of crimes. Most people subscribe to forms of negative retributivism or mixed theories that, by definition, encompass nonretributive values.

Second, it is not an option simply to direct judges to take retributive and consequentialist considerations into account as appears to them warranted. As section I made clear, that won't work. No form of retributivism by itself, or combined only with instrumental crime prevention considerations, can resolve the multiple offense paradox, adequately specify criteria for assessing blameworthiness, or take account of practical operational issues. In any case, directing judges simply to choose purposes case by case would recreate the problems, and dangers, of unconstrained discretion that indeterminate sentencing presented and the retributivist revival sought to address. Just as book reviews often reveal more about reviewers than about books, fully discretionary sentencing inevitably reveals more about judges than about offenders.

A just punishment system would acknowledge competing normative claims. It would be limited by retributive notions of proportionality that take account of offenders' blameworthiness. It would be fair, using procedures and standards that are transparent, consistent, and even-handedly applied. It would treat offenders with equal respect and concern, allowing each to be assessed according to appropriate criteria in his or her individual circumstances and situation. It would be parsimonious, imposing no unjustifiable human suffering.

Proportionality, fairness, equal treatment, and parsimony can all be subsumed within a broader concept of respect for human dignity. That term has, however, wrongly, a bad name in some intellectual circles. This is largely because of particular contexts, and ways, in which it is used and because it is often used polemically to express strong opposition to something the speaker abhors. Harvard psychologist Steven Pinker, for example, in 2008 wrote that "the problem is that 'dignity' is a squishy, subjective notion, hardly up to the heavyweight moral demands assigned to it." The context was his frustration that religious members of the second President Bush's Council on Bioethics decried abortion, birth control, and fetal tissue research as violations of human dignity, which he found troubling and dogmatic. Pinker's reaction, however, was overblown. He should have objected not to the words "human dignity" but to their use in that context as conversation-stopping "polar words."

Federal Court of Appeals judge Thurman Arnold in 1937 invented that term, observing that epithets such as communist and fascist stopped discussions entirely or shifted their focus to whether the terms were or were not being used polemically. Calling someone sexist, homophobic, racist, anti-Semitic, or Islamophobic has the same effect in our time. Opposing fetal tissue research as a violation of human dignity is a polemical parallel to opposing full legalization or restriction of abortion as a violation of human dignity. Characterizing positions on abortion as pro-life and pro-choice is equivalent. Use of polar words is emotionally satisfying to advocates but not conducive to dispassionate discussion, problem-solving, or reconciliation of the implications of competing principles and values.

Lawyers are troubled by the term's absence from American constitutional law. Harvard law professor Carol Steiker observed in 2014 that "Dignity remains largely a constitutional cipher, lacking a home in any specific amendment of the Bill of Rights or a substantial or well-theorized role in American constitutional jurisprudence." She argued that the concept may be better used to express a general social value than to characterize an individual right and has "collective" value in explaining why shaming, extreme punishments, and many mandatory sentencing laws are morally objectionable.

Human dignity easily could have become an implied element of American constitutional jurisprudence, as it has in many other countries. In another human rights setting, the US Supreme court implied the constitutional right of privacy that underlies its recent decision on gay marriage. The court has, however, for at least 40 years shown little solicitude for human rights in the criminal justice system.

"Human dignity," is no more amorphous than "privacy," "due process," "equal protection," and "cruel and unusual," terms with which American courts and lawyers have successfully grappled for two centuries. That courts have not yet developed a jurisprudence of human dignity does not mean that they cannot or should not. Law reviews abound in articles considering the possibilities.

Philosophers have not until recently begun to develop robust understandings of human dignity, but that is changing. Berkeley philosopher Meir Dan-Cohen argued in 2002 that all of the substantive criminal law, a much broader subject than punishment, should be reconceptualized to replace its traditional emphasis on the "harm principle" with emphasis on "what may be called the *dignity principle:* the view that the main goal of the criminal law is to defend the unique moral worth of every human being."

Jeremy Waldron in 2014 in "What Do the Philosophers Have against Dignity?" surveyed writing by philosophers troubled by historic associations of dignity as a quality associated with social rank and religiosity. He was unconvinced that the concept is inherently too vague to be useful and offered a platform, free of those associations, on which he and others might build: "To respect someone you have to pay attention to them and their situation . . . As a foundational idea, human dignity might ascribe to each person a very high rank, associated with the sanctity of her body, her control of herself, the demands she can make on others, and her determination of her own destiny, values, and capacities."

Waldron's insistence that attention be paid to people and their situations—"morality requires us to do this anyway," he wrote—is not very different from Ronald Dworkin's insistence that people be treated as equals and with respect and concern. That is how a just punishment system should deal with people convicted of crimes. This is part of what Carol Steiker seems to have meant when she observed that "respecting the individuality of offenders in sentencing implicates both collective and individual dignity interests." The US Supreme Court in *Woodson v. North Carolina,* 428 U.S. 280 (1976), acknowledged, though only concerning capital punishment, that "individualizing sentencing determinations generally reflects simply enlightened policy" and that not doing so would be to treat "all persons convicted of a designated offense not as uniquely individual human beings but as members

of a faceless, undifferentiated mass." That is self-evidently right, making the
Supreme Court's mean-spirited Eighth Amendment jurisprudence of disproportionate punishments other than capital punishment, which I mentioned
earlier in this chapter, a moral anomaly.

Human dignity provides a useful framework for thinking about punishment. Kant and Bentham understood this better than many contemporary
writers do. Kant argued that convicted murderers should be executed even in a
dissolving island society in which all inhabitants would soon embark on ships
to live in other places; not doing so would fail to acknowledge the murderer's
nature as an autonomous human being capable of moral choice. However,
Kant observed, the murderer should be treated with respect: "Death is judi-
cially carried out upon the wrongdoer, although it must still be freed from any
mistreatment that could make the humanity in the person suffering it into
something abominable" (p. 116).

Bentham insisted that punishment is justifiable only when its benefits exceed the detriments experienced by the offender. In making that determination, he further insisted that punishments be individualized to take account
of the offender's "sensibilities," those personal characteristics that would make
a punishment worse for one person than for another. His notion of what this
encompassed was exhaustive; he identified 36 kinds of pertinent sensibilities.
His Rule 6 for determining amounts of punishment provides:

> It is further to be observed, that owing to the different manners and
> degrees in which persons under different circumstances are affected by
> the same exciting cause, a punishment which is the same in name will
> not always either really produce, or even so much as appear to others
> to produce, in two different persons the same degree of pain: there-
> fore, *That the quantity actually inflicted on each individual offender may
> correspond to the quantity intended for similar offenders in general, the
> several circumstances influencing sensibility ought always to be taken into
> account.* (p. 169; emphasis in original)

Taken together, Kant's and Bentham's views, not unlike Dworkin's and
Waldron's, require that offenders be treated with respect and concern and in
ways that accord with their dignity as human beings.

Proportionality, fairness, equal treatment, and parsimony are values that
characterize a punishment system that respects human dignity. Determining
just punishments in individual cases is intrinsically difficult. Nuanced
differences between defendants and suspects, and among offenses, often lead

practitioners to want to handle seemingly similar offenses in different ways. Issues of social and racial injustice are salient in every courtroom. Whether social and economic disadvantage should provide a defense to criminal charges or an appropriate basis for systematic mitigation of punishment is one. Whether evidence of social, racial, ethnic, or religious bias in the operation of criminal justice systems should be taken into account at sentencing is another. Gratuitous punishment, suffering that serves no useful purpose, is a third.

English philosopher Matt Matravers in 2011 explained why retributive principles by themselves are insufficient justifications for punishment. He observed that "The issue is not one of reconciling [punishment] practices to desert . . . but rather it is one of thinking about the requirements of liberal justice as a whole." Thought of in that way, it is clear—as the multiple offense paradox and myriad subjective differences between seemingly comparable offenses and offenders demonstrate—that values other than blameworthiness and crime prevention should be taken into account.

Incorporation of fairness, equal treatment, and parsimony values into a comprehensive jurisprudence of punishment raises three major matters. First, these additional values are not simply side constraints on the pursuit of retributive or consequentialist aims. Ronald Dworkin in 1977 wrote of "rights as trumps." Fairness, equal treatment, and parsimony should be treated as trumps on punishments that might otherwise justly be imposed. Any just punishment must be consistent with all of them.

Retributive or consequentialist reasoning may sometimes appear to justify punishments that other values forbid. Retributivists, for example, often argue that the logic of utilitarianism justifies punishment of innocent people if that will minimize human suffering. Critics of retributivism point out that its "do the crime, do the time" injunction implies breathtakingly severe punishments and is irreconcilable with the bulk discount: if 3 months is a just punishment for one drug sale or shoplifting conviction, then 300 months should be right for 100.

When such issues arise, the retributive or consequentialist logic must give way: knowing convictions or punishments of innocent people and imprisonment of people for 25 years for minor offenses are irreconcilable with respect for human dignity limits embodied in fairness, equal treatment, and parsimony. The human rights denials inherent in knowing conviction or punishment of the innocent are self-evident. Imposition of 25-year prison terms for trifling crimes, no matter how many, warrants elaboration. It violates fairness values. Prosecutors possess enormous discretion and seldom charge or insist on guilty pleas to all instances of equivalent crimes: Why in this case? It denies equal treatment by implying that trifling crimes in any number warrant as much or more censure as individual instances of much more serious crimes; no number of shopliftings is as serious as a rape, an aggravated assault, or a sizable white-collar crime. It denies equal treatment by ignoring the underlying psychological or situational reasons why people commit large numbers of minor crimes. More importantly, it implies that the offender's interest in living an autonomous life is unimportant, even though 25 years is more than half of a human being's best years and lengthy imprisonment obliterates most ex-prisoners' prospects for a good life.

Other countries' legal systems take human dignity seriously in relation to punishment, as Yale historian James Whitman demonstrated in 2004 and again in 2016. The German constitution declares dignity to be a fundamental principle that governs all applications of law. The German Constitutional Court, for example, has forbidden many prison practices that are commonplace in the United States as violations of human dignity. In *lebenslange Freiheitsstrafe*, 21 June 1977, 45 BverfGE 187, it declared life without parole sentences unconstitutional in part because they are incompatible with human dignity: no human being should be denied the possibility of hope for a better future life. Other European courts have reached the same conclusion in interpreting their national laws. Similar ideas underlie the shorter maximum prison sentences—often 12 or 14 years for any offense or set of offenses other than murder, and much shorter for most offenses—authorized in continental European than in Anglo-Saxon legal systems, as Dirk Van Zyl Smit and Sonja Snacken showed in 2009. Similar ideas underlie the ad hoc rationalizations— crushing sentences, mercy—that, as chapter 5 shows, are offered in other countries to explain the bulk discounts received by people convicted of multiple offenses.

Second, the multiple values the practice of punishment implicates are not simply alternatives from which judges may pick and choose; all set independent limits. American criminal codes usually provide that the purposes of the criminal law, punishment, or sentencing include at least imposition of deserved punishment, deterrence, incapacitation, and rehabilitation. Those lists serve as buffets from which judges may choose and provide no criteria for making the choices. Matt Matravers in 2019 proposed something like a buffet when he called for a "plural" rather than a "mixed" account of punishment in which censure and deterrence are independent governing principles: "The results may well be counter-intuitive (one might end up threatening more severe hard treatment for less serious, but harder to detect, crimes than for more serious, more easily detected, crimes)," but, he observes, "it is not inconsistent so long as censure and deterrence are independent."

This is not very different from Henry M. Hart's classic refutation in 1958 of the *Model Penal Code*'s primarily rehabilitative purposes.[14] He observed that deterrence, rehabilitation, incapacitation, norm reinforcement, satisfaction of the "community's sense of just retribution," and "even socialized vengeance" all have roles to play and that judges and parole boards must take account of them case by case as they are pertinent. Note, however, a fundamental contextual difference. Matravers wrote at a time when retributivism has long been widely seen as relevant, including by him, as a principled justification for punishment. When Henry Hart wrote 60 years earlier, indeterminate sentencing and consequentialist approaches were unchallenged. Retribution was germane for Henry Hart not as a general guiding principle but only sometimes, usually in connection with sensational cases, as acknowledgment of public opinion.

Matravers's example of serious crimes punished less severely than lesser ones and Henry Hart's elaboration illustrate and underlay the core problems of indeterminate sentencing that retributive theorists in the 1970s sought to redress. Punishing lesser crimes more harshly than greater ones defies common morality and undermines basic social norms. Conferring authority on individual judges to choose among and apply irreconcilable purposes assures outcomes based more on differences in judicial idiosyncrasies, personalities, and ideologies than on differences among offenses and offenders. Broad discretions are especially susceptible to influence by conscious racial and class bias, negative stereotypes, and unconscious or implicit bias.

Third, a comprehensive jurisprudence of just punishment that respects human dignity would require individualized, subjective assessments of offenders' blameworthiness. American philosopher David Luban observed in 2007 that subjectivity lies at the heart of human dignity: "Having human dignity means having a story of one's own.... Human beings have ontological heft because each of us is an 'I,' and I have ontological heft. For others to treat me as though I have none fundamentally denigrates my status in the world. It amounts to a form of humiliation that violates my human dignity."

---

14. Both Matravers and Henry Hart explicitly refer to the purposes of the criminal law rather than of punishment, but appear to subsume punishment's within the criminal law's purposes. H. L. A. Hart (1968), by contrast, distinguishes between the—for him, preventative—purposes of the criminal law and the general justification of punishment.

William James in *The Varieties of Religious Experience* (1902) offered a similar, more general, metaphorical observation about the need to take individuals seriously: "Any object that is infinitely important to us and awakens our devotion feels to us also as if it must be *sui generis* and unique. Probably a crab would be filled with a sense of outrage if it could hear us classify it without ado or apology as a crustacean, and thus dispose of it. 'I am no such thing,' it would say; 'I am MYSELF, MYSELF alone.'"

Plutarch quotes the fourth-century B.C.E. philosopher Bion of Borysthenes, who observed of boys playing by a stream on a summer day, "Though boys throw stones at frogs in sport, yet the frogs do not die in sport but in earnest." What happens in punishment happens to the person punished. The frog's perspective, Luban's subjective perspective, cannot justly be ignored. A just sentencing system must harness the tension between the requirement of fairness that there be general standards that apply to all and the requirement of justice that all ethically important grounds for distinguishing between individuals be taken into account.

A comprehensive jurisprudence of just punishment would consist of principles of proportionality, fairness, equal treatment, and parsimony. Blameworthiness and proportionality play central roles. No sentencing system could be said to be just unless it set rigid upper limits, keyed to blameworthiness, on the severity of punishment and unless values of fairness, equal treatment, and parsimony are respected.

Human dignity underlies the case for fairness, which largely concerns process, the case for parsimony, which requires avoidance of gratuitous harm, and the case for treatment as an equal, which requires consideration of an offender's circumstances and situation. This jurisprudence of just punishment allows judges to make individualized assessments of blameworthiness, and insists that gratuitous harm not be done. It recognizes the complexity and myriad differing circumstances of human lives. It cannot resolve fundamental issues of social and racial injustice but empowers judges to make individualized assessments of offenders' particular circumstances and blameworthiness within the constraints set by the other principles.

The proposed jurisprudence provides solutions to the multiple offense paradox. The bulk discount is morally necessary. Without it, punishments would be so severe that they would be incompatible with human dignity and so mechanical that they would fail to treat offenders and their interests with equal respect and concern. Every human being has but one life to live, lives it within particular circumstances, and makes countless mistakes. To ignore that is to ignore that we are human.

The recidivist premium to the contrary is morally unjustifiable. If the potential aggregate severity of sentences for multiple current convictions calls for imposition of something much less, for mercy or avoidance of crushing sentences, the burdens of recidivist premiums call out even more loudly. Depriving individuals of a large part of their remaining lives is as wrong when it is done piecemeal as when it is done at one time. Other objections to the recidivist premium are familiar ones. Imposition of increments of additional punishment because of earlier convictions is double counting, effectively punishing offenders a second time for their prior offenses. Punishing a subsequent offense more severely than an otherwise comparable first offender is punished for the same offense breaks the link between blameworthiness and deserved punishment.

The proposed jurisprudence of just punishment provides a firm foundation for operation of the parsimony principle. Indiana University philosopher Richard Lippke in 2017 argued that "parsimony" is redundant, an empty concept, because both retributive and utilitarian theories explicitly reject punishment more severe than is theoretically justifiable. Parsimony is better understood, however, as deriving not from punishment principles but from respect for human dignity. Bentham was adamant that punishments that serve no purpose are morally intolerable.

Bentham's view was bedded within utilitarianism. It is better viewed as coming from outside as Australian criminologist John Braithwaite and Oxford philosopher Philip Pettit do when they describe "dominion," the capacity to live a life of one's choosing, as the value most at stake in thinking about both crime and punishment.

The requirement that all people be treated with equal respect and concern can help address the problem of "just deserts in an unjust society." Punishments of people living fundamentally disadvantaged lives, or who are powerfully affected by mental disabilities or acute problems of drug dependence, should be determined in terms of the choices and possibilities available to them and not on the false premise that the hard realities of their lives are different than they are, or do not matter.

There is one important problem, however, that the proposed jurisprudence cannot solve: determination of ordinally deserved punishments or of the anchoring points of penalty scales that are necessary for any system of ordinally proportionate punishments to work. Those judgments depend on cultural attitudes toward crime, criminals, and punishment that vary widely and that no mechanical or theoretical fix can resolve. Palpable differences between places exist in such matters: think only of contrasts in punishment severity and imprisonment rates between the United States and Scandinavia or between Maine and Mississippi. Gaining general acceptance of ideas that no one should be punished more severely than he or she deserves, and that more serious crimes normally should be punished more severely than lesser ones, is a more achievable goal, and an important step in the right direction.

The issues discussed in the preceding paragraphs require fuller exploration and elaboration. I discuss them in greater detail in other chapters. The important thing to recognize, however, is that they raise problems that retributive punishment theories now in use cannot adequately address by themselves but that a normative framework incorporating principles of proportionality, fairness, equal treatment, and parsimony can.

Moving toward a comprehensive jurisprudence of just punishment will require partial abandonment or substantial amplification of most retributive and mixed theories of punishment. This change may not be as unlikely as some may believe. It will require a paradigm shift, which Thomas Kuhn in 1962 demonstrated seldom happens in the physical sciences until prevailing ways of thinking change enough to be able to absorb unfamiliar, seemingly heretical ideas. However, that is what happened when retributive punishment theories replaced consequentialist ones in the minds of most policymakers, philosophers, and lawyers in the 1970s. Robert Nozick in 1981 in *Philosophical Explanations* explained how such things happen:

> When a philosopher sees that premisses he accepts logically imply a conclusion he has rejected until now, he faces a choice: he may accept this conclusion or reject one of the previously accepted premisses. . . . His choice will depend on which is greater, the degree of his commitment to the various premisses or the degree of his commitment to denying the conclusion. It is implausible that these are independent of how strongly he wants certain things to be true. The various means of control over conclusions explain why so few philosophers publish ones that (continue to) upset them.

It is time for proponents of retributive and mixed theories of punishment to adopt new "premisses" of proportionality, fairness, equal treatment, and parsimony.

3

Proportionality

AT THE HEART of all retributive theories is the idea that punishments should be proportionate to the seriousness of the crimes for which they are imposed. That idea's influence, however, is waning; it is beset by challenges. Some are theoretical or conceptual and mostly of interest to scholars. Others involve trade-offs between seemingly conflicting aims to punish individuals justly and prevent crime effectively. In earlier times, disagreements centered on imposition of otherwise unwarranted prison sentences in order to rehabilitate offenders and imposition of anomalously severe punishments in order to evidence judges' determination to suppress acute crime problems.[1] In our time, incapacitation is the hot topic. Some offenders who have committed minor crimes, and on proportionality reasoning deserve modest punishments, for example, may rightly or wrongly be considered especially dangerous, and be candidates for preventive detention. The most discussed trade-offs concern use of predictions of dangerousness as bases for detaining some presumed-to-be-innocent suspects before trial and punishing some convicted persons more severely than they deserve.

The theoretical and policy challenges can be explored in their own terms, and solutions can be sought. The bigger question, though, is whether the challenges are epiphenomenal and portend displacement of retributivism as

---

1. These issues are no longer much written about. Nigel Walker (1969), Norval Morris (1974), and Francis Allen (1981) discussed them at length. No doubt some judges continue to believe both practices make sense; the empirical evidence shows that neither achieves its goals. Imprisonment for rehabilitation fell from fashion with the collapse of support for indeterminate sentencing in the 1970s; a substantial body of research shows in any case that rehabilitative programs are less effective in prison than in the community (e.g., MacKenzie 2006; Petersilia and Rosenfeld 2008). The sizable literature on deterrence shows that ad hoc increases in punishment severity have few if any discernible effects on crime (e.g., Nagin 1998, 2013, 2018).

the most intellectually influential normative framework for thinking about punishment.

Only time will tell. My best guess is that the challenges are more a reflection of changes in prevailing ways of thinking than of sudden realization that retributive ideas offer less practical guidance than was widely understood. If that is right, proportionality theory will become less central and other normative considerations will be given greater weight.

I. Whence Proportionality?

From Immanuel Kant and Georg Wilhelm Friedrich Hegel two centuries ago to Andreas von Hirsch, Paul Robinson, and other positive retributivists in our time, it is axiomatic: punishments must be made as proportionate as is humanly possible if they are to be just. For negative retributivists, for whom the seriousness of crimes sets upper limits on just punishments, anything greater is by definition unjust. Many nonretributivists such as H. L. A. Hart also think proportionality important, although for different reasons. In 1968 he observed, "The guiding principle is that of a proportion within a system of penalties between those imposed for different offences where these have a distinct place in a commonsense scale of gravity." Hart's argument was not that proportionate punishment is in itself conceptually essential but that most people intuitively believe it to be important; failure to respect that intuition risks undermining the criminal law's legitimacy in citizens' eyes, and with that risks weakening its influence on their behavior and beliefs.

Retributivist writers offer diverse explanations for why proportionality matters. Kant and Hegel regarded it as an a priori moral imperative. Human beings are rational actors capable of making moral choices; punishing offenders in proportion to their wrongdoing acknowledges that capacity and expresses respect for their humanity. Doing anything else is to treat people as if they are animals. Hegel, for example, insisted that the offender be treated "as a rational being. He is denied this honour if the concept and criterion of his punishment are not derived from his own act; and he is also denied it if he is regarded simply as a harmful animal which must be rendered harmless, or punished with a view to deterring or reforming him" (p. 126).

Some contemporary philosophers, such as Michael Moore in 1993, invoked the widely shared moral intuition that wrongdoers deserve to be punished. John Kleinig in 1973 and Douglas Husak in 1987 argued that punishment for blameworthy behavior is "fitting" in much the same way as commendation is due for praiseworthy behavior. Many American philosophers in the 1960s and 1970s, including Jeffrie Murphy, Herbert Morris, and Andreas von Hirsch, justified the proportionality principle on the basis of what were variously described as benefits and burdens, equilibrium, and social contract theories. The shared gravamen was that offenders enjoy the benefits of living in a secure, ordered society but selfishly reject the burdens of law-abidingness. Proportionate punishments assure that illicit gains, satisfactions, or unfair benefits are disgorged and equilibrium is restored. Another group of writers including Antony Duff, Joel Feinberg, Jean Hampton, Herbert Morris, and Andreas von Hirsch focused on retributive punishment's communicative properties. These include condemnation of wrongdoing, affirmation of crime's wrongfulness, acknowledgment of victims' losses or suffering, and facilitation of offenders' reattachment to good values. Some writers' names appear in more than one list. That is because some analyses that seemed promising in the early years of retributivism's revival were soon abandoned. Few people long remained satisfied by a priori Kantian and Hegelian reasoning or by the proposition that offenders' illicit gains, satisfactions, or unfair benefits adequately express the essential wrongfulness of many crimes including rapes and other serious violence.

Interest in retributive theory revived in English-speaking countries in the 1970s. For at least a century before that, ideas about the rehabilitative and incapacitative effects of punishment were overwhelmingly influential. Few people, as I demonstrated in chapter 2 with quotations from Sheldon Glueck, Jerome Michael, and Herbert Wechsler, took retributivism seriously.

Jerome Michael and University of Chicago philosophy professor Mortimer Adler, in *Crime, Law, and Social Science* (1933), encapsulated prevailing ways of thought before the 1970s: the "criminal law provides for the official treatment of criminals. . . . [T]he consequences [of conviction] take the form of sentences to the various modes of treatment." They discuss two "incompatible" theories of punishment: the "punitive" (retributive) and the "non-punitive" (consequentialist). They conclude that "the punitive theory is a fallacious analysis and that the non-punitive theory is correct. . . . The infliction of pain is never justified merely on the ground that it visits retributive punishment upon the offender. Punitive retribution is never justifiable in itself."

The eclipse of utilitarianism and revival of retributivism appeared to be sudden. In retrospect, they were not. Roots of change were evident much earlier. C. S. Lewis, in a 1949 article, "The Humanitarian Theory of Punishment," offered a searing critique of rehabilitative justifications of punishment and urged their replacement by the "traditional or Retributive theory." Anthony

Burgess's dystopian 1962 novel *A Clockwork Orange* about the use of aversive conditioning to restrain violent impulses offered, he wrote in 1986, "a moral lesson, and it is the weary traditional one of the fundamental importance of moral choice." Legal scholars, most trenchantly Francis Allen in 1959 and Kenneth Culp Davis in 1969, decried dangers and abuses of indeterminate sentencing, its broad discretions, and its rehabilitative presuppositions.

Philosophers chimed in. John Rawls in a celebrated 1955 article, "Two Theories of Rules," and his student Edmund Pincoffs in 1966 in *The Rationale of Legal Punishment*, argued that consequentialism is fine for legislators, but judges should pay attention to blameworthiness. And, far from least, H. L. A. Hart's 1959 presidential address to Britain's Aristotelian Society, setting out an analytical framework that could accommodate both utilitarian and retributivist ideas, argued that proportionality and equal treatment have roles to play even in utilitarian accounts of punishment.

In this chapter, I mostly discuss the fundamental challenges proportionality theory faces. I continue in section II by discussing current disquiet. In section III, I say more about proportionality theory's origins including Kant's and Hegel's recognition of important limitations. Section IV discusses problems proportionality theory cannot satisfactorily address, especially in relation to scaling and linking offense seriousness and punishment severity. If these problems cannot be solved, punishments can at best be said to be roughly or approximately proportionate, which fatally undermines the plausibility of positive retributivism. Section V suggests ways to ameliorate current problems and anticipate future ones should a paradigm shift be underway.

There are two big questions. First, can proportionality theory provide satisfactory answers to core conceptual questions about crime seriousness, punishment severity, and links between them? Alas, it cannot.[2] Second, should it be consigned to the dustbin of history? The answer here is more positive. Proportionality theory by itself is not enough. Combined with values of fairness, equal treatment, and parsimony, however, it provides a powerful normative framework for thinking about and establishing just punishment practices and policies.

That retributive considerations by themselves cannot provide adequate guidance for thinking about so complex and multifaceted a phenomenon as punishment should not be surprising. It is odd that anyone ever thought

---

2. Nor, as chapter 5 explains, can it provide meaningful guidance for thinking about punishment of that large majority of offenders who are convicted of more than one offense, or who have previously been convicted, or both.

that they could. The English political philosopher Isaiah Berlin in 1958 in "Two Concepts of Liberty," his inaugural lecture as Chichele Professor of Social and Political Philosophy at Oxford, published in 1959, showed that the implications of equally valid first principles often conflict. No one disagrees that maintenance of public order and conditions of security that allow citizens to live lives of their choosing is important, but its pursuit will always be in tension with other equally or more important goals. The theorist's job is to show how they can justly be reconciled. The policymaker's and practitioner's jobs are to do it.

II. Disquiet

Writers on punishment routinely describe proportionality as a fundamental requirement of justice. Rutgers University philosopher Douglas Husak, long one of America's leading criminal law theorists, in a 2020 article observed: "Sentencing according to the principle of proportionality is crucial if the state is to treat offenders as they deserve." The term has served for a half-century as a metonym for retributive ways of thinking, as shorthand for the proposition that punishments should be based on, or limited by, offenders' blameworthiness, rather than on their rehabilitative prospects or reoffending probabilities, other putative effects of what is done to them, or consonance with public demands for vengeance.

Recent developments call the salience of proportionality theory into question. Policymakers in common-law countries seem unmoved by the proposition that justice forbids imposition of disproportionately severe punishments.[3] To a lesser extent but perceptibly, something similar is happening in Scandinavia. The *Criminal Justice Act* 2003 in England and Wales created a presumption favoring imposition of indeterminate prison sentences on people convicted of any of 153 offenses, some, such as having carnal knowledge of a sheep, not of self-evidently enormous gravity. The recent Canadian Conservative government of Stephen Harper enacted a slew of severe mandatory minimum sentencing laws. Recent Australian governments have enacted a plethora of laws limiting parole release eligibility to achieve comparable ends. Innumerable three-strikes, mandatory minimum sentence, and similar laws in the United States mandate longer prison terms for some affected crimes than are routinely imposed for palpably more serious wrongdoing. In

---

3. Detailed documentation can be found in Ashworth and Roberts (2016: England and Wales); Doob and Webster (2016: Canada); Freiberg (2016: Australia); Tonry (2016a: United States).

Scandinavia, University of Helsinki professor Tapio Lappi-Seppälä observed in 2020, "Informed and principled argument about the penal value of different offense types has been replaced by references to the demands of the general sense of justice," as evidenced by the media and public opinion, especially concerning violent and sexual crimes.

No doubt influenced by these and related developments, and the belief that they respond to, or are reconcilable with, public preferences, scholars have begun to question the usefulness of the principle of proportionality. Nicola Lacey and Hanna Pickard, for example, referring to "powerful emotional dynamics" of populist crime politics, in 2015 asked whether "appeals to proportionality are little more than empty rhetoric." Douglas Husak in a 2019 article, ceding ground to crime control politics, endorsed subordination of concerns for proportionality and equal treatment to efforts to prevent crime by means of incapacitative use of risk predictions: "Retributivists should preserve the role of desert while weakening its strength. . . . If we have good reason to inflict different amounts of punishment on two offenders who have committed equally serious crimes, we should not be worried that our decision does not preserve proportionality."

Setting real-world concerns aside, other philosophers doubt that retributive proportionality theory can convincingly answer fundamental questions. "Make the punishment fit the crime," anyone can glibly say. That is easier to say than to do. Little conceptual attention has been paid to "metrics" of crime seriousness or punishment severity. Without them we have no basis for explaining why one crime is more serious than another, for example why armed robbery is more or less serious than acquaintance rape, or why one punishment is more severe than another. Without those explanations, it is impossible, except on the basis of intuition—which varies widely between individuals—and policy decisions, often influenced by political self-interest, public emotion, and media coverage, to say why any particular offense deserves any particular punishment. Danish philosopher Jesper Ryberg, in a 2020 essay, "Proportionality and the Seriousness of Crimes," observed that proportionality theory's inability to deal satisfactorily with scaling of crime seriousness calls it into question "as the plausible principle of penal distribution." Swedish philosopher Göran Duus-Otterström in 2020 described insoluble problems in scaling punishment severities and cautioned, "Such are the difficulties . . . that critics of retributivism must be forgiven for thinking that the problem is insuperable." British philosopher Matt Matravers, in a 2020 essay, "The Place of Proportionality in Penal Theory," wrote, "The problems of determining metrics for crime seriousness and sentence severity, and of fixing the scales of punishment . . . pose a serious challenge to the principle of proportionality."

Here is the bottom line. Neither retributive theories in general nor "the principle of proportionality" can satisfactorily explain how much punishment ("hard treatment" in the disciplinary argot) should be imposed for a particular crime or how much and what kinds of suffering any particular offender deserves to endure.

Proportionality theory does, however, support two less comprehensive injunctions that, I believe, most people—citizens, scholars, and practitioners alike—accept. First, no one should be punished more severely than he or she deserves.[4] Second, all else being equal, people who commit more serious crimes should be punished more severely than people who commit less serious ones, and vice versa. Converting that agreement into real-world policies and practices, however, is not easy.

Prevailing ways of thinking do not take shape in vacuums. Even assuming, as research by the English criminologist Julian Roberts, Americans John Darley and Paul Robinson, and many others has repeatedly shown, that most people believe offenders should be punished as much as, or no more than, they deserve, how crimes are ranked by seriousness, and punishments by severity, depends on prevailing attitudes, beliefs, and practices. Lacey and Pickard illustrate that these vary substantially by comparing punishment practices in Scandinavian countries, among the developed world's least severe, and in the United States, by a wide margin, the most. Comparisons of contemporary practices in Massachusetts (120 state prisoners per 100,000 population in 2017) and Maine (134) with those in Oklahoma (704) and Louisiana (719) provide a comparable American demonstration. So over time does comparison of American prison sentence lengths in the 1970s and the 2010s.[5]

---

4. Much apparent agreement is, alas, likely to be knee-jerk and unconsidered. Endorsing positive abstract principles—fairness, equality, mercy, proportionality—is easy, and comforting to the endorser's self-image. The proportionality principle, however, is inherently comparative: whether a particular punishment can reasonably be said to be just requires comparisons with punishments of others for similar and different crimes. The slip is between comparative and one-off casuistic reasoning. Probably few people urge especially severe punishments in individual cases, or judges justify them, on the basis that "X should be punished more than he deserves because . . ." Much more common are decontextualized, noncomparative statements; whatever X received was deserved because of the seriousness of his crime, antisocial personality, fecklessness, "dangerousness," or past criminality.

5. Mean times served by people released for the first time from state prisons in 1980 were 63 months for murder, 33 months for rape, and 25 months for robbery (Cahalan 1986, Table 3.25). By the 2000s, those numbers more than doubled: in 2009, murder averaged 158 months; rape, 92 months; and robbery, 53 months (Bureau of Justice Statistics 2011). These

The two injunctions provide contours for a just punishment system but provide no substantive guidance for specifying upper limits on deserved punishments or what crimes are more serious than others and by how much. Those specifications inevitably vary with prevailing beliefs, but once made provide bases for saying that particular punishments are too severe.

Achievement of general acceptance of the two injunctions is not an unworldly aspiration even if in our time their invocation is mostly rhetorical. Conventional beliefs change, even concerning contentious and emotional topics. Some American southerners before the Civil War and during the Jim Crow period opposed racial inequality on moral grounds. Theirs eventually became the prevailing view. Early feminists and sympathizers, notably including Mary Wollstonecraft in *A Vindication of the Rights of Women* (1792) and John Stuart Mill in *The Subjection of Women* (1869), argued, again against the odds, that subordination of women is wrong. That became the prevailing view. Consensual homosexual behavior remained a criminal offense in England until 1967 and in some American states until 2003. That is unimaginable now. Other countries' criminal law systems, for example in the Scandinavian countries, are committed to ideas of proportionality as an upper limit on deserved punishment and of equal treatment of comparably situated offenders. Someday that may be true in the United States. Even if a paradigm shift in thinking about punishment is underway, the two injunctions will have roles to play.

III. Origins

Few people disagree with the Mikado's declaration that the punishment should fit the crime. It is not easy to explain what that means or to know when it happens. Punishments can meaningfully be said to be proportionate only if we can explain why some crimes are more serious than others, why some punishments are more severe than others, and how specific crimes should be linked to particular punishments. The contemporary literature has comparatively little to say about any of these matters. Kant and Hegel discussed them centuries ago.

---

numbers understate actual times served; prisoners released in any year overrepresent people serving short sentences and underrepresent people serving long ones. Because many more people in recent years are serving sentences of life, life without parole, and mandatory minimum terms measured in decades, the underestimates were greater in 2009.

For nearly a half-century, most writers on punishment theory have described themselves as retributivists of one sort or another and described the principle of proportionality as a requirement of justice. Details vary, but all retributivists agree that the seriousness of the crime should be the sole or a primary determinant of punishment's severity. UCLA philosopher Herbert Morris, for example, in a classic 1981 article, referred in passing to "principles that are familiar dictates of retributivism—that only the guilty may be punished, that the guilty must be, and that the punishment inflicted reflect the degree of guilt."

Conceptualizations of "degrees of guilt" differ. Kant referred to offenders' "inner wickedness." Andreas von Hirsch in *Doing Justice* (1976) famously wrote of their "just deserts." Others refer to blameworthiness, wrongfulness, or moral culpability. All of these terms encompass the nature and gravity of the criminal behavior and the offender's mental state and awareness at the time.

In this chapter I usually refer to blameworthiness, by which I mean something akin to Morris's degrees of guilt or Kant's inner wickedness. I assume that offenders should be punished for harms they intended or foresaw. Foresight encompasses harms the offender knew or expected would happen. Reasonable people might differ on whether recklessness as defined in the 1962 *Model Penal Code* ("conscious disregard" of a "substantial and unjustifiable risk") counts as foresight. For sure, if the offender knew the risk was substantial and unjustifiable; otherwise, not.

Mine is not the mainstream view.[6] English philosopher Matt Matravers in a 2019 essay, "Rootless Desert and Unanchored Censure," observed that crime seriousness "is usually taken to be a composite of harmfulness (or endangerment, as not all crimes lead to actual harm) and culpability." In the mainstream view, he writes, harm "is equated with the actual harm done or

---

6. I am not alone: e.g., Alexander and Ferzan (2018). Many philosophers, however, accept the legitimacy of the emotional intuition that consequences matter. Thomas Nagel (1979) offers examples to show that we blame ourselves and others do also when harms occur that are caus ally related to our behavior (e.g., the minor auto repair not made that causes an accident). From this, he concludes that people may fairly be deemed more blameworthy when harm results than when it doesn't. Jeremy Waldron (2008) and David Enoch (2008) deconstruct legal treatments of moral luck in far more detail, distinguishing among moral, legal, and plain luck, but like Nagel accept as morally germane the widely held intuition that resulting harms matter. The critical question, though, is not whether people should or do feel guilty when their actions cause harm, or should be held civilly liable for the costs of those harms, but whether they should serve as the bases for authoritative moral censure, conviction, and punishment.

threatened and 'culpability' is a matter of the blameworthiness of the agent (for example, whether he acted intentionally or only recklessly)."

The key phrase is "the actual harm done" which sometimes may not have been intended, foreseen, or even foreseeable by the offender or anyone else. A trivial example is the pickpocket who intends the minor misdemeanor of stealing pocket change from a person of seemingly modest means but whose hand emerges holding a $20,000 Rolex watch; in most legal systems, that is a serious felony. A decidedly nontrivial example is the mugger who steals a woman's purse and pushes her aside to get away. If she falls and hits her head on the sidewalk or is otherwise seriously hurt, the harm could be substantial. If she falls and has a miscarriage, the actual harm done can be prosecuted as a homicide in many American states. The loss of the fetus is a calamity and a tragedy, but would almost never have been something the assailant sought, foresaw, or consciously risked. In neither hypothetical is there any doubt that the offender's behavior proximately caused the harms. Punishing the offender for them, however, makes him or her strictly liable and erases the distinction between crimes and torts. This is odd; criminal laws in Western countries almost never allow strict liability to serve as a basis for convicting people of crimes punishable by prison sentences. The self-evident reason is that it is unjust to impose severe punishments on people who are neither "wicked" nor morally blameworthy.

Tort law is different. Negligent, reckless, and intending actors are liable for harms they cause. They take their victims as they find them, including, for example, the assault victim who has a "glass jaw," or for other reasons experiences greater than normally foreseeable suffering or loss. There, however, the issue is only who should bear consequential and incidental costs. Likewise for victim compensation and social insurance schemes. Their aims are to provide assistance and support to victims to help them get on with their lives. The offender's mental state and awareness or nonawareness of risk are irrelevant to deciding what assistance and support are needed.

Kant to my knowledge did not discuss serendipitous harm.[7] However, he insisted that punishment be calibrated to the seriousness of the offense:

---

7. Thomas Nagel (1979, n. 22 [p. 60]) uncontroversially observes that for Kant a good will, even if ineffectual in achieving good things, "would sparkle like a jewel in its own right" and from that infers, "He would presumably have said the same thing about a bad will: whether it accomplishes its evil purposes is morally irrelevant." That implies that Kant would have approved neither of punishment of people whose purposes were not evil nor of punishments more severe than their evil purposes warrant.

But what kind and what amount of punishment is it that public justice makes its principle and measure? None other than the principle of equality (in the position of the needle on the scale of justice), to incline no more to one side than to the other. Accordingly, whatever undeserved evil you inflict upon another within the people, that you [deserve] . . . But only the *law of retribution (jus talionis)* . . . can specify definitely the quality and the quantity of punishment. (p. 115)

Analysts, however, have seldom delved into the questions of what makes one "undeserved evil" worse than another, how "the quality and the quantity" of punishment required by "the principle of equality" are to be determined, and how crime seriousness and punishment severity should relate to one another.

Kant recognized that the answers are not obvious. Much of his discussion concerns homicide and other grave crimes for which he believed death was inexorably called for. He acknowledged that application of the principle of equality is more difficult for lesser crimes. In those cases, the offender deserves "what he has perpetrated on others, if not in terms of its letter at least in terms of its spirit" (p. 140). Kant also observed that the nature and severity of deserved punishments should sometimes take account of offenders' personal circumstances, particularly class distinctions, which makes the link between crime and punishment even less certain.[8] This at least raises the question whether punishment severity should be understood objectively, or subjectively in terms of individualized effects on particular people.

Hegel's conception of the measure of deserved punishment closely resembles Kant's: "What the criminal has done should also happen to him." However, he acknowledged that, save for crimes deservedly punishable by death, relations between crimes and punishments cannot be mechanical:

An insuperable difficulty arises. . . . It is very easy to portray the retributive aspect of punishment as an absurdity (theft as retribution for theft, robbery for robbery, an eye for an eye, and a tooth for a tooth, so that

---

8. Kant ([1797] 2017) expressed particular concern that "the existence of class distinctions would not allow for [application of] the retributive principle" and proposed harsher punishments for privileged offenders. Thus, "someone of high standing given to violence could be condemned not only to apologize for striking an innocent person socially inferior to himself [the usual sanction], but also to undergo a solitary confinement involving hardship; in addition to the discomfort he undergoes, the offender's vanity would be painfully affected, so that through his shame like would be fittingly repaid with like" (p. 115).

one can even imagine the miscreant as one-eyed or toothless); but the concept has nothing to do with this absurdity. (pp. 127–28)

Instead, he wrote, "Thought cannot specify how each crime should be punished; positive determinations are necessary for this purpose." Cultural norms change: "With the progress of education, however, attitudes toward crime become more lenient, and punishments today are not nearly so harsh as they were a hundred years ago. It is not the crimes or punishments themselves which change, but the relation between the two" (p. 123).

Kant published only a few pages on punishment; Hegel several times more but still not many. They were writing in detail about a subject that, except for people such as Jeremy Bentham and Cesare Beccaria who rejected their retributive premises, had previously been discussed only in broad generalizations.

Kant and Hegel were positivist retributivists who believed that deserved punishments not only may but must be imposed and that anything greater, or less, is per se unjust. Hegel was explicit: "An injustice is done if there is even one lash too many, or one dollar or groschen, one week or one day in prison too many or too few" (p. 245). Negative retributivists such as Norval Morris relax both the horizontal and the vertical proportionality requirements but insist that any punishment more severe than positive retributivism would allow is per se unjust.

IV. Fundamental Proportionality Questions

Efforts have been made to answer the three questions raised by the first passage I quoted from Kant. There are no satisfactory answers. Kant and Hegel were right: the best we can do is make "positive determinations" about punishment that take account of the "spirit" of proportionality.

A. Crime Seriousness

Efforts to specify the relative seriousness of crimes founder on three problems. First, there is no conventional or widely accepted metric of seriousness. Second, the competing realities problem: victims' and offenders' conceptions and experiences of a single crime are sometimes very different. Third, the moral luck problem—that crimes may cause an intended harm or a lesser or greater one—often breaks the link between blameworthiness and harm.

1. *The Missing Metric.* We lack any widely agreed measure or metric of what makes one category of crime, or one particular crime, more or less serious

than another. In other domains, metrics are common. The Richter scale measures the strength of earthquakes. The Saffir-Simpson scale measures hurricane force. The metric, imperial, and United States customary unit systems measure lengths, weights, and volumes. Likewise in many realms of day-to-day life. Acuteness of medical need determines emergency ward priorities. Once an hourly pay rate is set, we know exactly what is due to people who work 17 or 37 hours. Nothing even vaguely comparable exists for crime.

No big deal, some might say. There is no need for a highfalutin metric. Everyone knows when one crime is more serious than another; intuitions are widely shared. Associate US Supreme Court Justice Potter Stewart in *Jacobellis v. Ohio*, 378 U.S. 184, 197 (1964), analogously explained that it would be difficult to define hard-core pornography, but it isn't necessary: "I know it when I see it." He was mocked. A half-century later, his observation is regularly trotted out, as here, to illustrate the limits and elusiveness of personal intuitions.

Widely shared intuitions about offense seriousness exist only at the extremes. Almost everyone agrees that robbery and rape are more serious than shoplifting, bicycle theft, or sale of marijuana. Agreement is harder to reach on whether rape is more serious than robbery or shoplifting than bicycle theft. When offense descriptions become finer-grained—intoxicated acquaintance rape compared with street robbery, or shoplifting by professionals compared with bike thefts by addicts—the widely shared intuitions dissolve. Intuitions are idiosyncratic and vary widely.

There are a number of possible metrics. One is objective: the amount of physical injury or property loss crimes cause in general or in specific cases. This, however, raises formidable problems of assessing, characterizing, scaling, and combining degrees of physical injury. Routine property losses present similar if lesser problems: they can be assessed in terms of the victim's loss, the offender's gain, or the property's market value. Comparisons of property losses—for example, $100 thefts, $10,000 embezzlements, and $10 or 100 million securities frauds—are especially difficult. American law professor Paul Robinson, when he was a member of the US Sentencing Commission, imaginatively albeit unworkably proposed that they be scaled above thresholds by use of square and cube roots. Log linear approaches are likewise imaginable. Offenses such as muggings, robberies, and many burglaries that involve both physical injury and property loss compound the difficulties.

A second possible metric is to use the average or actual costs of victimizations of different crimes, but this raises, among many others, the formidable problem of estimating the monetary costs of physical and psychological injuries. A third possible metric, a bit nebulous, is crimes' effects on victims' capacities to live a satisfying life. A fourth, even more nebulous, is the extent to which crimes invade victims' core interests.

Little work has been done on any of them; on most, almost none. Many economists have carried out aggregate cost-of-crime and cost–benefit studies. Almost all use data collected by Vanderbilt University economist Mark Cohen on damage awards for pain and suffering in private tort actions to estimate the intangible costs of crime.[9] This is inherently arbitrary and unrepresentative; few crimes result in tort actions and those usually involve notorious crimes, sympathetic victims, and deep-pocketed defendants. Table 3.1 shows the severity rankings that emerge from Cohen's analysis; it has been used by countless social scientists to compare the costs and benefits of prevention programs.

Two patterns stand out. Intangible costs, mostly based on estimated pain and suffering, are the primary driver of offense seriousness. Many of the rankings are counterintuitive: robbery, a combination of assault and theft, is less serious than assault alone; drunk driving is more serious than robbery, assault, burglary, and auto theft; arson is more serious than anything except child abuse and rape. Offense scales based on economic analyses inevitably depend on the variables included in the model and how they are estimated. The findings do not provide a credible basis for developing scales of offense seriousness.

Andreas von Hirsch and Nils Jareborg in 1991 proposed a "living standards" metric that takes account of crimes' effects on victims' "means and capabilities" for living a satisfying life. Crimes that significantly impede a victim's ability to support him or herself, or to maintain prior living standards, for example, are more serious than crimes that do not. Theft of an automobile from a wealthy person who owns several imposes lesser burdens than stealing the only car of a family of modest means. Burning down a

---

9. Other methods have been used to calculate the costs of crime, but a 2017 US General Accountability Office survey concluded that "there is no commonly used approach for estimating the costs of crime, and experts face multiple challenges when making estimates" (p. 2). The other most commonly used method investigates people's willingness to pay additional taxes to reduce crime by specified amounts (e.g., Cook and Ludwig 2000). A 2004 study, for example, found that survey respondents said they would be willing to pay an additional $100 to $150 per year to reduce specific violent crimes—such as assault or armed robbery—by 10 percent (Cohen et al. 2004). Dominguez-Rivera and Raphael (2015) provide an especially comprehensive and well-informed overview.

Table 3.1 Crime seriousness, by average economic cost
(1993 constant dollars)

Crime	Lost Productivity	Medical, mental health costs	Social services	Property loss	Quality of life	Total*
Child sexual abuse	2100	6290	1100	0	89,800	99,000
Adult rape, sexual assault	2200	2700	27	100	81,400	87,000
Child physical abuse	3400	3490	2100	26	57,500	67,000
Arson	1750	1118	0	15,500	18,000	37,500
Assault, injury	3100	1567	46	39	19,300	24,000
Robbery, injury	1500	1565	44	1400	13,800	19,000
Drunk driving	2800	1482	0	1600	11,900	18,000
All assault	950	501	16	26	7800	9000
All robbery	950	436	25	750	2300	8000
Motor vehicle theft	45	5	0	3300	300	3700
Burglary	12	5	5	970	300	1400

*Total includes an additional invariably small item, not shown: fire and police services.
Source: Cohen (2005, Table 3.1).

vacation home usually causes less dislocation than burning down a primary residence.[10] If offenders are aware of salient differences between victims, it is at least plausible to say that greater harm was intended or foreseen in one case than another. Sentencing policies often provide, for example, increased penalties for crimes against elderly, infirm, financially dependent, and otherwise vulnerable victims.

That kind of case-level analysis is not, however, what von Hirsch and Jareborg had in mind. They propose that assessments of "standard harms" associated with different crimes be used to develop seriousness

---

10. These examples are taken from a presentation by von Hirsch at the University of Minnesota Law School in 1992.

scales.[11] This may slightly sharpen intuitive analyses, but not by much except for a few types of crime such as sale of marijuana or minor property crimes that are unlikely ever to affect anyone's living standards and thus would seldom warrant other than minor punishments. The living standards analysis offers no insights concerning sexual offenses, serious violence, or major property crimes that are likely to differ from widely shared intuitions.

Standard harms analysis provides a basis for saying that homicide is uniquely serious and that rape is more serious than auto theft, or burglary than shoplifting, but few people would disagree. It would usually call for punishing property crimes involving larger amounts more severely than property crimes involving significantly lesser amounts, but few people would disagree about that either. It provides little basis for deciding whether intoxicated acquaintance rape is more serious than street robbery or burglary than auto theft. Individuals have opinions and beliefs about the harms typically associated with different crimes, but they inevitably vary depending on the idiosyncratically different weights individuals give to different kinds of harm.

All that is left are intuitions of the sort that lead legislators to authorize higher penalties for some crimes than for others, sentencing commissions to rank offense seriousness, and judges to distinguish among individual offenders. Public opinion surveys and laboratory experiments on people's views about the seriousness of crime provide little additional guidance. They find broad agreement across time and space in assessments of the relative gravity of a small number of serious crimes.[12] However, findings do not remotely approach the level of detail needed to develop comprehensive scales of offense seriousness.

2. *Conflicting Realities.* Offense definitions are general, but victims' and offenders' experiences of crimes are specific. To a person with a glass jaw, a barroom assault may cause excruciating pain, life-threatening injury, and permanent disfigurement. The assailant may have intended only insult and minor if any pain or discomfort. To an offender, the measure of the seriousness of a crime is the wrongfulness of what he or she set out to do, foresaw, or consciously risked. The measure of the seriousness of a crime to a victim is what

---

11. Husak (1994) and Ryberg (2004) explore implications and possible methods for incorporating the living standards approach into characterizations of crime seriousness as, in considerably greater detail, does Ryberg (2020).

12. High points, e.g., of a half-century's work: Sellin and Wolfgang (1964); Sebba (1978); Robinson and Darley (2007); Adriaenssen et al. (2018).

happened, and with what consequences. A crime that results in great pain, hospitalization, extended recuperation, or ongoing mental health problems is more serious to a victim than an identical crime without some or all those consequences. Pickpocketing involving pocket change is different than when it involves Rolex watches. Closely comparable crimes may have starkly diverse effects: one victim may simply recall an unpleasant experience; one may suffer continuing anxiety, miss work, and incur sizable counseling bills; one may suffer posttraumatic stress disorder, never recover, and eventually commit suicide. Bystanders mostly see, and care about, the victim's reality. So, often, do prosecutors and judges. Criminal law mens rea doctrine, however, requiring consonance between what offenders sought to do and what happened, usually focuses on the offender's reality.

3. *Moral Luck.* The moral luck problem is that an offender may intend, foresee, or recklessly disregard a specific harm but what happens is always to some degree serendipitous. A would-be assailant may produce no harm at all if an attempt fails and the intended victim was unaware of it; some harm if only lesser, incidental damage results; the intended harm; or a greater one. Criminal law doctrines address some of these problems, but not enough.[13] They embody diverse mixes of utilitarian and retributive considerations and provide standards for convictions, not punishments.

There is no consensus view about serendipitous harm among people who write about moral luck. American philosopher Thomas Nagel in 1979, with English philosopher Bernard Williams in 1981 an instigator of the modern literature, accepts the legitimacy of the emotional intuition that consequences matter. So do other influential philosophers (e.g., Susan Wolf in 2001 and Jeremy Waldron in 2008). However, equally influential writers disagree (e.g., Sanford Kadish in 1994, Joel Feinberg in 1995, Larry Alexander and Kimberly Ferzan in 2018). Some paradigmatic hypotheticals appear to many retributivists to be easy. Few disagree with Oxford University criminal lawyer Andrew Ashworth's 1988 view that an intending murderer who fails only because a gun misfires or because the victim moves at the critical microsecond, is as blameworthy as if he had succeeded. From Bentham onward, however, most common-law jurisdictions and most utilitarians, including the drafters

---

13. Examples: transferred malice doctrine (the shot misses the intended victim but hits someone else); homicide doctrines such as felony murder and equation of intent to commit grievous bodily harm with intention to kill that make assailants criminally responsible for greater than intended harms.

of the *Model Penal Code*, have favored punishing attempts less severely than completed offenses.

Utilitarian views of moral luck are, however, beside the point for purposes of retributive proportionality theory. In principle, retributive views such as Ashworth's concerning unsuccessful completed attempts should be two-edged, as he explained in 1993. Harm and culpability both matter, he wrote, but the only pertinent harm is what was intended, foreseen, or recklessly risked. Serendipitous harms should not be taken into account. If causing less harm than was intended or foreseen should not diminish imputation of blame, causing unintended, unforeseen greater harms should not increase it.

Matravers's mainstream "actual harm caused" view, that crime seriousness is a composite of harmfulness and culpability, offers an ironic "punishment of the innocent" parallel to a standard retributivist critique of utilitarianism. The critique is that utilitarians should approve of punishment of innocent people if that will produce a net decrease in human suffering. H. J. McCloskey's classic 1965 hypothetical involves the rape of a white woman, apparently by a black man, in the American south during the Jim Crow period. A sheriff believes he can prevent racial violence in which many people may be injured or killed if he frames an innocent black man. The question is whether he should do that. Most utilitarians say no, arguing either that only morally blameworthy offenders may be punished[14] or that occasional punishments of the innocent would inevitably be discovered, nullifying any beneficial effects and undermining the criminal law's legitimacy and effectiveness.

Some utilitarians, Anthony Quinton observed in a 1969 essay, contend that knowingly punishing an innocent person when necessary to prevent greater aggregate suffering might be considered not "punishment," but some other kind of state action. Three analogies might be offered to support this view. None succeeds. The first is civil commitment of people determined to be risks to themselves or others. This, however, is prospective not retrospective in focus, does not involve blaming of blameless people, and is premised on good

---

14. H. L. A. Hart (1968) was perplexed that Bentham endorsed the insanity offense on the rationale that insane people cannot be deterred. Hart characterized this as a "non sequitur"; the audience for deterrent punishments is the general population, he wrote, not only mentally disturbed people such as the offender. Hart was a much keener analyst than I could ever be, but he seems to have overlooked that Bentham also endorsed ignorance-of-the-law and intoxication defenses on the rationale that affected offenders could not have known that what they did was a crime. Bentham appears to have anticipated Hart's distinction between the separate questions of who may be punished and how much. The non sequitur disappears if insane offenders are not liable to punishment because they are not blameworthy and can therefore not be convicted.

faith judgments about worrisome disabilities of the individuals affected. The second is the distinction in many European legal systems between "sanctions," which are punishments proportioned to blameworthiness, and preventive "measures," which sometimes but rarely are imposed. Postconviction preventive detention of people believed to be unusually dangerous is the extreme example of a measure. Both sanctions and measures, however, are premised on convictions for blameworthy behavior.[15] Third, and a bit far-fetched, punishment of innocents as a form of crisis intervention might be viewed as "collateral damage" akin to the killing of civilians in warfare. The comparison is its own refutation.

Hart characterized the "not punishment" argument as use of an impermissible "definitional stop" that simply evades the problem. To the person affected, punishment is punishment, whatever its rationale or name. Bion of Borysthenes's observation, which I quoted earlier, "boys throw stones at frogs in sport, yet the frogs do not die in sport but in earnest," is pertinent. The frog's experience is what, anthropomorphically speaking, matters morally.

The parallel argument concerning punishment for serendipitous harm is that increments of increased severity beyond what offenders otherwise deserve are not really "punishments" but something else, perhaps state impositions meant to acknowledge emotional reactions, protect the law's legitimacy, or prevent crime. If Hart is right in ruling out the definitional stop to justify punishing innocent people, and he is, neither retributivists nor anyone else should be able legitimately to offer a similar justification for punishing people for harms they did not intend, foresee, or consciously risk.

Many people appear to believe, however, all else including the offender's blameworthiness being equal, that serendipitous harms make crimes more serious. The victim's bad luck is the offender's. Of a thousand equally blameworthy drunken drivers, 999 may arrive safely home without incident and one be involved in an accident causing injury or death. At him or her the

---

15. Italian historian Michele Pifferi (2012, 2016) provides the fullest account of the origins of the sanctions/measures distinction. Netherlands psychologist Jan De Keijser (2011) and Andreas von Hirsch (2011) examine normative issues relating to the use of measures in detail. The distinction arose early in the twentieth century as Europeans and Americans debated the merits of indeterminate sentencing premised on the view that rehabilitation of most offenders and incapacitation of the incorrigible should be the primary aims of punishment. Americans opted for indeterminate sentencing. Europeans chose to retain a primary emphasis on retributive punishments with measures reserved for offenders believed to present extraordinary risks. As a practical matter, postconviction preventive detention is seldom used (e.g., in Germany: Weigend 2016); and in some countries has been abandoned (e.g., in Scandinavian countries: Lappi-Seppälä 2016).

book is usually thrown and demands for punishment are adamant. Cases involving no harm are a different matter. Public furors seldom occur when unsuccessful attempts are punished less severely than successful ones, or when drunken drivers who get home safely are not charged with attempted homicide. All thousand are guilty of drunken driving, and could appropriately be prosecuted and punished for that offense, but unless the one involved in the accident was otherwise more blameworthy than the rest, he or she should be dealt with in the same way. Doing otherwise is to punish by lottery. Of course, if the drunken driver intentionally or knowingly caused the accident, or consciously risked it, that is a different matter.

I have been unable to find any sustained analysis of other analytical models for characterizing crime seriousness. Other relevant works may exist, of course, but none of the few writings that attempt exhaustively to survey the relevant literature—for example, Victoria Greenfield and Letizia Paoli in 2013 or Jesper Ryberg in a 2020 essay—mentions them. We lack a metric of crime seriousness and face the confounding problems of different realities and moral luck.

B. Punishment Severity

How much hard treatment is due any particular offender? Efforts to develop scales of punishment severity founder on interpersonal comparisons of suffering. In physical sciences, objective scales are easy. Fahrenheit and Celsius scales give different values to a temperature degree, but once specified we know exactly what 17 degrees means. No equivalent system exists or could exist for retributive punishment systems. Physical measurement systems are essentially arbitrary. Once values are set, they can be used. The issues and values punishment raises and implicates are too numerous and complex to be measured by means of arbitrary measures.

Nor do ordinary market mechanisms suffice. Markets set values in many realms of day-to-day life. Diamond prices, controlling for demand, vary in understood ways with carats, colors, and imperfections. Buyers' willingness to pay determines values in wholesale fish markets. Once an hourly pay rate is set, we know exactly what workers are owed. All of these measures are imperfect, of course, and reflect consideration of complex interacting details, but all provide widely accepted indicators of importance or value. None of these, however, offer useful analogies for just systems of punishment because there can in principle be no markets. The question is not what the market will bear but what punishment is just. The two minimum requirements of retributive justice—that no one be punished more severely than he or she deserves and that all else being equal more serious crimes be punished more severely than lesser ones—make it necessary that there be close relations between crimes and punishments.

Market mechanisms cannot achieve that for two reasons. First, punishment processes are not markets; the goal is not a negotiated price but a punishment that is just relative to those received by others for equally, more, and less serious crimes. Second, there are no equivalents in criminal courts to willing sellers and buyers. Prosecutors and defense lawyers can and do negotiate, of course, but the dice are loaded. Prosecutors have always had more power than defenders and can refuse to negotiate or insist on unjustly severe punishments. Mandatory minimum sentence and similar laws have increased their power in our time. Federal Court of Appeals judge Gerald Lynch observed in 2003 that "the prosecutor, rather than a judge or jury, is the central adjudicator of facts (as well as replacing the judge as arbiter . . . of the appropriate sentence to be imposed)." Even were powers balanced, results would depend on negotiators' skills; differences in outcomes in closely comparable cases are inevitable. Those are the reasons why broad-based, anything-goes plea bargaining of the sort the US Supreme Court approved in *Bordenkircher v. Hayes*, U.S. 357 (1978), exists only in the United States.[16]

There is nothing remotely comparable to a Celsius degree or a market rate to indicate whether offenses are scaled correctly or designated punishments are the right ones. The American federal sentencing guidelines grid is illustrative. One axis sets out 43 levels of offense seriousness and specifies for each a range of recommended punishments, mostly prison sentences. The US Sentencing Commission simply assumed that objective durations of confinement are the coin of punishment. Any seemingly objective measure of severity, including years in prison or dollars, however, will have substantially different effects on different people.

There is no widely agreed metric of punishment severity. Financial penalties are illustrative. Fixed amounts burden the poor more than the rich, but so do fines scaled to income and wealth. Taking comparable shares of income, net worth, or both from the poor and the rich makes the poor poorer and leaves the rich richer and better able to replenish what they have lost. Even if—and no existing system of fines, including day fines, does this—all of offenders' assets above what is required for a subsistence

---

16. *Bordenkircher* is discussed in chapter 2 at note 6.

standard of living were taken, rich offenders' social capital makes financial recovery and resumption of previous living standards much easier and
more likely.

Confinement presents comparable problems. A stay in the same prison for
the same period imposes vastly different burdens on a middle-aged breadwinner,
a claustrophobe, a seriously mental ill person, a terminally ill person, a young
gang member for whom prison time is a rite of passage, and a career offender
for whom it is a cost of doing business. The commonest solutions are to ignore
the problem or base punishment severity on the suffering of an average person.
Unusual suffering can then be seen as either a regrettable externality or something the offender, aware of his or her personal vulnerabilities, knowingly risked,
as American philosopher Richard Lippke suggested in 2020. Either view begs
the question.

Social scientists have repeatedly shown for at least a half-century that
common intuitions about punishment severity are often wrong. Most people
probably believe, for example, that imprisonment is inherently more severe
than a community punishment. Scottish criminologist Nigel Walker learned,
however, in talking with inmates in an Oxford prison in the 1960s, that many
preferred a 1- or 2-year prison sentence to a fine. They might have the fine
hanging over them for a long time, be unable to pay it, and wind up in jail
for nonpayment anyway, they said; better just to serve time and put it behind them. Stanford criminologist Joan Petersilia repeatedly in the 1980s and
1990s found that many offenders preferred a short prison term to a period
of intensive probation in the community; the risks of failing a drug test or
breaching a probation condition that would result in revocation were too
high. University of Minnesota law professor Richard Frase showed in 2005
that the single most common reason judges give for sentencing offenders to
prison when Minnesota guidelines do not call for it is that offenders preferred
it, for the same reasons Petersilia's informants gave. *Ranking Correctional
Punishments*, a 2010 book by criminologists David May and Peter Wood,
gives many more examples of studies showing that offenders often prefer imprisonment to a community punishment.

There is no literature to my knowledge on the metric of punishment, or
on how to measure or characterize the suffering of an average person, or a particular individual, while being punished. Retributivists distinguish between
authoritative state censure, condemnation, or blaming that occurs when an
offender is found guilty and the hard treatment that punishment entails.
Communication of censure can be standardized; hard treatment cannot. In
the United States, imprisonment is the hard treatment invariably assumed

for nontrivial crimes by individuals.[17] Whether that is because imprisonment restricts prisoners' mobility, autonomy, or liberty; diminishes their quality of life; reduces their life chances; humiliates them; stigmatizes them; degrades them; causes psychological suffering; or something else is seldom discussed or considered.

Imprisonment does some of those things to all inmates and all of them to some, but that does not make the metric question unimportant. Nor does it make all those effects justifiable. If, for example, restriction of mobility were accepted as the essence of punishment, alternatives to imprisonment such as home detention or confinement in comfortable but secure accommodation in conditions permitting exercise of all privileges of citizenship except mobility would be available. All of the other effects would be unwanted externalities to be avoided or ameliorated. Prophylactic measures might include full-wage employment in confinement or by day release, extensive family including conjugal visits, adequate medical and mental health services, extensive educational, vocational training, and recreational opportunities, and nondisclosure of records of criminal convictions.

This is not as far-fetched as most Americans might imagine. It is at least the aspiration and to varying extents the reality in many Swiss, Dutch, German, and Scandinavian prisons. Federal District Court Judge James E. Doyle in *Morales v. Schmidt*, 340 Fed. Supp. 544 (1972), reasoning that people are sent to prison as punishment, not for punishment, held that prisoners retain all rights of citizenship except those entailed in restriction of mobility. The decision was quickly overturned by a higher court.

Two scant punishment theory literatures nibble at the edges of a punishment metric. One explores ways to substitute other forms of punishment for imprisonment. The other considers whether interpersonal differences in suffering should be taken into account.

1. *Interchangeability of Punishments.* Paul Robinson, Andreas von Hirsch and colleagues, and Norval Morris and I attempted long ago to devise systems for equating periods or amounts of community punishment to periods of imprisonment. None of us succeeded. Andreas von Hirsch, Paul Wasik, and

---

17. The next few paragraphs pertain primarily to the United States and, to a lesser extent, other English-speaking countries in which imprisonment is extensively used and prison terms are often long. In much of Western Europe, most sentences to imprisonment are immediately suspended, only 4 to 20 percent of convicted offenders receive unsuspended prison sentences, the vast majority of prison sentences are for 2 years or less, and day fines, community service, mediation, and electronic monitoring are extensively used as prison alternatives (Aebi et al. 2014; Lappi-Seppälä 2016).

Judith Greene in 1989 proposed a limited system for replacing imprisonment with community punishments, but only when the latter are as burdensome as the putatively equivalent term of imprisonment. That necessarily limits substitution to only the most minor of crimes.

Morris and I in 1990 published a book reporting on our attempt to develop a "punishment units" scheme in which all punishment forms could be expressed. Our aim was to devise a system in which offenders would be sentenced to a specific number of units, say, 120. Each of 1 month's imprisonment, 2 months' probation, 2 weeks' home confinement, a fine of 5 days after-tax income, and 24 hours of unpaid community service might be valued as 10 units. Any punishment or combination of punishments that totaled 120 units would do. Judges would specify the pertinent purposes "at" rather than "of" sentencing. By this we intended that the judge think about, and be required to explain, what he or she hoped to accomplish by imposing that specific sentence on that particular person.

We gave up. The insuperable problem was that in American political and legal culture, then and now, only imprisonment counts. Some state sentencing commissions experimented with punishment units and invariably considered or established equivalences that limited substitution to only the shortest prison sentences. Washington State, for example, made 24 hours' community service equivalent to 1 day of confinement; 240 hours could thus substitute for 10 days' confinement. By contrast, successful community service programs in the United States, England, and Scotland substituted 240 hours service for 6 months' imprisonment. The rationale, as Douglas McDonald explained in 1986, was that anything longer was administratively infeasible. In the end, a bit lamely, Morris and I urged increased use of community punishments that were "roughly equivalent" to imprisonment.

Paul Robinson in various writings between 1987 and 2017 also developed a punishment units scheme. Like von Hirsch, Wasik, and Greene in 1989, he would permit substitution of community punishments for imprisonment only when they were as burdensome as a prison sentence would have been. As a practical matter, this limited his scheme to choices among community punishments or between highly burdensome community punishments and very short prison sentences. Some notion of suffering ordinarily resulting from imprisonment as the generic metric of punishment severity is implicit in Robinson's and von Hirsch, Wasik, and Greene's proposals. Adam Kolber in 2009 appears to have meant something similar when he used the word "distress."

2. *Subjective Measures of Suffering.* Kolber provoked a furor among punishment theorists when in an emperor's-new-clothes argument he insisted that severity of punishment, on any coherent account, should be assessed in relation to the suffering or distress of individual offenders. He made two main claims in a 2009 *Columbia Law Review* article: "First, a successful justification of punishment must take account of offenders' subjective experiences when assessing punishment severity. Second, we have certain obligations to consider actual or anticipated punishment experience at sentencing." A few people agree. It is fair to say, however, that his claims mostly provoked spirited objections.[18]

The objections are peculiar to our time. Only modern retributivists assume that punishment decisions should take no account of individual differences. Kant assumed that punishments should be adjusted to take account of their differing effects on individuals and provided several examples.[19] Bentham insisted that the offender's "sensibilities" be considered ("sensitivities" in our time). That is, the punishment must take account of how it would affect that particular individual. People have different sensitivities and react in different ways to the same experience, including experiences of punishment.[20] Nigel Walker in his 1991 book *Why Punish?* observed that retributive theories of punishment, taken seriously, would require the omniscience of Saint Peter or Islam's Recording Angel to calculate what any flawed human being deserves in light of every detail of his or her existence that relates to assessment of moral blameworthiness relating to the specific crime.[21]

---

18. Agreeing: e.g., Ashworth (1983); Masur, Bronsteen, and Buccafusco (2009); Hayes (2016). Disagreeing, vehemently: e.g., Markel and Flanders (2010); Lippke (2020). Matravers (2020, p. 91) suggests that the issue is a false one: "There is a difference between 'equal treatment' and 'treatment as an equal' (Dworkin 1977, p. 227). Disregarding fundamental differences between individuals that materially affect their experience of a punishment fails to notice this distinction and in subjecting them both to identical (equal) treatment, fails to treat them as equals (that is 'with the same respect and concern')."

19. I provided one example in note 8 to this chapter.

20. Bentham ([1789] 1970) devoted three substantial chapters of *An Introduction to the Principles of Morals and Legislation* to tailoring of punishments to individual characteristics: "Of Circumstances Influencing Sensibility," "Of the Proportion between Punishments and Offences," and "Of the Properties to be Given to a Lot of Punishment."

21. Walker's view—assess this offender's blameworthiness in relation to this crime on the basis of comprehensive knowledge about him and his life—is different from the cosmic whole-life view of desert that W. D. Ross (1930) described. Assessments of offenders' overall moral desert would be based on examination of all of their previous lives to determine whether they have qualities that warrant good or bad things and the extent to which they have already received good things and endured bad ones. Kolber (2020) exhaustively examines Ross's and others' similar analyses.

As with scaling of offense seriousness, so with punishment severity. We lack any commonly agreed metric. Human beings will muddle through. Crimes will be committed and punishments will be imposed, but proportionality theory can provide only the most general guidance on what those punishments should be.

C. Linking Crimes and Punishments

Linking crimes and punishments, even assuming we could scale both in morally convincing ways, founders on cardinal, or absolute, desert. British philosopher Antony Duff in 2001 observed of efforts to specify absolute desert: "There is no Archimedean point, independent of all existing penal practice, from which we could embark on such an enterprise." Joel Feinberg observed in 1965: "There is no rational way of demonstrating that one criminal deserves exactly twice or three-eighths or nine-twelfths as much suffering as another." Hegel declared that "it is impossible to determine by *reason* . . . [what] the just punishment for an offence is" (p. 245; emphasis in original).

Even if as individuals we believe we know, others believe differently. We could vote on a range of possibilities for a particular offense, or average everyone's intuitions, but the result would be an arithmetic amalgam, little more morally compelling than drawing straws. The fallback, as Andreas von Hirsch reiterated in 2017, is to switch to ordinal, or relative, desert, develop broadly supported intuitive scales of offense seriousness and punishment severity, and draw lines between the two: specify the crime and follow the lines. This works mechanically but sidesteps the questions of how severely the most and least serious crimes deserve to be punished and how much more punishment one crime deserves compared with another.

V. Rough Equivalence

Proportionality is at the core of retributive theory but by itself cannot specify the contours of a just punishment system or a just punishment. Utilitarian proportionality in principle can do both. Bentham's rules for determining punishments of individuals for specific crimes are complex, but with perfect knowledge of how deterrence works and of individuals' sensibilities, could in principle indicate uniquely appropriate punishments. Retributive proportionality theory, by contrast, can provide no general or specific guidance until judgments are made about the most severe punishments that may be imposed in general and for specific kinds of crimes. Those judgments vary widely with time and place and reflect diverse historical, cultural, and political influences.

Punishments will not be proportionate in the retributive sense unless policymakers and practitioners want them to be. In recent decades in some English-speaking countries, they have often not much cared. Many, probably most, people in Western countries, however, would say they support the two retributive injunctions that no one be punished more severely than he or she deserves and, all else being equal, that more serious crimes should be punished more severely than less serious ones. Assuming those avowals are substantive, and not merely rhetorical, proportionality theory has roles to play, but subject to conditions.

A. The Top of the Punishment Scale

The first concerns maximum punishments. Limits have to be set, negotiated; there is no place to look for an objective indicator. Andreas von Hirsch and Norval Morris argued about this for decades. Morris argued in 1974 that relatively broad agreement can be reached, in any place and time, about punishments that are too severe and, sometimes, too slight for particular crimes; those limits of "not undeserved punishment" set the boundaries within which a just sentencing system must operate. Von Hirsch in 1976 proposed 5 years' imprisonment as the maximum for all but exceptionally serious crimes, with proportionately lower caps for the less serious. He repeatedly expressed frustration with Morris's view and urged him to be more concrete. They never reached a meeting of the minds. That is not surprising. Von Hirsch is a positive retributivist, committed to proportionality. Morris was at heart a consequentialist who, like H. L. A. Hart, believed that the law must reflect widely shared public attitudes and beliefs if it is to retain its legitimacy.

Nicola Lacey and Hanna Pickard are right; in times and places where broad agreement about punishment severity does not exist, commitment to proportionality will remain mostly rhetorical. That is not true everywhere. In many western and northern European countries, statutory maximum punishments for most crimes are in low single digits (in years) and for the most serious, except sometimes murder, are often 10, 12, or 14 years. Because maximums by definition apply to the most serious crimes, and most crimes are not very serious instances of their kind, much lesser punishments are normally imposed. Low caps and modest proportionate punishments in such places are not likely to be controversial.

The psychological dynamic is different in the United States and England and Wales where maximum statutory punishments for many crimes are expressed in decades or lifetimes and sentences of 10 or more years are common. American sentencing commissions, as Dale Parent and Justice Stephen Breyer separately in 1988 and 1999 showed for the Minnesota and federal guidelines, ducked principled questions when setting sentence lengths. They undertook statistical analyses of sentencing patterns a year or two before they began work and based guidelines largely on what they learned. They usually ignored statutory maximums and achieved crude proportionality; former sentencing patterns presumably roughly paralleled prevailing attitudes about crime seriousness, at least among judges and parole boards. Even that approach, however, did not work for long in Minnesota. In the aftermath of several notorious murders in the early 1990s, the legislature in a stroke doubled the lengths of presumptive sentences for many crimes, as Richard Frase showed in 2005.

The empirical approach rests uncomfortably within a proportionality frame. In principle, articulable normative rationales should underlie scaling of crime seriousness and punishment severity. American punishment practices, for victim reality reasons, punish violent crimes more severely than systematic analyses starting from normative premises would justify. The empirical approach may nonetheless be the likeliest to succeed. In principle, were it politically possible, it would be better to negotiate an overall cap and seriousness rankings on the basis of general principles or criteria.

B. Rough Equivalence

Matt Matravers observed in his 2020 essay "The Place of Proportionality in Penal Theory" that "as anyone who has graded papers in legal theory—and many other domains—knows, it is a rough and ready business in which one seeks for rough equivalence and not precise differences," and suggested that may be the best to be hoped for concerning punishment. Norval Morris and I in our effort to facilitate substitution of community punishments for imprisonment similarly concluded that rough equivalence is the only achievable goal.

That is a weak aspiration, but it may be the best we can do. And not so bad. Any classification of crimes is necessarily a classification of legal definitions that apply to wide ranges of behavior. Robberies, for example, involve different combinations of offenders, victims, locations, threats, weapons, injuries, and property values and may be accomplished or unsuccessfully attempted.

Each difference can vary in character and intensity. Some of those differences can be captured to some degree by creating subcategories of offenses, but major differences between events falling within the same category will remain. Particular punishments likewise vary objectively in nature, intensity, and detailed characteristics, and subjectively in their effects on individuals. And, every punishment decision must be made by an individual or group of individuals with distinct personalities, beliefs, and idiosyncrasies. No system of rules or punishment standards can encompass all the material differences. If an overall cap and a morally persuasive system of offense seriousness ranking has been set, rough equivalence in treatment of different cases is probably the best human beings can do.

C. Varieties of Retributivism

For the reasons set out in this chapter and in writings by others whom I have quoted, no punishment system based on positive retributivist premises is achievable. Reasonably principled systems based on negative retributivist principles may be. Norval Morris's "limiting retributivism" proposals, first fully set out in his 1974 book *The Future of Imprisonment*, are more timely now than when he made them. He called for setting maximum punishments for every type of crime, and sometimes, for the most serious or emotionally galvanizing, minimums. Within those limits, the presumptively appropriate punishment, following the parsimony principle, would be the least severe allowable. That presumption could sometimes be overridden when there were valid, evidence-based reasons to believe a more severe punishment would be an effective crime preventative. Morris believed the state of the empirical evidence when he wrote did not justify increasing punishments for deterrent, incapacitative, or rehabilitative reasons.

The National Academy of Sciences Committee on Causes and Consequences of High Rates of Incarceration concluded in 2014 that the evidence concerning deterrence and incapacitation is little better in our time. Current evidence concerning rehabilitation is more encouraging. Well-managed, targeted, and funded programs can reduce reoffending. This provides no justification, however, for imprisoning people, or imprisoning them for longer than they otherwise would be. Treatment programs are more effective in the community than in prison. It often provides justification for diverting people from prison.

Proportionality theory by itself cannot provide adequate guidance for creating just systems of punishment. The theoretical implications are clear.

Lots of careful work needs to be done to enrich understanding of what makes particular crimes more serious than others and particular punishments more severe than others. Little has been done so far and it has not provided useful tools. Scaling decisions will continue largely to result from negotiations among people who have different intuitions, but those negotiations can be better informed and more sensitive to normative considerations than they now are. Theorists could help.

The policy implications are also clear: punishments should always be the least severe possible under the circumstances. Numerical sentencing guidelines did not exist in the United States when Morris wrote. They do in 2020, in the federal system and 16 states. They set ranges of ostensibly appropriate sentences for particular categories of crimes. Positive retributivism can provide little useful principled guidance on fixing punishments within those ranges. The necessary conceptual work has not been done. Morris's limiting retributivism can provide guidance: impose the least severe presumptively appropriate punishment unless there are good, evidence-based—not intuition-based—reasons to do something more. When there are mitigating circumstances relating to the offender or the offense, do less. Should paradigms shift, the proportionality implications are the same: do least harm to wrongdoers, and only for good evidence-based reasons.

4

Deep Disadvantage

MOST PEOPLE'S MINDS harbor incompatible ideas about punishment. One is severe: criminals should be punished. The other is sympathetic: there but for God's grace go I. Punitive passions call for condign punishment. Sympathy calls for compassion. Among those most needing it are people who have lived deeply disadvantaged lives. The criminal law cuts them no slack.

Here, an illustration, is Associate Supreme Court Justice Elena Kagan's description of the life of Evan Miller in *Miller v. Alabama*, 567 U.S. 460 (2012), the decision that declared mandatory life imprisonment without parole for offenders under age 18 unconstitutional:

> [I]f ever a pathological background might have contributed to a 14-year-old's commission of a crime, it is here. Miller's stepfather physically abused him; his alcoholic and drug-addicted mother neglected him; he had been in and out of foster care as a result; and he had tried to kill himself four times, the first when he should have been in kindergarten.

Evan was involved in a brutal murder; punitive passions pulsate. Who, thinking about their own early lives, or their children's, can read about Eric's without shuddering?

Commission of commonplace crimes has long, probably always, been understood to be probabilistically related to a congeries of socioeconomic and other characteristics of individuals. Oliver Wendell Holmes Jr. observed in 1881 in *The Common Law* that if punishment "stood on the moral grounds which are proposed for it, the first thing to be considered would be those limitations in the capacity for choosing rightly which arise from abnormal instincts, want of education, lack of intelligence, and all other defects which are most marked in the criminal classes."

Desperate people experience stronger temptations to steal than do comfortable people. Deeply disadvantaged young people in socially disorganized areas are more tempted by the attractions of gang membership and street-corner drug dealing than are Harvard undergraduates. Many people sell sex or drugs or commit property crimes because that is the least worst—or only—way they can obtain enough money to survive.

Individuals do, of course, make good and bad moral choices, but the conditions in which they are made vary enormously. *Chicago Sun-Times* columnist Mike Royko 40 years ago made the point in describing the criminal calculations of two Chicago boys:

> You take some teenager in an affluent suburb. He has just returned from playing tennis or football after school. . . . He walks into a seven- or eight-room house in which he has his own room, equipped with a stereo and maybe his own TV set, and a closet full of nice clothes . . .
>
> After having dinner with his father, who has a well-paying job, and his mother, who might work but also might be home every day, he goes in his room, looks in the mirror and asks himself: "What is in my heart? Do I want to join a gang and go out and mug somebody and pursue a life of violence and crime? Or do I want to go to college and become a CPA?" Goodness, thank goodness, usually prevails over evil. So the lad does not go out and join the Blackstone Rangers . . .
>
> A similar decision is made by a youth in one of the city's many slum areas. His home is a dismal flat or a congested housing project. Income is his mother's welfare check. School is a place where the most important thing you learn is not to turn your back on strangers. Security and social life are the other kids on the street—the gang . . .
>
> So he looks in the cracked mirror and asks: "What is in my heart? Do I want to become a CPA, or a physician, or a lawyer? Do I want to earn $50,000 or more per year? Do I want to go to Northwestern or Georgetown or maybe Yale? Hell no. I *want* to pursue the life of crime and violence. I *want* to go out and mug somebody. I *want* to wind up doing 10 to 20 in Stateville so I can be with my friends. I want this because it is in my heart and has been there since I was born." (emphasis in original)

We know why the inner-city youth does not plan to be an accountant and why the suburban youth is unlikely to join a street gang. We also know why the inner-city youth's prospects are so bleak. People from deeply disadvantaged backgrounds face harder choices and larger temptations than do the rest of us. Decisions to commit crimes or join gangs are not always simply feckless failures to resist temptation. Often they are the regrettable but understandable choices of people whose lives provide few opportunities, satisfactions, or pleasures.

Before the retributivist revival of the 1970s, few people writing about punishment philosophy seem much to have worried about social injustice. Before that, troubling cases could be and often were dealt with sympathetically. Indeterminate sentencing was premised in large part on the beliefs that many people's crimes have social and psychological causes and that a just punishment system should try to address them. Criminal justice policy had not yet become highly politicized. Prosecutors were little less likely than judges, juries, and probation officers to sympathize with troubled offenders. Charging and bargaining decisions have always been made behind closed doors; prosecutors did and do as they wish. Juries and judges could and can acquit sympathetic defendants or convict them of lesser charges. The jury's capacity to add a measure of compassion to the cold application of legal rules, to acquit when the law calls for conviction, to convict of a lesser offense rather than a greater one, was long said to be its fundamental virtue.[1]

Harvard Law School dean Roscoe Pound in a 1910 article, "Law in Books and Law in Action," asserted that "jury lawlessness is the great corrective of law in its actual administration. The will of the state at large imposed on a reluctant community, the will of a majority imposed on a vigorous and determined minority, find the same obstacle in the local jury that formerly confronted kings and ministers." Less conspicuously, judges could take sympathetic circumstances into account when individualizing sentences. So could parole boards when making release decisions.

Prevailing ways of thinking in our time are less sympathetic. Prosecutors are more hardboiled. Informal accommodations are harder to justify. Sentencing laws and guidelines make it difficult. Few people now celebrate jury nullification. Judges' instructions do not mention the jury's power to nullify or, lest it influence consideration of guilt, what sentence might or must be imposed.

---

1. As leading criminal law scholars have long argued: e.g., Holmes (1899); Pound (1910); Michael and Wechsler (1940); Kadish and Kadish (1971); Butler (1995).

Judicial nullification is more commonly viewed as a regrettable breach of the judge's obligation to enforce the law than as an admirable effort to do justice.

Few scholars have written about special problems of justice in conviction or punishment of deeply disadvantaged offenders. The principal works until recently were a handful of law review articles in the 1970s and 1980s, judge David Bazelon's *Question Authority* (1978), brief discussions by philosophers in writings primarily devoted to other topics, and William C. Heffernan and John Kleinig's 2000 collection *From Social Justice to Criminal Justice: Poverty and the Administration of Criminal Law*. There has been a small recent resurgence of interest, starting with a 2011 *Alabama Civil Rights and Civil Liberties Law Review* symposium, "Rotten Social Background in the Twenty-First Century." A handful of mostly younger writers have taken the topic on, offered new arguments, and developed fresh ideas.

Federal court of appeals judge David Bazelon in 1976 catalyzed the early literature when he proposed creation of a social adversity defense: defendants should be acquitted if the jury decided their mental or emotional processes or self-control were so impaired that they could not justly be held responsible for their acts.[2] Most legal scholars then and now have disagreed, arguing that the crux of the problem is not overwhelming temptation but insufficient moral probity, not irresistible impulses but impulses not resisted, not undeterrable offenders but undeterred ones. A few academic lawyers have become somewhat more sympathetic in recent years, but only to the extent of recognizing a partial defense or approving informal reductions in sentences.

Philosophers have long been more sympathetic. Jeffrie Murphy, in an influential 1973 article, "Marxism and Retribution," rejected his own retributive "benefits and burdens" theory of punishment because of the social adversity problem. A large proportion of defendants in criminal courts, he noted, are deeply disadvantaged, and cannot reasonably be said to enjoy the benefits of living in a secure, ordered society. That being so, their punishment cannot be justified until "we have restructured society in such a way that criminals genuinely do correspond to the only model that will render punishment permissible—i.e., make sure that they are autonomous and that they do benefit in the requisite sense."

Andreas von Hirsch observed in 1976 in *Doing Justice* that "as long as a substantial segment of the population is denied adequate opportunities for a

---

2. The most discussed work on a social disadvantage defense after Bazelon's is a landmark 1985 article in the *Journal of Law and Inequality* on "Rotten Social Background" by University of Alabama law professor Richard Delgado.

livelihood, any scheme for punishing must be morally flawed." The most influential punishment theorist in our time, British philosopher Antony Duff, in *Trials and Punishments*, in 1986, offered an ideal retributive punishment theory but concluded that "punishment is not justifiable within our present legal system; it will not be justifiable unless and until we have brought about deep and far-reaching social, political, legal, and moral changes in ourselves and our society." English philosopher Ted Honderich observed in *Punishment: The Supposed Justifications* in 1989 that "[t]here is nothing that can be called the question of [punishment's] moral justification which is left to be considered," if "the great question of the distribution of goods in society" is not adequately addressed.

Bazelon and the philosophers were mostly right and the other legal scholars were mostly wrong. Juries and judges should have greater leeway to acquit defendants on the basis of deep disadvantage, though this raises complex moral issues, and judges should be encouraged to mitigate their sentences when they believe it appropriate to do so. In this chapter, I explain why. The first section takes a small step to the side to consider why changes in prevailing beliefs about punishment befuddled efforts to think more sympathetically about disadvantaged offenders. The views of many, probably most, legal academics, practitioners, and policymakers have reflected the punitive temper of recent times. In attempting to tailor punishments to fit crimes, many people forgot that just punishments must also fit offenders. Things may, however, be changing.

The second section summarizes contemporary evidence on the causal influences of individual differences and environmental conditions on offending. It shows beyond peradventure of doubt that offending by the deeply disadvantaged involves much more than simple failures to resist temptation.

The third section discusses proposals for a "social adversity" or "rotten social background" defense. The arguments in favor are substantially stronger than those against, but, as a practical matter, even if such a defense were recognized it would probably result in few acquittals. It might, however, give disadvantaged offenders greater leverage in plea bargaining and increase the likelihood that they receive mitigated sentences.

The fourth section discusses informal mitigation of punishment at sentencing. Few people disagree in principle that judges should, in appropriate cases, mitigate the severity of sentences to take account of material differences in offenders' circumstances and characteristics. Many believe that a deeply disadvantaged background is a material characteristic. Unfortunately, informal mitigation of punishments is not enough. The severity and rigidity of American sentencing laws often deny judges the necessary authority. The moral challenges presented by deeply disadvantaged offenders cannot adequately be addressed without creation of a social adversity defense.

I. The Zeitgeist

Before retributivism gained currency in the 1970s, sympathetic handling of deeply disadvantaged defendants presented no special problems. It didn't always happen, of course, but it could be done easily and inconspicuously. If prosecutors decided not to file charges or judges or juries chose not to convict, that ended the matter. The American Bar Foundation Survey of case processing in state courts in the 1950s showed that all those ameliorating practices were common. If there was a conviction, the judge and the parole board could individualize sentences in sympathetic ways. Section 1.02(2)(e) of the 1962 *Model Penal Code* provided that one purpose of sentencing is "to differentiate among offenders with a view to a just individualization in their treatment." The *Code* gave officials authority to individualize punishment decisions by establishing presumptions in favor of probation in all cases and of parole release at the earliest possible time.

Attitudes and practices changed in the 1970s when legislatures began to abolish parole release, enact determinate sentencing laws, and authorize sentencing guidelines, and changed more in the 1980s and 1990s when mandatory minimum sentence and similar laws came into vogue. Offense severity became the primary consideration. Philosophers, fellow-traveling academic lawyers, and policymakers focused on the conviction offense or offenses as the primary basis of punishment decisions. That was understandable—the rise of retributivism was in large part a response to what were widely believed to be too broad and often abused discretions under indeterminate sentencing— but it was a fundamental mistake. It shifted attention away from individual offenders' blameworthiness as manifested in the circumstances of their lives and of their offenses and refocused it almost entirely on the seemingly objective but often misleading indicator of offense seriousness. Andreas von Hirsch's pioneering *Doing Justice* (1976) enthusiastically approved. In principle, though, and in the eyes of Saint Peter or the Recording Angel, decisions about deserved punishments would take account of all the aggravating and mitigating details that make one offense more or less serious than another and all the facets of an offender's life and characteristics that make his or her actions more or less blameworthy. Recent American policies and practices to the contrary often base sentences primarily or solely on the statutory definitions of the offenses of which defendants are convicted.

The problems presented by deeply disadvantaged defendants became harder to deal with because prevailing ways of thinking about crime and punishment among academics shifted toward retributivism and among policymakers shifted toward greater severity. Judge Bazelon's proposal for a social disadvantage defense was essentially consequentialist: more would be gained from occasional acquittals, he said, than would be lost. His scholarly opponents, pre-eminently University of Pennsylvania law professor Stephen Morse, were mostly retributivists. To many contemporary practitioners, policymakers, and academics, especially people who came of age in recent decades, retributive ideas appear to be timeless and self-evident and contemporary punishment patterns and practices appear to be normal. They aren't.

Most people's thinking on any subject reflects the ethos of their times, as historian David J. Musto showed about attitudes and policies concerning drug use in *The American Disease: The Origins of Narcotic Control* (1973), historian Grant Gilmore showed about the arts in *The Death of Contract* (1974), historian Jaroslav Pelikan showed about depictions of the historical Jesus in *Jesus Through the Centuries* (1985), and I showed about attitudes toward crime and criminals in *Thinking about Crime* (2004).

After conventional thinking about sentencing and punishment shifted away from consequentialism and toward retributivism, most criminal law scholars, practitioners, and policymakers came to view criminal cases as morality plays in which only the seriousness of the current offense and the criminal record much matter. If a mentally competent defendant caused a criminal harm, mens rea requirements are met, and no established affirmative offenses apply, that is all that matters. Juries and judges seem to believe they have no legitimate choice except to convict and judges that they must impose proportionately severe or mandated punishments: the defendant, after all, culpably failed to resist temptation and committed an offense. That it was an especially strong or overwhelming temptation does not signify.

Legislators and prosecutors likewise. It is difficult to imagine that anyone thinking about human frailty, what they would want for themselves or their children, or what it would be like to spend years, decades, or a lifetime in a concrete box would vote to enact a three-strikes, mandatory minimum sentence, or life without parole law. Legislative majorities in every state did, usually enthusiastically. Prosecutors throughout the United States equally enthusiastically filed charges triggering the unprecedentedly harsh new laws.

Things may, however, be changing. One of the most important lessons from the historical literature on conventional ways of thinking is that they oscillate. Classical periods in the arts inevitably ossify and are followed by revisionist romantic periods which ossify in their turn and are followed by new forms of classicism. David Musto showed that public and political responses to alcohol and drug use follow similar cycles. As use increases, and associated problems become more evident, condemnatory and moralistic objections increase. Changing ways of thinking disperse throughout the population and in due course lead to decreases in use. For a generation after drug use peaks, attitudes continue to harden, harsher laws are enacted, and practitioners become more severe. Then things change: attitudes become less unforgiving, severe laws are moderated, and enforcement declines and becomes less punitive.

I showed in *Thinking about Crime* that the historical patterns Musto documented concerning drug policy recurred in our time. Use of most illicit drugs peaked in 1979. The harshest laws were enacted between 1984 and 1996, and almost none after that. After 1996, many states and the federal government moderated their drug laws, drug treatment received greater support, and practitioners enforced drug laws less vigorously.

Public and political attitudes about crime and punishment seem to be following the same pattern. Crime rates peaked in 1991 and have since declined steadily and dramatically. Few harsh laws have been enacted since the 1990s. Conservative and liberal activists and politicians have joined hands in support of reduced use of imprisonment, increased investment in treatment programs, and modification of harsh laws. Newly elected prosecutors in a number of American cities say they intend to reduce racial disparities, make court processes fairer, and ameliorate overuse of pretrial detention, fines, and fees.

Whether these changes portend decisive shifts in prevailing ways of thinking remains to be seen. If so, arguments for changes in handling of criminal charges against deeply disadvantaged offenders may fall on fewer deaf ears. Increased receptiveness of some legal scholars and philosophers to that possibility, discussed in section III, may signal that minds are opening.

II. Crime and Disadvantage

Proponents of a social disadvantage defense, such as law professor Richard Delgado in a 2011 article, "The Wretched of the Earth," typically support their arguments by pointing to factors such as single-parent households, socially disorganized neighborhoods, and inferior schools that are correlated with offending. Things go rhetorical after that. "Unremitting, long-term exposure to conditions of threat, stress, and neglect indelibly mark the minds and bodies of those exposed," Delgado wrote. The evidence is, however, much stronger than mere inferences from correlations. This can be seen by juxtaposing findings on causes and correlates of offending by developmental psychologists with those by urban sociologists.

Developmental psychologists investigate the antecedents and causes of prosocial and antisocial behavior. They want to be able to distinguish between causes and correlates. Most rely heavily on prospective longitudinal cohort studies that document the lives of groups of people over extended periods. It has long been recognized, for example, that "birds of a feather flock together" among delinquent children who do poorly in school. What was for long not known was why. Do reasonably successful students befriend delinquent peers and then began to fail, or do already failing students seek other forms of validation and find it among delinquent peers? Knowing the answer has important implications for running schools and enhancing children's life chances or, in the terms of the discipline, altering developmental trajectories.

Developmentalists distinguish between "risk" and "protective" factors in explaining developmental trajectories, and design interventions that aim to make positive outcomes more likely. All else being equal, risk factors such as low intelligence, impulsivity, attention deficit disorders, single-parent households, inconsistent parental discipline, socially disorganized neighborhoods, inferior schools, deviant peers, and criminal parents or siblings increase the likelihood of crime, delinquency, school failure, early pregnancy, drug and alcohol abuse, and mental health problems.[3] Protective factors such as good parenting skills, cognitive-skills training, mental health services, improved educational opportunities, and prosocial peers can offset risk factors and reduce the likelihood of dysfunctional futures.

I discuss developmental psychology to make two points relevant to imputation of personal culpability to deeply disadvantaged people. First, developmental trajectories are established in early childhood, at ages at which no one would attribute moral responsibility to young people for the trajectories that will characterize their later lives. A celebrated 1993 article by Duke University neuropsychologist Terrie E. Moffitt, one of the most cited specialists in developmental psychology, identified two categories of offenders who can be identified in early childhood. She called them "life-course persistent" and

---

3. For an exhaustive compilation of the relevant research, see Farrington, Kazemian, and Piquero (2018).

"adolescence-limited" offenders; the terms refer to patterns of delinquency and criminality in later life.

Moffitt's typology rests comfortably with knowledge about lifetime offending. "Age/crime curves," Cambridge psychologist David Farrington showed in "Age and Crime," a classic 1986 article, characterize all human groups. Sizable majorities of teenagers, especially boys, engage in behavior which, if coming to police attention, would justify arrest and prosecution. Property offending peaks in the mid-teenage years and violent offending 1 or 2 years later, and then rapidly declines. For most people a process of natural desistance occurs as maturity, employment, meaningful sexual relationships, and conventional aspirations make the risks associated with criminality apparent. These are Moffitt's adolescence-limited offenders. Life-course persistent offenders typically begin offending at younger ages and continue to offend well into adulthood. There is no meaningful sense in which they choose to become life-course offenders. The circumstances of their lives determine the choice for them.

Second, offending trajectories can often be altered through identification of risk factors and strengthening of protective factors. Whether those analyses are undertaken and acted upon, and whether appropriate interventions are developed and competently executed by responsible adults, are also not matters about which responsibility can reasonably be imputed to children. As the poet William Wordsworth put it, the child is father of the man. The deeply disadvantaged defendants for whom Judge Bazelon would have made a social adversity defense available are often people who, when young, were launched on grievous trajectories into which no one constructively intervened. Fourteen-year-old Evan Miller, the appellant in *Miller v. Alabama*, did not choose the life fate decreed for him.

The causal influences on offending of individual differences and community characteristics are vividly demonstrated by work that combines developmental psychology and urban sociology. Table 4.1 is drawn from a classic 2000 article by Swedish sociologist Per-Olof H. Wikström and Dutch-American developmental psychologist Rolf Loeber. It shows percentages of Pittsburgh boys who admitted committing serious delinquent acts through age 18. The table demonstrates the relative influences of individual differences (the psychologists' turf) and community characteristics (the sociologists'). It demonstrates the overwhelming causal influence of deep disadvantage.

The vertical axis divides the boys into three groups on the basis of individual characteristics associated with offending: high protective scores (i.e.,

Table 4.1 Serious offenses by risk score and neighborhood
context, percentages

Risk and Protective Score	Housing Type				
	Above Average	Average	Disadvantaged, Private Housing	Disadvantaged, Public Housing	N
High Protective	11.1%	5.1%	16.7%	37.5%	155
Balanced Risk and Protective	27.3	40.1	38.5	60.7	651
High Risk	77.8	71.3	78.3	70.0	222
N	142	556	188	142	

Source: Wikström and Loeber (2000, Table 6).

low offending probability), balanced scores (moderate probability), and high-risk scores (high probability). The horizontal axis divides the boys into four groups on the basis of where they lived: above-average neighborhoods, average neighborhoods, disadvantaged private housing neighborhoods, and disadvantaged public housing neighborhoods.

Two patterns leap out. First, individual differences matter. No matter what the neighborhood, 70–80 percent of children with high-risk scores admitted serious delinquency. Second, however, living in a disadvantaged public-housing neighborhood mattered much more for low and moderate risk children:

(i) In above-average neighborhoods, individual differences are strongly associated with offending probabilities: only 11 percent of low-risk children admitted offenses compared with 78 percent of high-risk children;

(ii) In disadvantaged public housing areas, neighborhood effects swamp individual differences: nearly 40 percent of low-risk, 60 percent of mid-risk, and 70 percent of high-risk children admitted offenses.

The vast majority of high-risk children admitted offenses, no matter where they lived. Almost irrespective of their individual characteristics, most boys living in disadvantaged public housing areas admitted offenses. Some did not, but they were exceptions to the rule. The likeliest explanations are that they had unusually capable parents or other caretakers, were unrepresentative of neighborhood demographics (e.g., the minister's, school teacher's, or doctor's children), had unusually strong superegos, or were just lucky.

Offending patterns are probabilistic and depend in substantial part on the circumstances of people's lives. To insist that the difference between those who do and those who do not offend is simply that some resisted temptation is to celebrate an idealized but unworldly conception of personal moral choice. It is to insist on heroic behavior by people who face overwhelming odds against them and from whom it is unrealistic, and unfair, to demand heroism.

Individuals do, of course, make moral choices, but the conditions in which they make them vary enormously. Most people understand this without looking at data of the sort presented in Table 4.1.

People from deeply disadvantaged backgrounds face vastly harder choices and larger temptations than the rest of us do. The moral of Royko's tales of two young men and the underpinning of Bazelon's social disadvantage defense is the belief that deep disadvantage is relevant to assessment of moral culpability.

Drug selling is an example that has put hundreds of thousands of disadvantaged young Americans behind bars in recent decades. The risks of street-level drug dealing make little sense to most people with reasonably good prospects of living a satisfying life. Especially in recent decades, the probabilities of imprisonment and a ruined life were enormously high and well-known. For disadvantaged people with little social capital and limited life chances, with substandard educations and few marketable skills, however, drug dealing can appear to present otherwise unparalleled opportunities. They overestimate the benefits and underestimate the risks.[4] This is compounded by peer influences, social pressures, and examples of successful local dealers who live self-indulgent, affluent lives and manage to avoid arrest.

This is at once a simple and a complicated problem. "Do the crime, do the time" can appear to be a simple and principled solution to crime. It ignores the complex circumstances of the lives of deeply disadvantaged people. Proponents of a social disadvantage defense and of mitigation of sentences for disadvantaged offenders are searching for a better solution.

---

4. Reuter, MacCoun, and Murphy (1990); Kleiman (1997).

III. *Excuse and Disadvantage*

Academics' attitudes concerning punishment of deeply disadvantaged offenders are beginning to change. Philosophers have long been sympathetic, though they have paid more attention to the state's moral authority to punish than to whether disadvantage sometimes lessens or in extreme cases negates blameworthiness. Through 2000, legal scholars were not sympathetic. Except for Judge Bazelon and Richard Delgado, most agreed with Stephen Morse that living a disadvantaged life may often be hard, but it doesn't excuse criminal offenses. Since then, increasing numbers of lawyers and philosophers have called for recognition of a partial responsibility defense, paralleling legal doctrines of provocation and diminished capacity, or for informal mitigation of punishment at sentencing. Few have endorsed Judge Bazelon's proposal for a complete defense.

Bazelon's proposal was prompted by two cases and one insight. He was the principal draftsman of *Durham v. United States*, 214 Fed. 2d 862 (1954), a decision of the Federal Circuit Court of Appeals for the District of Columbia that reformulated the insanity defense to center on whether the defendant's behavior was the "product" of mental disease or defect. The traditional standard in *M'Naghten's Case*, [1843] All ER Rep 229, was much more complex, requiring that the "accused was labouring under such a defect of reason, from disease of the mind, as not to know the nature and quality of the act he was doing; or if he did know it, that he did not know he was doing what was wrong." *Durham* sought to permit expert testimony on the defendant's mental condition while allowing the jury to decide whether, because of that condition, the defendant should be deemed not legally responsible for his or her actions.

The second case was *United States v. Alexander*, 471 F.2d 923 (D.C. Cir. 1972), in which the defendant, a black man, responded with lethal rage to a victim's race-baiting taunts. The defendant's lawyers sought to introduce evidence about his deeply disadvantaged background and his experiences as a victim of racial maltreatment to explain and excuse his actions. The trial judge refused. The appellate court approved the refusal. Bazelon dissented.

The insight came from University of Chicago law professor Norval Morris, who observed in a 1968 article in the *University of Southern California Law Review* that an "adverse social and subcultural background is statistically *more* criminogenic than is psychosis" (his emphasis). His point was that commission of serious crimes can more accurately be predicted from knowledge of a person's background and circumstances than from knowledge of his or her psychiatric diagnosis. The insanity defense is premised on the proposition that people should not be convicted for actions over which they lack capacity for self-control. Morris contended that the empirical evidence would equally, or more convincingly, support recognition of a social disadvantage defense.

Morris took it as given that a social disadvantage defense would raise insuperable analytical and political problems. Less empirical justification existed for an insanity defense, he wrote, and proposed that it be abandoned. Bazelon flipped the argument and drew the opposite conclusion: because of the fundamental importance of moral responsibility, there should be an insanity defense and there should also be a social disadvantage defense.

Bazelon proposed in a 1976 article in the *University of Southern California Law Review* that testimony be permitted in appropriate cases concerning the influence of deep disadvantage and that the jury be directed "that a defendant is not responsible if at the time of his unlawful conduct his mental or emotional processes or behavior controls were impaired to such an extent that he cannot justly be held responsible for his act." The aim was for the jury—"the traditional representative of our consensual sense of morality"—to decide. Anticipating the criticism that juries should not be allowed such great discretion, he observed that juries are often given broad discretion to interpret and apply open-textured terms and concepts such as reasonableness, seasonableness, foreseeability, and negligence. The ultimate factual questions in many tort, contract, and criminal cases turn on reasonableness.

Bazelon predicted that few defendants would be acquitted on the basis of social disadvantage, for the same reasons that few insanity defenses succeed. The usual explanations concerning insanity are that juries do not believe the factual claims underpinning the defense, worry that false claims may let calculating criminals get away with premeditated murder, and fear that defendants are dangerous and will harm others if acquitted. If defendants were occasionally acquitted on the basis of social disadvantage, Bazelon argued, it would show that jurors believed they should be excused and draw attention to the seriousness of the underlying social problems.

If Bazelon's speculations are right, as I believe they are, recognition of a social adversity defense would seldom result in acquittals. It would, however, have three other positive effects. First, it would make an important moral statement: in a just society, no one should be exposed to such extreme levels of material, psychic, and developmental deprivation that a social adversity defense is necessary.

Second, by emphasizing the powerful influence of deep disadvantage on offenders' lives, it would conduce judges to mitigate the severity of the punishments they impose on such offenders. Unsuccessful claims of self-defense or subjectively experienced but objectively insufficient provocation are often viewed as valid bases for mitigation. *Model Penal Code* section 7.01(2)(d), for example, provides that one reason not to impose a prison sentence is that "there were substantial grounds tending to excuse or justify the defendant's criminal conduct, though failing to establish a defense." Recognition of a social adversity defense, even when unsuccessful, would lay a comparable foundation for mitigating punishment severity.

Third, deeply disadvantaged defendants' positions in plea bargaining would be strengthened. Even if few such defenses are likely to succeed, a large proportion of deeply disadvantaged defendants could potentially offer them. Prosecutors prefer not to risk acquittals in cases in which there are foreseeable evidentiary problems or plausible affirmative defenses. Defendants are often offered plea bargaining concessions in such cases. Establishment of a social disadvantage offense would make concessions more often available to deeply disadvantaged offenders.

Bazelon's proposal and arguments elicited a prompt response in the same journal from University of Pennsylvania law professor Stephen Morse. He offered three main objections. The first is that some individuals exposed to deepest disadvantage do not become offenders, thereby refuting the claim that the experience is necessarily causal. The second is that a social disadvantage defense would imply that affected offenders lack capacity for moral choice, and no legal system should do that, especially when the individuals concerned would often be members of minority groups. The third, the gravamen of the difference between them, is that situations in which a capacity for moral choice is eliminated are already dealt with adequately by traditional criminal law defenses of insanity, necessity, duress, and provocation. Morse's view was that deeply disadvantaged defendants should be acquitted or be convicted of lesser charges only in cases in which one or more of those defenses applied. Otherwise not.

This disagreement exposes a fundamental difference in views about the rule of law. When people use the phrase "justice according to the law," it is an open question which of the two nouns should take priority. For Morse, it was more important that laws be consistently applied than that just results be obtained in individual cases. He did not want to allow juries to apply their collective sense of justice: "The problem with this view is that although juries are representatives of the moral standards of the community, each jury is not a totally independent 'legislature' free to decide what those moral standards should be. Juries do not create community moral standards; they apply them after being instructed on the law by the judge." Bazelon, by contrast, was not troubled: "I view nullification as an important means of bringing to bear on the judicial process a sense of fairness and particularized justice." Juries composed of a diverse group of lay people are more likely to understand pressures that affect disadvantaged people than are highly educated judges from privileged backgrounds, living privileged lives, or both. If jurors' collective sense of injustice tells them that a defendant should not be convicted, they should not be compelled to act in a way they believe to be unjust.

There are easy answers to Morse's three points. First, ignoring seemingly overwhelming pressures on a class of offenders because a few somehow manage to overcome them is unjust. It is not reasonable to expect ordinary people to be heroes or to demonstrate superhuman self-control even if a few are or do. Existing affirmative defenses are based on exactly those rationales. In most jurisdictions, defenses of necessity, duress, self-defense, and provocation focus not on heroism or extraordinary self-possession but on what a reasonably prudent person would have believed under the circumstances or how such a person would have acted. If 60–70 percent of medium and high-risk young Pittsburgh men living in public housing admit committing offenses by age 18, it is not easy to explain why a reasonable person under those circumstances would not have. A reasonable person, as an empirical matter, should be an ordinary or average person. As an empirical matter, the 60–70 percent of young Pittsburgh men did what most young men in their circumstances would have done.

Second, that a few deeply disadvantaged poor or minority defendants are not convicted when they could have been would not in the real world stigmatize all disadvantaged or minority individuals. Negative stereotyping of minority and disadvantaged people, unconscious bias, and statistical discrimination are grievous problems that too often result in wrongful convictions, but a few acquittals would not change them.

Third, the long-established affirmative defenses of insanity, duress, necessity, and provocation would by their definitions not be available to most defendants to whom Judge Bazelon's defense would apply. If they were, his proposal would have been redundant and there would have been no reason other than a penchant for analytical tidiness for Morse or anyone else to object. Richard Delgado in 1985 worked systematically through the established affirmative offenses and concluded that none of them would easily encompass deeply disadvantaged people whose behavior satisfied conventional mens rea standards.

Morse's three points are premised on the view that it is absolutely undesirable if mentally competent people who should be convicted under existing black letter laws might sometimes not be convicted. That happens all the time when prosecutors decide not to file charges or dismiss charges to elicit guilty pleas, when procedural or evidentiary problems preclude admission of essential evidence, and when judges or juries rightly or wrongly decide the prosecution's burden of proof has not been met. It is a defendant's good fortune. Usually, except sometimes from envy or resentment, bystanders celebrate others' good fortune. People win lotteries, receive unexpected inheritances, escape without a scratch from devastating car crashes, and are exposed to infectious diseases they do not contract. Good luck happens. H. L. Mencken defined puritanism as "the haunting fear that someone, somewhere, may be happy." Morse's worry seems to have been that some defendant, somewhere, sometime, may get lucky.

Wrongful convictions are unambiguously undesirable. Innocent people are blamed, punished, and stigmatized and people close to them are harmed. Acquittals because of a successful disadvantage defense or because a prosecutor's burden of proof was not met cause no comparable harms. Bystanders with an avenging angel's view of the criminal law may be offended, but there is no reason to incorporate that view in the law. Ronald Dworkin explained in *Law's Empire* (1986) why citizens' preferences that others suffer harm, or satisfactions when they do, should not matter.[5]

Sentencing is and always has been a human process. Individuals must make weighty decisions about other people's lives. Judges and juries usually take that responsibility seriously and want both to apply the law in what is generally understood to be an appropriate way and to do justice to the people whose lives are in their hands. When those aspirations conflict, concerns for justice sometimes do, and should, defeat concerns for literal application of legal standards. That is why juries and judges in eighteenth-century England, as historian Douglas Hay showed in *Albion's Fatal Tree* (1975), often acquitted people of property and other crimes punishable by death and why, in twentieth-century America, as I showed in a 2009 *Crime and Justice* essay, judges and prosecutors often nullified mandatory sentencing laws.

---

5. I discuss Dworkin's argument that negative preferences based on invidious considerations should not count in chapter 5. They are a form of schadenfreude, an unattractive human tendency that we all recognize but few celebrate.

Discussion of a deep disadvantage defense has percolated through the criminal law literature since 1976. Some recent work explores new ideas, but most rehashes familiar arguments. There are three main strands.

One, most prominently associated with Antony Duff, focuses on the state's moral authority to punish deeply disadvantaged offenders rather than on whether they deserve to be convicted and punished. He argued in *Punishment, Communication, and Community* (2001) that people who are treated as responsible members of a community are obligated to comply with its criminal law and may justly be tried and punished. Individuals are, however, sometimes excluded from participation in a community's political life, from having a fair opportunity to acquire economic and material benefits that others enjoy, and from receiving the respect and concern due to citizens. Offenses by people who have been excluded are not necessarily justified or excused, but the state lacks authority to call them to account. Duff's work provoked a sizable number of responses.[6] I do not discuss them in detail because their subject is state authority, not justice in punishment.

It would be but small solace to disadvantaged offenders to learn that the state lacks moral authority to punish them, but will do it anyway. Duff in *Trials and Punishments* (1986), his first major discussion of the topic, observed that the state lacks moral authority to punish but did not conclude that deeply disadvantaged offenders may not be punished. Instead, he endorsed traditional deterrence-premised approaches. Other philosophers who doubt the state's moral standing to punish disadvantaged offenders take similar positions.[7]

The second strand consists of proposals made since 2000 for recognition of new mitigating defenses based on deep disadvantage that, if proven, would result in conviction for less serious offenses. Stephen Morse, for example, in articles in 2000 and 2003, moderated his previous hard-line position and

---

6. E.g., Matravers (2006); Holroyd (2010); Tadros (2011); Chau (2012); Howard (2013); Garvey (2014). Others consider whether the state has authority to punish disadvantaged offenders on behalf of all its citizens or only law-abiding ones and whether authority is lost by complicity in allowing the structural conditions of deep disadvantage to exist or by hypocrisy in enforcing laws.

7. Cornell law professor Stephen Garvey (2014, p. 55) argues that states that treat people as second-class citizens by excluding them in one or more of Duff's senses "can no longer claim to have the authority to punish" them but can claim "the weaker authority to coerce [them] in order to elicit [their] obedience." Benjamin Ewing (2018, p. 52) similarly argued that despite lacking moral authority to punish, the state may "subject such offenders to non-condemnatory setbacks in order to pursue various purposes of punishment without engaging in a morally compromised practice of condemnation." Distinctions without differences? People subjected to "coercion" or "non-condemnatory setbacks" are likely to wonder how what is being done to them is different from being punished.

proposed that fact finders be authorized to return verdicts of "guilty but partially responsible" for offenses committed by people suffering from "diminished rationality" or acting in the presence of a sufficiently "hard choice." Elisabeth Lambert in a 2018 article elaborated Morse's proposal, describing research findings that show that people exposed to economic scarcity often experience declines in cognitive functioning. She reasoned by analogy that deep disadvantage may sometimes cause comparable cognitive impairment which, if shown, would permit mitigation of punishment.

Ohio State law professor Joshua Dressler, in articles in 2005 and 2009, similarly replaced his earlier opposition to a social adversity defense with a proposal for recognition of two generic partial excuses, one based on diminished capacity, and one on diminished opportunity. His rationale was that judges should and traditionally sometimes did take account of deep disadvantage informally by mitigating punishments at the sentencing stage, but widespread adoption of sentencing guidelines and mandatory sentencing laws makes that difficult or impossible. The proposed partial excuses would reopen that door.

These proposals are no doubt improvements on flat rejection of a social adversity defense, but they are half-measures. They do not make a comparably powerful moral statement about the social injustice of extreme deprivation. They do not authorize judges and juries to acquit deeply disadvantaged defendants when they believe that characteristics of their lives make a conviction unjust. They would, however, strengthen defendants' plea bargaining leverage. They would also, by focusing the judge's attention on deep disadvantage, make informal mitigation at sentencing more likely.

The third strand of recent writings acknowledges the pressures deeply disadvantaged people face and identifies competing considerations that, when balanced, may sometimes justify exculpation or mitigation. Indiana University philosopher Richard Lippke in a 2014 article argued that it may be unjust to expect people facing "chronic temptation structures" to exhibit extraordinary self-constraint over extended periods. He would take account of whether the circumstances of offenders' lives constitute chronic temptation structures, the strength of their moral reasons not to offend, and the strength of their reasons to offend. Rutgers University philosopher Stuart Green in a 2010 article offered three different considerations: "(1) the kind of unjust deprivation, if any, to which the offender has been subjected; (2) the kind of unfair advantage or disadvantage to which the victim has been subjected; and (3) the particular offense committed." Both proposals are narrow and place primary emphasis on the seriousness of the crimes involved, implicitly limiting their reach to minor ones. In the end, those are some of the kinds of considerations that would influence the gestalt calculations Judge Bazelon envisioned juries making.

Were I a legislator or a judge, I would support Bazelon's proposal. Inevitably there are hard cases of the sort that he had in mind for which current laws do not provide. It would be open and honest to authorize acquittals when fact finders conclude that defendants' behavioral controls or cognitive processes have been so impaired that they cannot justly be convicted. A social adversity defense would acknowledge judges' and jurors' understandable human reactions to difficult cases and allow them to be dealt with openly and without jury nullification or judicial circumvention.

There are few negatives. As Bazelon believed, human skepticism and emotional reactions to serious crimes and seemingly dangerous defendants would limit acquittals to small numbers of cases. In the parallel situation of insanity defense claims, juries have traditionally been loath to vote for acquittals. They are rare. For serious violent crimes, jurors' concerns in insanity cases about credibility, cupidity, and dangerousness are likely to recur in deep disadvantage cases. For less serious assaults, property crimes, and drug crimes, they may weigh less heavily—but so what? If the fact finder in any case, violent or not, concludes that the offender's life circumstances substantially or completely excuse his or her actions, what is the loss? Judges or juries will have behaved in a way they believe to be just and acknowledged that that defendant was affected by extraordinary pressures.

IV. Social Adversity in Mitigation

In earlier times in the United States, judges routinely took offenders' circumstances and characteristics into account when making sentencing decisions. They still do in other Western countries. Sentencing laws and guidelines in contemporary America, however, make individualized sentencing much less possible. That is why Joshua Dressler shifted from resolute opposition to a social adversity defense to support for a partial responsibility approach. It is also why the possibility of mitigated sentences is not by itself an adequate solution to the moral problems posed by deeply disadvantaged offenders.

The arguments for mitigation for socially disadvantaged defendants are straightforward. Socially disadvantaged defendants are subject to more powerful environmental and subcultural pressures to commit offenses than are most other people, are especially likely to have experienced deeply deprived childhoods, and for those reasons deserve to be punished less severely than others not affected by those forces. Taken seriously, retributive punishment ideas require that fact-specific individualized culpability be taken into account and serve as the, or a, principal measure of deserved punishment. Mitigation of penalties for many deeply disadvantaged offenders should occur as a natural consequence of a fact-specific and subjective assessment of culpability.

Mitigation of sentences of disadvantaged offenders, especially minority offenders, is the norm in the legal systems of other Western countries. In *Bugmy v The Queen* [2013] HCA 37, ¶12, the High Court of Australia observed: "An Aboriginal offender's deprived background may mitigate the sentence that would otherwise be appropriate for the offence in the same way that the deprived background of a non-Aboriginal offender may mitigate that offender's sentence." The Supreme Court of Canada in *R. v. Gladue*, [1999] 1 S.C.R. 688, endorsed mitigation of punishments of disadvantaged offenders generally. It also observed that the disadvantaged backgrounds of many aboriginal defendants tend to mitigate or reduce their culpability and noted that restorative rather than punitive dispositions are often appropriate for them. Many disadvantaged minority offenders in America occupy the same social space as do aboriginal offenders in those countries.

Contemporary American criminal justice policies, however, allow little latitude for individualizing punishment decisions concerning deeply disadvantaged offenders. Mandatory minimum, three-strikes, career criminal, and similar laws do not allow it. Sentencing guidelines systems often forbid judges to "depart" because of offenders' personal characteristics and circumstances. Ironically, these policies mostly date from the 1980s and sought to avoid differentially harsher punishment of disadvantaged and minority offenders. The premise was that allowing personal characteristics to be taken into account would result in less severe punishments of more privileged offenders.

In retrospect, those policies are perverse. Relatively few convicted offenders, especially in state courts, have privileged backgrounds. Most are economically and socially disadvantaged and disproportionately many suffer from mental health problems and drug dependence. The policies forbade special treatment of offenders from deprived backgrounds who achieved personal success. The minority offender from a broken home and a devastated neighborhood who nonetheless managed a reasonably stable domestic life, obtained a solid education, and established a stable employment record was as ineligible for a mitigated sentence as a privileged offender. Those policies treat many disadvantaged and minority offenders unfairly. Yale Law School academics Kate Stith and Steve Y. Koh observed of federal sentencing guidelines in 1993 that "denying judges the opportunity to mitigate sentences on the basis of social disadvantage has worked *against* poor and minority defendants" (their emphasis).

In any decent society, judges imposing sentences should be able to take account of morally significant differences between offenders. In the United States, they mostly can for minor offenses not affected by mandatory and similar sentencing laws or sentencing guidelines systems. For more serious offenses, often they cannot. The beginnings of obvious solutions are to repeal mandatory and similar sentencing laws, establish a deep disadvantage defense, and make it clear that deep disadvantage is an appropriate reason to impose less severe punishments than would otherwise occur.

Failure to acknowledge and allow for the effects of deeply disadvantaged lives on some offenders and their offenses is deeply unjust. Remember Evan Miller and others who have lived horrifyingly similar lives.

5

Multiple Convictions

MOST THEORETICAL WRITING about punishment centers on first offenders convicted of a single offense. Little has been written about the sizable majority of defendants who are convicted of several offenses at the same time or have previously been convicted of others. That is not a small oversight.

Efforts to address it expose fundamental conceptual problems. The biggest is the multiple offense paradox. Efforts to offer principled accounts of the sentencing of multiple offenses founder on it. In Western legal systems, individuals sentenced following multiple convictions receive a "bulk discount" that results in a lesser total punishment than if each conviction had resulted in the punishment normally imposed on a first offender convicted of a single offense. By contrast, sentences of people convicted of separate offenses in successive proceedings usually include "recidivist premiums" that result in harsher punishments, often much harsher, than first offenders receive for the same offense.[1]

Here is an example. If conviction of a single burglary normally results in a 1-year prison sentence, convictions of five at the same time would at most normally result in 2 or 3 years altogether. Dealt with in separate proceedings, the first burglary would again receive a 1-year sentence but the second through the fifth might receive sentences of 2, 3, 4, and 5 years respectively. Sentenced simultaneously, the aggregate punishment would be 2 to 3 years; sentenced successively, 15 years. Those numbers are hypothetical but, as I show below,

---

1. The terms of art are usually attributed to Kevin Reitz (2010). The practices they describe were discussed earlier by others but not in depth. An emerging literature was catalyzed by Oxford conferences organized by Julian Roberts on previous (Roberts and von Hirsch 2010) and multiple convictions (Ryberg, Roberts, and de Keijser 2017).

they realistically illustrate the results of the multiple offense paradox. Both practices are ubiquitous and comport with intuitions that are widely shared.

Mainstream punishment theories differ substantially, but most offer relatively straightforward explanations of what punishments are warranted for people convicted of a single offense, and why. Positive retributivists argue that ordinal scales of offense seriousness provide reasonably adequate guidance. Negative retributivists argue that offense seriousness sets maximum and sometimes minimum justifiable punishments; within those bounds other considerations may be taken into account. Proponents of mixed theories would allow judges to choose among alternative purposes, usually subject to retributive limits; sometimes, as in Enrico Ferri's positivism, not.

Because life is complicated, and we lack perfect knowledge, applications of any theory confront factual ambiguities that must be resolved even concerning sentencing of an individual convicted of one offense. Nonetheless, the different conceptions of contemporary retributive and mixed theories are clear enough. No one today espouses purely consequentialist theories.[2] Even Bentham did not. He proposed an excruciatingly detailed system for determining optimal deterrent punishments, but he also approved a wide range of affirmative defenses—insanity, infancy, ignorance and mistake of law, intoxication—that proscribe any punishment at all. I mostly discuss retributive and mixed theories.

The multiple offense paradox is perplexing. In legal systems characterized by the expediency principle,[3] a prosecutor presented with credible evidence

---

2. In earlier times, people did. Baroness Barbara Wootton (1959, 1963), for example, proposed elimination of consideration of mens rea at the trial stage, with the focus instead to be on whether the defendant caused the harm. Blameworthiness would be taken into account at the dispositional stage at which harm reduction and prevention would be primary considerations. H. L. A. Hart, among many others, took her and others' similar proposals seriously, making them a primary topic in *Punishment and Responsibility* (1968).

3. Prosecutors in "expediency principle" countries, including all common-law and some European jurisdictions, have authority to exercise discretion in deciding whether, when, and how to initiate a prosecution, and for what. Prosecutors in "legality principle" countries, including Germany, Italy, Finland, and Sweden, are in theory required to prosecute all cases for which available evidence would justify a conviction or to follow office policies and rules in applying generally applicable diversion policies (Asp 2012; Corda 2016; Lappi-Seppälä 2016; Weigend 2016). For a variety of reasons—infrequent use of imprisonment, short sentences, low maximum authorized sentences for single or multiple offenses—the multiple offense paradox raises much less acute issues in legality principle countries. There is no bright line in practice between systems characterized by the two principles but the distinction captures central tendencies. Fundamental differences in exercise of prosecutorial and judicial discretion are observable when, say, English and American practices are compared with those in Sweden and Finland.

of 10 drug sales, burglaries, assaults, or thefts committed over 6 weeks could file all simultaneously, thereby triggering the offender-friendly bulk discount, or file them separately, thereby triggering the offender-unfriendly recidivist premium. Most jurisdictions and ethical prosecutors presumably try to avoid arbitrariness by observing conventions when such choices are made. However, such gross potential differences testify to the power and consequences of the inconsistent intuitions that punitive punches should be pulled when cases are handled together but swung harder when cases are dealt with separately.

In chapter 2, I sketched the elements of a way to think about punishment that addresses the multiple conviction paradox while acknowledging ideas about blameworthiness and the need to deal with offenders respectfully and humanely. The fundamental problem is that most writers discuss punishment in isolation from other applicable values and principles. As Isaiah Berlin insisted, however, difficult problems often implicate competing normative principles that must first be acknowledged and then reconciled. Implications of equally valid first principles often conflict. The way forward becomes clearer when we recognize that any morally tolerable system of punishment must take account not only of offenders' blameworthiness but also—at least—of other normative principles centering on fairness, equal treatment, and parsimony.

Sentencing systems in Western countries vary enormously in the extent to which they do this. Scandinavian, German-speaking, and southern European countries probably come closest. The English-speaking countries, with their reliance on plea negotiation, mandatory minimum sentencing laws, frequent use of imprisonment, and lengthy prison terms, are furthest away. Partly those differences are products of national histories and cultures, but partly also they result from conventional ways of thinking about punishment in the English-speaking countries that are especially incomplete, inconsistent, and mechanistic.

Building upon negative retributivist and mixed theories, in this chapter I propose a framework for addressing the multiple offense paradox within just sentencing systems. Section I draws on empirical data that unchallengeably demonstrates that the typical person being sentenced has been convicted of multiple current offenses, or previously been convicted of others, or both. The paradigm case is not a first offender convicted of a single offense. Section II surveys efforts—in my view unsuccessful—to justify the recidivist premium and somewhat more successful but ad hoc efforts to justify the bulk discount. The latter, however, as is made clear in a 2017 essay by Jesper Ryberg and a 2018 book by Larry Alexander and Kimberly Ferzan, cannot be justified in

Table 5.1 Multiple charges, most serious felony, 75 largest US counties, 2009

Most Serious Charge	No Other Charge	Other Charges
All felonies	45%	55%
Violence	37%	63%
Murder	39%	61%
Rape	32%	68%
Robbery	39%	61%
Property	47%	53%
Motor Vehicle Theft	48%	52%
Burglary	33%	67%
Drugs	46%	54%

Source: Reaves (2013, Table 2).

retributive terms. Section III sets out a framework for sensibly addressing the multiple offense paradox in a just sentencing system. Were I czar, I would mandate the bulk discount because it respects other important human dignity values and forbid the recidivist premium because it does not.

I. Multiple Convictions, Past and Present

Almost all writing about punishment theory treats the first offender convicted of a single offense as the standard case. Those cases, however, make up significantly less than half of convicted offenders.[4] Tables 5.1 and 5.2 illustrate this. They present 2009 US data, the most recent available, on current charges and prior convictions of felony defendants in the state courts of the 75 most populous counties. Table 5.1 shows that 55 percent of all felony defendants' cases involved multiple charges, including 61–68 percent of violent crimes and 53 percent of property crimes.[5]

---

4. The following discussion understates the proportion of cases involving offenders convicted of multiple offenses on one occasion or successively. The US data refer only to people charged with felonies in 2009 (and thus ignore the far larger numbers charged with misdemeanors). Many individuals, however, are prosecuted for felonies on multiple occasions over a period of years. One-year counts underrepresent the number of separate occasions when individuals with prior convictions are prosecuted. If multiyear data were available and combined, cases involving defendants without prior convictions would be a lower percentage of total cases than the single-year data reveal.

5. The American experience is paralleled elsewhere. Professor Anthony Doob in private communication reported that Statistics Canada data for 2014 show that nationally 60 percent of

Table 5.2 Prior convictions and arrests, most serious felony, 75 largest US counties, 2009

Most Serious Charge	No Prior Convictions	Misdemeanor Convictions Only	One Felony	2 to 4 Felonies	4-plus Felonies	Prior Arrests
All felonies	40%	17%	13%	19%	11%	75%
Violence	47%	16%	13%	16%	8%	69%
Murder	52%	9%	13%	14%	13%	66%
Rape	49%	15%	14%	12%	10%	66%
Robbery	48%	13%	13%	17%	9%	70%
Property	44%	16%	11%	16%	13%	72%
MV Theft	38%	14%	11%	20%	17%	78%
Burglary	39%	17%	13%	18%	13%	77%
Drugs	34%	16%	13%	22%	15%	80%

Source: Reaves (2013, Tables 7 and 10).

Table 5.2 presents data on prior convictions and arrests. Overall, 60 percent of felony defendants had at least one prior conviction; 43 percent had prior felony convictions.[6] Thirty percent had two or more prior felony convictions. Eleven percent had more than four. For specific offenses, 48 percent of murder defendants had prior convictions, 53 percent of all violent crime defendants, 56 percent of property crime defendants, and 66 percent of drug defendants.

These data do not indicate total percentages of all multiple-conviction defendants, that is, both those subject to multiple current charges and those charged with a single current felony but who had previously been convicted. Some defendants charged only with one felony no doubt had prior convictions, but it is difficult to estimate how many. The last column in Table 5.2 is the closest I can come. It shows that 75 percent of all felony defendants had previously been arrested, ranging from two-thirds for murder and rape to

---

convictions involved more than one offense, ranging from 55 percent in Quebec to 72 percent in the Yukon. Roberts and de Keijser (2017) report that the Sentencing Council of England and Wales estimates that approximately 40 percent of sentencing decisions involve multiple crimes.

6. Home Office data on sentenced offenders in England and Wales in 2005 reveal higher percentages: 88 percent of those convicted of indictable offenses had prior convictions and 76 percent of those convicted of summary offenses (Roberts 2008, Table 5.2).

nearly 80 percent for motor vehicle theft, burglary, and drugs. The first-time defendant with a clean record exists, but is not the standard case.

The real-world salience of the multiple offense paradox varies widely between countries. In the United States, prior convictions can increase sentences under state guideline systems by 1.7 to 14.4 times, as Table 5.3 shows.

Some states' guideline systems, Minnesota's, for example, as Richard Frase shows in a 2017 essay, impose a recidivist premium even on first-time defendants convicted of multiple offenses, counting the most serious as the first offense and treating the others as if they were subsequent offenses. Other guidelines systems treat first-time offenders differently; sentencing for each is governed by the guidelines, usually with a presumption that sentences will be served concurrently. States without guidelines are characterized by similar diversity; no national data are available. "Career criminal," "dangerous offender," "habitual offender," and three-strikes laws based on the number and not necessarily the seriousness of convictions result in decades-long sentences up to life without the possibility of parole for people with prior convictions.

In other English-speaking countries, a "totality" principle operates to reduce sentences in cases involving multiple current offenses. A 2014 article by Julian Roberts and Jose Pina-Sanchez shows that increases in punishment severity attributable to prior convictions in England and Wales are not substantial. The totality principle is expressed in various ways, sometimes focusing on avoidance of "crushing" punishments, other times on assuring that

Table 5.3 Mean prison sentence increase for criminal history, all offenses, US sentencing guidelines systems

Jurisdiction	Average Percentage Increase for Criminal History
District of Columbia	170%
North Carolina	220%
Federal Courts	250%
Minnesota	470%
Oregon	720%
Pennsylvania	770%
Washington	800%
Utah	980%
Kansas	1440%

Source: Frase et al. (2015, Table 2.2).

punishments for any number of lesser offenses, such as theft, are not greater than punishments for more severe ones, such as rape. Other efforts are made to create mechanisms and doctrinal justifications for limiting the effects of previous convictions. I discuss these doctrines and policies in some detail in section II.

Prison sentences are comparatively rare in Scandinavian countries. Terms are usually short, reductions of one-third are automatic or nearly so, criminal history is given comparatively little weight, and maximum sentences for individual and multiple offenses top out at 12 to 21 years (most are much shorter). The scope for a recidivist premium is necessarily much smaller, as Tapio Lappi-Seppälä showed in 2016. The situation is much the same in most other western European countries.

II. *Multiple Offenses in Theory*

Many retributivists, including George Fletcher in 1978 and Richard Singer in 1979, and many others since, insist that previous convictions are irrelevant. Any additional punishment concerning them is double counting, they say, a violation of double jeopardy principles, additional punishment for crimes on which the book has been closed: "Did the crime, did the time." That logic would abrogate the recidivist premium, but also implies elimination of the bulk discount.

Many writers, however, bow to a widely shared intuition that previous convictions somehow aggravate a later crime's seriousness or the offender's blameworthiness.[7] That intuition influences every Western country's sentencing practices, though to widely different degrees. Prior convictions are hugely important in the United States, as Table 5.3, the plethora of mandatory minimum sentence and similar laws, and every statistical analysis of sentencing patterns attest. In Scandinavian countries governed by statutory sentencing principles, the role of prior convictions is limited and specified, but exists. English law authorizes increases only for prior offenses that are "recent" and "relevant." Other English-speaking countries allow increases

---

7. Ashworth and Wasik (2017) and Ewing (2019), however, offer a reason why imposition of the recidivist premium is often unjust: time in prison complicates people's later lives in ways that make achievement of law-abiding lives especially difficult. This accords with the initially tentative (e.g., Nagin, Cullen, and Jonson 2009) but now consistent (e.g., Mears and Cochran 2018) finding that all else being equal, spending time in prison makes people more not less likely to commit subsequent offenses.

subject to loose, subjective case law limits. Australian law requires deference to the "intuitive synthesis" that sentencing judges are expected to make.

A. Recidivist Premiums

Previous convictions received little theoretical attention when retributivism came into fashion in the United States in the 1970s. Before that, during a century of indeterminate sentencing, consequentialist ideas predominated.[8] Previous convictions were but one among many considerations that might be germane to individualization of punishment in a particular case. When intellectual fashions changed, most scholarly writing focused only on what H. L. A. Hart called the general justifying aim of punishment. In the earliest days of the retributivist revival, only Norval Morris, Andreas von Hirsch, and Paul Robinson wrestled with the distributive questions of how severely and in what ways individual offenders should be punished.

Concerning prior convictions, four positions emerged:

Prior Convictions Are Irrelevant. They should be given no weight in
    sentencing later crimes, as George Fletcher and Richard Singer argued.
    The deserved punishment has been suffered; the debt to society has
    been paid. Increased punishment for a subsequent crime because of a
    previous conviction is unjust.
Prior Convictions Increase Culpability. People with previous convictions
    are more culpable than first offenders, Andreas von Hirsch argued in
    Doing Justice (1976), and deserve to be punished more severely.
First Offenders Should Receive Discounts. Changing his mind, von Hirsch
    in a 1981 article proposed a system of "progressive loss of mitigation."
    Punishments for first and a small number of additional convictions
    should receive discounts from what is otherwise deserved. That is be-
    cause the offenses may have resulted from extraordinary, unlikely to
    recur, circumstances or otherwise been out of character. The discount
    should diminish with subsequent convictions as those presuppositions

---

8. In 1920s to 1950s America, indeterminate sentencing embraced the aims of utilitarian (primarily deterrent) and positivist (primarily rehabilitative and incapacitative) punishment theories
and others, with at most a nod to retribution, as evidenced by the purposes clause of the *Model
Penal Code.* It lists deterrence, reformation, and incapacitation but gives no role to retribution
except in setting upper limits (American Law Institute 1962, section 1.02 (2): "The general
purposes of the provisions governing the sentencing and treatment of offenders are: . . . (c) to
safeguard offenders against excessive, disproportionate or arbitrary punishment."

lose plausibility. After the discount lapses, previous convictions should be disregarded.

Judges Should Decide Case by Case. Punishments for particular crimes should be set within a range of "not undeserved" punishments, Norval Morris argued in *The Future of Imprisonment* (1974), usually at the low end of the range. Previous convictions are among a number of considerations that might justify more severe sentences up to but not above the deserved upper limit.

Theoretical and policy dimensions of criminal history received little sustained attention until Oxford criminologist Julian Roberts invigorated the subject in a 1997 *Crime and Justice* essay and subsequent writings. Policymakers and practitioners in the United States merrily set and applied policies that increased punishments on the basis of prior convictions. Most sentencing commissions made criminal history one axis of a grid that set out presumptive or advisory sentence ranges; so far as I know (I worked with seven commissions as they developed guidelines), none of those policies were based on sustained normative ponderings but resulted instead from back-of-an-envelope calculations and ad hoc intuitive judgments. A few habitual offender statutes permitting lengthy or life sentences for third-time felons survive from earlier times. Every state enacted mandatory minimum sentencing laws. Between 1993 and 2006, 26 states enacted three-strikes-and-you're-out laws. Many of those states and others enacted "career criminal" or "dangerous offender" statutes that authorized or required longer sentences for defined categories of recidivist offenders.[9]

In England and Wales matters have been similar, as David Downes and Rod Morgan recount in successive editions of the English *Oxford Handbook of Criminology*.[10] For part of the twentieth century, a habitual offender statute allowed long-term confinement of (mostly) recidivist property offenders. Before 1991, judges had discretion to take previous convictions into account as they thought appropriate. The *Criminal Justice Act 1991* for a time limited the weight they could be given, but the relevant provision was repealed in 1993. Three provisions of the *Crime (Sentences) Act 1997* predicated mandatory minimum prison sentences on prior convictions. The Labour Government that took office in 1997 continuously promoted a policy of incremental increases

9. I provide details and sources in Tonry (2016*b*).

10. Downes and Morgan (1994, 1997, 2002, 2007, 2012); Morgan and Smith (2017).

in punishment for each successive conviction. A Home Office commission headed by John Halliday proposed in its 2001 report that laws be enacted prescribing additional punishments in respect of recent and relevant prior convictions and authorizing indeterminate confinement for "dangerous" offenders. The *Criminal Justice Act 2003* enacted those proposals.

There matters stood when Julian Roberts, in *Punishing Persistent Offenders: Exploring Community and Offender Perspectives* (2008) and a series of edited essay collections, continued his efforts to focus attention on multiple and previous convictions. In *Punishing Persistent Offenders*, he shows that offenders, judges, other officials, and ordinary citizens agree that previous convictions justify additional punishment. Interviews of convicted English offenders showed that they believed recidivist premiums are appropriate and that they expected judges to impose them. Data on judges' sentencing patterns showed that they do sentence recidivists more severely; surveys of practitioners and officials heavily showed that they approved (ranging from 51 percent of probation officers to 90 percent of police and prosecutors). To gauge public views, Roberts arranged for a representative Market and Opinion Research International (MORI) survey of United Kingdom residents to include questions about the seriousness of hypothetical cases; the offenses were identical and the cases differed only in the extent of offenders' prior criminal records. The results showed that respondents believed criminal history is important and should influence sentencing.

So there is the problem. Many philosophers and other theorists believe that punishments should be based only or primarily on the offender's blameworthiness in relation to the current offense or offenses. Most practitioners and the general public believe that prior offending matters.

1. *Classical Views.* Neither Kant and Hegel nor Bentham explicitly discuss prior convictions but all three would have opposed the recidivist premium. Kant's and Hegel's principle of "equality" takes account only of the seriousness of the offense for which punishment is due. Bentham's view that all punishment is evil, his insistence that no punishment be more severe than deterrent considerations require, and his insistence that punishments be tailored to offenders' "sensibilities" leave little or no room for the premium.

Punishment for Kant is a "categorical imperative." Its imposition, irrespective of good or bad effects, is a moral requirement. Punishments may have preventive effects, he believed, but they are irrelevant to determination of deserved punishments. Punishments must be strictly apportioned to the seriousness of the crime: "What kind and what amount of punishment is it that public justice makes its principle and measure? None other than the principle of equality. . . . Only the *law of retribution* (*jus talionis*) . . . can specify definitely the quality and quantity of punishment" (p. 115). Hegel is equally adamant: "An injustice is done if there is even one lash too many, or one dollar or groschen, one week or one day in prison too many or too few" (p. 245).

Taken together, these passages describe views not very different from those of contemporary positive retributivists. The equality they insist on requires punishments that may change over time as cultural attitudes change, but that must be closely attuned to the seriousness of the offender's wrongdoing, and to nothing else. Whether a recidivist premium imposed following a second conviction is conceptualized as additional, delayed punishment for the first crime, or as additional punishment for the second, it violates the equality principle.

Bentham also would have opposed the recidivist premium. Because punishment like any other intentional infliction of pain is evil, it must therefore be parsimonious, in no case more than is necessary to achieve its aims. Because individuals have different personalities, vulnerabilities, and sensitivities, they are affected in different ways by the same objective experience. Punishment accordingly must take account of its likely effects on individuals.

The recidivist premium has a steep hill to climb to be justified in Benthamite terms. If its end is to prevent crime, it cannot be justified on the basis of current evidence on deterrence and incapacitation.[11] No informed person can say with a straight face that we know that the additional pains suffered by offenders because of the premium prevent greater additional suffering by victims.

2. *Contemporary Defenses.* A handful of ideas permeate recent efforts to justify the recidivist premium. One is that being convicted the first time imposes special duties on offenders to reflect on their wrongdoing and become better, law-abiding people. A second is that reoffending demonstrates defiance or disrespect of the court, the state, or the law. A third is that reoffending demonstrates bad character. A fourth is that the criminal law's legitimacy depends on acknowledgment of the widely held intuition that recidivists should be punished more severely than first offenders.

---

11. The National Academy of Sciences Committee on Causes and Consequences of High Rates of Incarceration (Travis, Western, and Redburn 2014, chap. 5) was highly skeptical that increases in punishment, including recidivists receiving premiums, have significant deterrent or incapacitative effects. So are recent authoritative surveys of the evidence (e.g., Chalfin and McCrary 2017; Chalfin and Tahamont 2018; Nagin 2018). I discuss those literatures in chapters 6 and 7.

These arguments face immediate difficulties. Liberal societies criminalize designated behaviors, not bad judgment, bad attitudes, bad character, or being the object of opprobrium. Allowing characterological assessments to count opens the door to stereotyped, idiosyncratic, and invidious judgments that are undesirable in any case and especially because they predictably redound to the detriment of the dissentient, the disadvantaged, the disreputable, and the disheveled. No one should be punished for living an unconventional life or, as Mr. Doolittle put it in *My Fair Lady*, defying middle-class morality.

The other conventional argument is that previous convictions can serve as a proxy for elevated risks of reoffending. This might be acceptable to consequentialists who, after all, are primarily concerned to minimize crime and the human and other costs associated with it. American indeterminate sentencing and the *Model Penal Code*, however, made prior convictions only one of many circumstances that might be taken into account.[12] To a positive retributivist, prevention is off-limits as a rationale for punishment. To most negative retributivists the use of reoffending predictions must be tightly constrained.[13]

a. Reoffending as Inattention to Moral Instruction. Rutgers law professor Youngjae Lee and Queens University philosopher Benjamin Ewing argue in different ways that recidivists' failures to take advantage of opportunities for moral learning justify the premium. Lee argues in a 2010 essay that something about the experience of being convicted creates a special relationship between offenders and the state that obligates offenders to do whatever is required to avoid committing additional offenses. Failure to satisfy that obligation justifies harsher subsequent punishment.

Lee's offenders walk naked into black judicial boxes subject to a criminal charge and exit with a punishment and an obligation not to reoffend. Every citizen, however, has an obligation not to offend. Each is a free moral

---

12. Sentence lengths for multiple current convictions are tightly limited (American Law Institute 1962, sects. 6.06, 6.07, and 7.06). All prison sentences are indeterminate with minimum and maximum terms; the parole board sets release dates under a presumption that all prisoners should be released when first they become eligible. When consecutive sentences are imposed, the code specifies that minimums and maximums for the most serious offense govern. The longest possible minimum is 10 years for the most serious felonies including murder and aggravated rape (1 year is the norm). The longest minimums for other felonies are usually 2 or 3 years (1 year is the norm). The longest possible maximum for a single offense other than murder is 20 years (for most, 5 or 10). All minimums and maximums are subject to 12 days per month reduction for good behavior. Good conduct thus can reduce a 20-year maximum to 12, 10 years to 6, and 5 to 3. The longest possible net minimum is about 6 years.

13. Chapter 7 explains why.

agent. Those who choose to offend are vulnerable to prosecution, conviction, and punishment. That's it. Unless Lee can convincingly explain where the offender's special obligation comes from, and he does not, the argument fails.

Ewing in a 2019 article argues that convictions remind offenders of their moral and legal obligations, the sources of their moral fallibility, and the need to guard against them. That reminder is important, he writes, "not because the failure to take advantage of it makes a person worthy of extra state condemnation, but because, all else equal, simply having the notice means having a better opportunity to avoid wrongdoing going forward." Being provided that opportunity, and not taking advantage of it, vitiates complaints "about the punishment that awaits them should they persist on the path of criminality."[14]

There are a number of problems with Lee's and Ewing's arguments. First, no rational offender would voluntarily agree to accept otherwise undeserved punishments or obligations different from those of other people. If the undertaking is implied, whether or not the offender agreed to it, some basis for the implication is needed. Even if some offenders, if asked, might agree to be subject to special obligations to be law-abiding or to make the most of their opportunities, their weak legal positions and the psychological pressures of court environments undermine claims that their undertakings could be voluntary in any meaningful sense. Second, all citizens are expected to know what criminal laws forbid and to abide by them; no explanation is given for why convicted offenders have different or greater legal obligations than others. Third, although Lee and Ewing explicitly reject the view that the premium should be imposed because offenders are defiant, disappointing, incorrigible, or of questionable character, that is what their arguments imply. Ewing observes that "recidivist crime . . . [may provide] stronger evidence of an underlying disposition to additional criminality—which is in turn either the product of, or constitutive of, worse moral character."

b. Reoffending as Culpable Omission. Lee argues that the recidivist premium can be justified on the basis of offenders' "omissions" to honor their

---

14. Ewing's analysis is less unforgiving than may appear. In the same article he explains that current American law in many ways—collateral legal consequences, criminogenic prison conditions, limited state support for reintegrative self-help in prison or in the community— diminishes offenders' opportunities to achieve law-abiding lives. He concludes that "the theory of 'prior convictions as moral opportunities' does not justify recidivist premiums in the criminal justice systems of America. . . . The most obvious practical implication of the theory is that if we wish to persist in punishing repeat offenders more harshly, we need to take more seriously than we currently do the challenge of making crime and punishment net moral opportunities of genuine value" (2019, p. 41). This is evocative of the conclusions of an earlier generation of philosophers about punishment generally (e.g., Murphy 1973; Duff 1986; Honderich 1989).

obligations to desist from future offending. Subsequent punishments can thus be deconstructed into the punishment deserved for the new offense and additional punishment for the culpable omission.

Lee's argument fails in its terms and as an analogy. Criminal law doctrines provide for omissions liability only in limited circumstances. The most common involve harms to others for whom an actor has an established duty of care, typically those of parents or caretakers for children, or of people who have undertaken contractually to care for others. Less commonly, courts recognize omissions liability in quasi-contractual circumstances in which a person has exclusive control over a vulnerable person and knows or has reason to know that the second person is in peril. Lee's argument involves no equivalent recognized or recognizable legal duty, nor any duty to a specific person. Basing the recidivist premium on a generalized obligation not to reoffend stretches omissions liability far beyond its traditional or any coherent reach. The predicates of Lee's premium are actions, not failures to act.

c. Apologies and Implied Promises. Christopher Bennett in a 2010 essay argued that punishment for an offense should be understood to involve an apology by the offender that implies an undertaking to desist from crime. Commission of a subsequent offense triggers the punishment deserved for it and additional punishment for failure to comply with the implied undertaking. The apology is understood to mean, "I am sorry I committed the first offense and caused or threatened harm to the victim, I recognize that it was wrongful and unlawful, and I promise not to do it or commit any other offense again." As an analogy, Bennett describes a protracted set of hypothetical interactions between a student and a professor in which a student fails to appear at meetings despite repeated commitments, implying that he does not know or care that each failed meeting is an unwarranted imposition and imposes opportunity costs on the professor.

The student may well feel guilty each time he or she fails to appear, apologize, and intend thereafter to appear on time. The professor may understandably feel aggrieved, and more aggrieved each time the student fails to appear. Many observers might feel the professor was entitled to refuse to make another appointment, extend a courtesy, or agree to a special request. Few would likely agree that the professor was entitled to penalize the student by reducing the course grade he or she otherwise deserved.

It is not easy to apply the inconsiderate student analogy to the criminal courts. Offenders are not required to apologize though sometimes they do, or otherwise express regret for their actions. Were apologies required, they could not fairly be described as voluntary, and if sincerely made, the appropriate recipient is the victim, not the judge or the state. Apologies in any case are backward-looking; they relate to what the offender did or the harm that was caused. Undertakings to desist from crime are unlikely in an apology, and gratuitous, and seldom likely to be of particular interest to victims, unless for some reason they are especially interested in offenders' future lives. If undertakings are made, victims, like the professor, are entitled to be disappointed if new crimes occur. Failure to honor an undertaking, though, would no more justify changing a deserved punishment than changing a deserved course grade. What is important about any new offenses is that they occurred, not that offenders failed to honor usually fictional apologies and implied undertakings. Failure to honor an implied promise, or an overt one, is not a criminal offense. People in a liberal society are entitled to be difficult, rude, eccentric, and disrespectful. There may be social costs to be paid, but neither vexatious behavior nor its consequences are the law's business.

d. Public Preferences. Julian Roberts justifies the recidivist premium partly on the basis of the widely shared view that recidivists should be punished more severely than first offenders. One argument is that, in a democracy, citizens' preferences should be respected. A second is that moral intuitions, partly probably a product of natural selection, are part of what makes us human, and punishment as a human process should respect those intuitions. A third is that the law's legitimacy in citizens' eyes depends on its being seen to operate consistently with widely held views. A fourth is that punishment, although usually understood as something done to an offender because of an offense, is also or to a significant degree a response to an offender's bad character as evidenced by repeat offending.

The public attitudes argument shifts focus from the offender to the audience, from what the offender deserves to what observers want to see done. The rule of law, however, calls on judges to make decisions based on the facts of the cases before them and to ignore external pressures. In other legal contexts, judges are ethically obligated to ignore political pressures, public emotions, and media attention and to decide the cases before them according to applicable laws. No one would believe it appropriate for a judge deciding a civil lawsuit about an automobile accident or a commercial dispute to base the decision on opinion surveys, media attention, or assessments of litigants' good or bad character. Criminal cases are no different. It is the defendant's liberty that is at stake, and the judicial task is to determine whether the defendant has committed the alleged offense and, if so, to determine the appropriate punishment. Retributivist accounts base the appropriate punishment on the offender's blameworthiness. Consequentialist accounts link punishment to

crime prevention or to maximizing happiness, dominion, or something similar. Economists' accounts tie appropriate punishments to economic efficiency. None of them ties it to satisfactions of bystanders.

Ronald Dworkin's discussion of personal and external preferences in relation to integration of Texas law schools in *Law's Empire* (1986) illustrates why
observers' preferences or satisfactions should not matter. The Supreme Court
in *Sweatt v. Painter*, 339 U.S. 629 (1950), considered whether the University of
Texas Law School could refuse to admit black applicants if a second state university law school was available to provide legal educations to them. Dworkin
distinguished between personal preferences, what one wants for oneself, and
external preferences, what one wants for others, and between positive and
negative versions of each. Then he asked, should the court take account of
white Texans' negative external preferences that black applicants be denied
admission? His answer was no: negative preferences based on invidious
considerations should not count. The schadenfreude some people enjoy in
other people's disappointments should not count.

The stakes involved in the recidivist premium—usually additional years
in prison—are greater than they were in *Sweatt v. Painter*. They involve infliction of suffering, not disappointment or denial of opportunity, and foreseeably burden a class of people who are already stigmatized. Making *Sweatt
v. Painter* an especially apt allusion, the inflicted afflictions disproportionately affect members of minority groups.

The existence of widely shared intuitions that recidivists should be
punished more severely than first-time offenders cannot justify the recidivist
premium. Decisions about justice in individual cases should not be influenced
by the results of surveys or plebiscites. That is little different from having the
audience in the arena vote on whether defeated gladiators live or die. In any
case, widely shared intuitions are seldom fixed. They vary over time and place
and between cultures. Intuitions at one time or place are often widely seen as
morally unacceptable later on or elsewhere. Examples include beliefs not so
long ago that husbands should be able to discipline their wives, that homo-
sexuality is the product of mental disorder, and that the sky will fall if black
people have equal access to public accommodations.

Legitimacy is important and worth worrying about. It is not, however,
obvious why offenders should be punished more severely in its pursuit, especially when most are socially and economically disadvantaged, and disproportionately many are members of minority groups. Public perceptions of the
legitimacy of the courts might be low for many reasons, including lack of transparency, mechanistic assembly-line case processing, widespread suspicions of

class and race bias, and political demagoguery. It is unlikely that the presence or absence of a recidivist premium is or could be a major contributor.[15]

e. Bad Character and Premeditation. Many of the arguments supporting the recidivist premium implicitly or explicitly turn on offenders' demonstrations of bad character. Julian Roberts is explicit: reoffending is a sign of antisocial tendencies that justify additional punishment. The following quotations from *Punishing Persistent Offenders* are illustrative:

> [R]epeat offenders are more culpable by virtue of their mental state at the time of the crime, in much the same way that offenders who plan their offending may be seen as more blameworthy.
>
> Having been convicted and sentenced, a person should desist from offending; committing further offences is evidence that the offender has elected an alternative moral course to that of a law-abiding citizen.

The first of those arguments is that recidivists are more culpable than first offenders in the same sense that people who commit crimes involving substantial planning and premeditation are more culpable than people who commit crimes impulsively. Planning and premeditation, however, may or may not signify enhanced culpability. It depends. Law professors often illustrate this by contrasting a mercy killing following repeated requests by a terminally ill loved one with an impulsive decision to kill a small girl by pushing her off a bridge railing. Both are intentional killings, but only the mercy killing is premeditated.

A small class of offenders—bosses of drug cartels, career members of organized crime groups, perpetrators of complex white-collar and organizational crimes—may be more culpable than most garden variety offenders because their actions reflect highly organized and extensive planning. The decisive characteristic, however, is not planning and premeditation per se but professionalism. Most offenders, however, are not drug cartel bosses, organized crime principals, or securities law violators but people living marginalized, chronically disorganized lives like those described in *Crime, Justice, and Protecting the Public* (1990), an English Home Office White Paper: "[M]uch

---

15. Roberts and Jan de Keijser (2014) in a different context express doubt that any credible empirical evidence supports Paul Robinson's (2013) "empirical desert" claim that public perceptions of the criminal law's legitimacy, and law-abidingness, will decline if legal rules and practices deviate from widely held views. There is equally little credible evidence that prohibition of the recidivist premium would create legitimacy deficits.

crime is committed on impulse, given the opportunity presented by an open window or unlocked door, and it is committed by offenders who live from moment to moment; their crimes are as impulsive as the rest of their feckless, sad, or pathetic lives."

Roberts separately argues that recidivists are especially culpable because they have chosen "an alternative moral course." It does not require legal training to recognize that the law is on a slippery slope when offenders' bad characters are used to justify harsher punishments.

f. Progressive Loss of Mitigation. Andreas von Hirsch's "progressive loss of mitigation" analysis, most fully developed in a 2010 essay, has two components. First, agreeing with many other retributivists, prior convictions cannot justify harsher punishments. Second, however, punishments for first and, to a diminishing extent, some subsequent offenses should be reduced because they may have occurred in extraordinary circumstances or otherwise have been out of character. Recent developmental and neuropsychological research documenting cognitive and impulse control differences between young people and adults buttresses his argument. So does research on the age/crime curve that shows that most people commit crimes as teenagers but rapidly desist as they mature. Steep declines begin in the late teens and continue into the twenties.

Von Hirsch's proposal has much to commend it. Empirical research on sentencing patterns shows that judges often do impose less severe punishments on first offenders. It is likely that most people have sympathy for others who are for the first time dealing with the intimidating, dehumanizing, and bureaucratic experience of being a criminal defendant. The developmental and neuropsychological findings and the age/crime curve provide good reasons to suppose that early crimes by younger people are often out of character relative to the characters they will have as mature adults. The research findings provide good reasons to reduce punishments for many younger offenders as, for offenders of any age, does the existence of extraordinary circumstances and the occurrence of acts that seem conspicuously out of character. Those considerations, however, need not depend on a progressive loss of mitigation theory. They can better be understood as mitigating circumstances that make an offense less blameworthy.

Viewed as a component of a retributive punishment theory, progressive loss of mitigation faces formidable challenges in the real world. First, many first offenses are not momentary lapses or brought about by extraordinary circumstances, but are products of planning and calculation. Second, as Table 5.1 showed, a sizable majority of offenders are charged with multiple offenses.

Many are convicted of more than one, raising the problem of how to apply progressive loss of mitigation to multiple current offenses. Collapsing multiple convictions into a constructive "first offense" could solve the problem, but not convincingly.

Third, many first offenses are not out of character except in a longitudinal temporal sense. Much offending by young people is done in groups, influenced by peer pressures and norms. Much offending is done by members of gangs or peer groups and reflects their cultures and expectations. Few first court appearances involve first offenses in the offender's life. A first drug crime arrest, for example, often follows hundreds of successful sales. A first prosecution for domestic violence, shoplifting, burglary, and many other offenses seldom occurs the first time the illegal behavior occurs.

Fourth, as Benjamin Ewing points out in a 2019 article, "if progressive loss of mitigation rests on the idea that subsequent offenses are progressively less likely to be out of character, then it is doubtful that we can save the view from collapsing into (or suffering from the same problems as) a culpability-based view rooted in character." I explain above why basing punishments on assessments of bad character is undesirable.

Many people who write about punishment theory find the progressive loss of mitigation analysis appealing because it justifies reduced punishments for many offenders. I have always thought it an unconvincing rationalization that tries to limit the significance of prior convictions while not too starkly contravening widely shared intuitions. It takes little imagination to recharacterize the mitigated first offender punishment as the norm and the subsequent increases as recidivist premiums.

B. Bulk Discounts

Multiple current convictions trigger a different and inconsistent widely shared intuition supporting the bulk discount. Data from many countries demonstrate that it exists almost everywhere.[16] Australian, Canadian, and English courts often apply a "totality" doctrine that sentencing for multiple offenses should be limited to, typically, the most severe punishment that could have been imposed for the most serious offense or should not exceed

---

16. E.g., Germany (Albrecht 1994); Australia (Lovegrove 1997); Finland (Hinkkanen and Lappi-Seppälä 2011); Sweden (Vibla 2017). Australian and Canadian appellate case law (Bottoms 2017), English case law and guidelines (Ashworth and Wasik 2017), and American sentencing guidelines (Frase 2017) offer similar demonstrations.

the normal sentence imposed for a qualitatively more serious kind of crime. These doctrines depend not on application of detailed rules and policies but ultimately, as Anthony Bottoms showed in a 2017 essay, on ad hoc decisions by trial and appellate judges. In the United States, the original *Model Penal Code* did not mention a totality principle but effectively observed one. It delegated to judges the decision whether to impose consecutive or concurrent sentences for multiple offenses but accorded little practical or legal significance to the decision.[17]

Various rationales have been offered for the bulk discount. I separately discuss policy arguments, offered usually by lawyers, and arguments by philosophers.

1. *Lawyers' Explanations.* There are four main ones. First, morbid psychology: judges should act sympathetically toward people whose multiple offenses were influenced by sympathy-inducing circumstances. Second, crushing sentences: no matter how many crimes were committed, justice requires limits on aggregate punishments. Third, interoffense comparisons: conviction and sentencing are blaming exercises and, no matter what the number of offenses, punishments should not imply equal or greater blame than do sentences imposed for palpably more serious offenses. People who commit burglaries are less blameworthy than people who commit rapes; people convicted of burglaries, no matter how many, should be punished less severely than people convicted of rape. Fourth, mercy: judges should be merciful when convictions for multiple offenses could result in unduly severe punishments.

a. *Morbid Psychology.* Andrew Ashworth argued in *Sentencing and Criminal Justice* (2015) that multiple offenses often are manifestations of a troubled, ongoing state of mind and in such cases should be merged and thereby benefit from the discount. Examples include offenses arising from a single incident, such as a burglary in which property was taken, an assault occurred, and an auto was stolen in escaping, or a series of offenses—six burglaries in a week or two—that may all be the product of a troubled mental state or dire personal circumstances. The rationale is presumably a psychological one which, for lack of a better term, I call "morbid psychology." People involved in a crime gone wrong panic, and do things they otherwise would not. People under circumstantial stress—a lost job, a loved one's death, a financial meltdown, an existential crisis, an acute

---

17. See note 12.

mental health problem—may commit a series of offenses that then seem to them to make sense but normally would not. Everyone has experienced stressful or emotionally charged times when things were said or done that were later regretted.

Several difficulties arise. One is to reconcile the morbid psychology argument for multiple current offenses with the progressive-loss-of-mitigation argument about successive offenses. The latter treats the absence of other offenses as plausible evidence for a presumption of reduced blameworthiness. The morbid psychology argument treats the occurrence of other offenses as plausible evidence of reduced blameworthiness. There is, however, no reason why they must be reconciled. Both can be viewed as fact-specific corollaries of the view that just punishments should take account of individuals' circumstances and situations.

Another is to reconcile the morbid psychology argument with criminal law doctrine that generally makes background psychological considerations irrelevant. Mens rea analyses disregard motive (the mercy killing), stressful circumstances (Jean Valjean), environmental conditions (social disadvantage), and heightened emotion (domestic or political violence), asking only whether the proscribed act and the required intention, knowledge, or recklessness have been proven. If so, end of story. Likewise, criminal law doctrine disregards mental states except concerning insanity, incompetence to stand trial, and diminished capacity. The morbid psychology argument by contrast calls for mitigation of sentences for mentally competent offenders for whom the required mens rea can be proven, posing the question why motives, most mental conditions, and other extenuating circumstances are irrelevant in the criminal law but dispositive at sentencing. The response is that sentencing is inherently discretionary and judges may properly be more compassionate at that stage.

Perverse incentives pose another difficulty. A traditional maxim insists that the criminal law should speak loudest when temptations are greatest. Bentham's utilitarian prescription calls for use of incremental punishments to provide marginal disincentives. Attempts should be punished less severely than completed offenses to provide incentives to desist. Punishments should be scaled to offense seriousness to provide incentives to commit less serious crimes. That logic applied to the burglary gone wrong or the short-term crime spree calls for increased penalties for successive crimes. The morbid psychology argument calls for decreases. A credible reconciliation is that the morbid psychology argument is concerned with individualized assessments of blameworthiness. Bentham's model, and much criminal law doctrine, are premised on assumptions about deterrent effects that are not supported by persuasive empirical evidence.

Even if those issues can be satisfactorily addressed, the morbid psychology argument arises only in some multiple-offense situations. It neglects the commonplace generalist offender charged with multiple offenses committed over an extended period. Such offenders are as likely to be affected by morbid psychology as are others who commit multiple offenses in a short period. It is not much of a stretch to extend the argument to include deeply disadvantaged people living in deteriorated neighborhoods. Joining gangs, selling drugs, and committing property crimes may seem sensible choices to people who would not feel that way if the circumstances of their lives were different. Remember Mike Royko's description in chapter 4 of the deeply disadvantaged and privileged youths' respective "choices" not to go to Yale or join a street gang.

b. Crushing Sentences. Uppsala University law professor Nils Jareborg in 1998 averred that human lives are short and no punishment should deprive an offender of a large fraction of what remains. Sentences that do are often referred to as "crushing." *R v M* (CA), (1996) 1 SCR 530, a leading Canadian case, establishes that a multiple-offense sentence is "unduly harsh" when the effect of the "aggregate sentence is . . . to impose on the offender a crushing sentence not in keeping with his record and prospects." The phrase recurs in the sentencing jurisprudence of other English-speaking Commonwealth countries.

An equivalent principle is implicit in statutory limits in some European countries on maximum aggregate sentences for individual and multiple offenses. The Norwegian mass murderer Anders Breivik, for example, received a prison term of 21 years because nothing longer was possible. Most European countries prevent crushing sentences through a combination of absolute limits (often 12 to 20 years) on any non–life sentence, substantially shorter maximums for most offenses, and near-automatic one-third remission (Americans call it time off for good behavior). Few people receiving life sentences in those countries serve more than 10 to 15 years. The *Model Penal Code* achieved something similar by authorizing judges to impose consecutive sentences, but constrained by the maximums and minimums for the most serious offense.

I found no literature that offers other than ad hoc criteria for knowing when a sentence is crushing. Retributive ordinal proportionality offers guidance for sentencing single offenses, but provides no obvious answers for multiple offenses other than summing up the separately deserved punishments for each. Consequentialists and negative retributivists can justify a crushing offense doctrine. Lengthy sentences cannot be justified on the basis of evidence about deterrent or incapacitative effects, except possibly for a tiny number of chronic dangerous offenders. There is convincing evidence that longer sentences have no greater deterrent benefit than shorter ones and that incapacitative effects are small to nonexistent. Natural desistance from crime, even among chronic offenders, occurs early in most lives, making long sentences ineffective in preventive terms. "Residual career lengths" are almost always short; few criminal careers extend beyond the early thirties and most end much earlier.[18] Traditional ideas about parsimony and use of the least restrictive alternative posit that no punishment is justifiable that exceeds its expected benefits.

Canadian and Australian cases that refer to crushing sentences offer no useful law-like generalizations for identifying them. Anthony Bottoms in 2017 discussed an Australian case, *Azzopardi v. R.* [2011] VSCA 372, in which a lengthy sentence for multiple offenses was shortened radically, but in a country in which sentencing jurisprudence celebrates the judge's intuitive synthesis, no useful generalizations emerge. Likewise in Canada, where the ultimate test is that sentences be "just and appropriate" or in England, where guidelines set starting points and ranges for subcategories of offenses such as robbery, theft, and sexual assault, but treat only sentences outside much broader "offense ranges" as "departures" requiring special justification.

c. Interoffense Comparisons. One indicator that an aggregate sentence is "unduly harsh," *R v M* (CA), (1996) 1 SCR 530, notes, is that it "is substantially above the normal level of a sentence for the most serious of the individual offences involved." Andrew Ashworth and Martin Wasik in a 2017 essay observed that "inter-offence proportionality is the dominant consideration," and accordingly that "several lesser offences should not combine to produce a sentence above that which is appropriate for a significantly more serious offence."

The unanswered question is why interoffense comparisons should trump an approach in which deserved sentences for each offense are simply totaled. The crushing offense analysis provides an explanation. John Darley and Paul Robinson in 1995 and Julian Roberts in 2008 showed that public opinion generally supports it.

---

18. These literatures are surveyed in the report of the National Academy of Sciences Panel on Causes and Consequences of High Rates of Incarceration (Travis, Western, and Redburn 2014, chaps. 3, 5).

One unnerving implication is that interoffense comparisons imply a characterological theory of punishment.[19] The proposition, for example, that no number of burglaries, common property crimes, auto thefts, or retail drug sales should be punished as severely as a robbery implies essentialist notions about offenders. The comparison is implicitly between "burglars" and "robbers"; the latter can justifiably be punished more severely. Proponents of interoffense comparisons would reply that they mean what they say: the comparison is between types of offenses not types of offenders. The relative seriousness of the offense and the blameworthiness associated with it are the basis for limiting sentence lengths.

d. Mercy and Compassion. The fourth rationale, Anthony Bottoms argued in 1998, is that a sense of mercy explains why judges sometimes reduce sentences. Judges sometimes say that is what they are doing. Nigel Walker, in *Aggravation, Mitigation, and Mercy* (1999), observed that judges invoke "mercy" when they have "a vague compassion for the offender but cannot articulate a precise justification for reducing the severity of the sentence." Walker showed, however, that mercy is an elusive concept in the context of sentencing. If an element of a case, for example, Jean Valjean's motive to steal food to feed his starving family, calls for a mitigated sentence, Walker observed, imposing one is an act of justice, not of mercy.

There is a fundamental question in any case whether judges have moral standing to grant mercy even if a victim or God did. Jeffrie Murphy, in an influential 1988 essay, "Mercy and Legal Justice," observed that "Judges in criminal cases are obligated to do justice . . . [There is] simply no room for mercy as an autonomous virtue with which their justice should be tempered." Judges have authority to enforce and apply the law; the source of their authority to be merciful is not obvious. Assuming such authority exists, its exercise is inherently subjective and idiosyncratic unless guided by standards. It is hard to see anything law-like or generalizable in granting judges ad hoc powers of mercy.

Some of these difficulties can be sidestepped by substituting "compassion" or "sympathy" for mercy. I have never understood why judges and lawyers feel more comfortable claiming to be merciful than claiming to be compassionate. As C. S. Lewis (1949) long ago observed, mercy implies reduction

---

19. Ryberg (2017) offers the additional objection that offense severity is a continuum, not a step ladder, and that without clear breaks inter-offense comparisons are not workable. That is reductionist. Step effects inevitably occur in categorizing phenomena in a natural distribution (for example, how does a teacher draw a line between a B+ and an A-?), and there are practical solutions. Sentencing guidelines grids provide examples.

in a punishment that is deserved. Compassion implies acceptance of human frailties and vulnerabilities.

Openly empowering judges to be compassionate is not much different from creating a presumption that judges be parsimonious. The motivations would be much the same, to avoid imposing unnecessary suffering. The *Model Sentencing Act* did this by calling always for imposition of the least restrictive alternative punishment. The *Model Penal Code* did it by creating presumptions against imprisonment and in favor of parole release. The principal likely objection to a license to be compassionate or to a parsimony presumption is that it would somehow be disrespectful to victims.[20] It has become conventional and politically correct to say that vindication of victims and acknowledgment of their suffering are goals of sentencing, but that cannot be right. In common-law systems, only the state and the defendant are parties in a criminal case.

The criminal law in any case often cannot "vindicate" victims by imposing punishments. Conviction and therefore sentencing are often impossible for uncontroversial reasons, for example, when the perpetrator is below the age of criminal responsibility, is incompetent to stand trial, or is acquitted on grounds of insanity. Harm to victims may result from offenders' morally innocent violent acts committed, for example, under a mistaken but reasonable belief of the need for self-defense. Defendants are acquitted for many reasons, including insufficient or inadmissible evidence, or simply that a judge or jury is not convinced of guilt beyond reasonable doubt. It would be exceedingly odd in any of those circumstances to say that the victim was treated unfairly or disrespectfully. It is similarly odd to say that the victim is treated unfairly or disrespectfully when a compassionate sentence is imposed.

A second objection to granting compassion licenses is that judges' subjective responses to offenders will produce disparities in punishments received by people convicted of comparable offenses. Positive retributivists might object. So be it. Negative retributivists and most consequentialists believe that sentencing is inexorably a human process and that decisions about punishment should always, within limits, take account of important individual differences.

---

20. From this comes the one exception Jeffrie Murphy allowed to his view that judges (and prosecutors and parole boards) lack authority to be merciful: "A judge or any other official may exercise mercy in a criminal case [only] as a vehicle for expressing the sentiments of all of those who have been victimized by the criminal and who, given those sentiments, wish to waive the right that each has that the criminal be punished" (Murphy 1988, pp. 179–80).

Each of the lawyers' arguments for the bulk discount is ethically attractive. All try to justify a practice that, unlike the recidivist premium, does no damage to offenders. The interoffense comparison argument comes closest to escaping the traditional retributive framework. The crushing sentence argument derives from equal treatment implications of human rights principles. Its proponents need in a generalizable way to explain why a sentence is crushing, and when.

2. *Philosophers' Efforts*. Judges and lawyers have been obliged to address multiple offense sentencing because such cases arise and courts must try to explain their decisions. Philosophers have only recently begun to consider the problem.

The default position for retributivist philosophers is that the bulk discount is not justifiable. So Larry Alexander and Kimberly Ferzan unqualifiedly concluded in a 2018 book. Jesper Ryberg in a 2017 essay attributed the underlying supporting intuition in part to "scope insensitivity," a psychological characteristic that makes human beings more sympathetic to concrete problems than to abstract ones, and to small numbers of troubling phenomena than to large ones. A drowned refugee child pulled from the sea or a father and daughter drowned trying to swim across the Rio Grande attract massive media attention and public sympathy; thousands of refugee children attract less. Stalin is said to have observed that one death is a tragedy, one million a statistic.

Few philosophers have attempted to justify the bulk discount. Two recent arguments deserve A's for effort but something less for persuasiveness. To make their cases, each abandons the mainstream retributive view that punishment is a blaming institution that should censure people in proportion to the blameworthiness expressed by their crimes.

a. *Making Amends*. Christopher Bennett in a 2017 essay argues that sentencing is inevitably and rightly discretionary. What counts is "making amends," a phenomenon not closely coupled to the seriousness or number of offenses. Bennett bases his argument on a vignette about one of two business partners who repeatedly over an extended period embezzled funds. Bennett considers what the victim would regard as adequate amends and concludes that it would seldom be the total amount of money involved, restitution in like kind, but something considerably less that expressed suitable remorse. Defendants being punished for multiple offenses, he argues by analogy, may receive discounted sentences if that punishment can reasonably be regarded as making amends.

There are substantial problems. First, people in close private relationships provide an inapt analogy for exercise of state power against—for this purpose—anonymous citizens. Second, unlike in the vignette, offenders' agreement is not a precondition to imposition of a punishment; it is far-fetched to view receipt of a punishment as a communicative act by the recipient. Third, "making amends" inexorably raises the question of who decides the amount of punishment. In the vignette, the victim must agree, but that cannot be right for the criminal court. Otherwise punishment decisions would depend on the luck of the draw in the identity of the victim. If the judge decides, the inevitable problems of subjectivity, idiosyncrasy, and inconsistency posed by "crushing sentences" and mercy arise, but more acutely. Fourth, "making amends" effectively abandons concern for proportionality and rule-of-law values including consistency, predictability, and transparency.

b. Character. Youngjae Lee in a 2017 essay, paralleling his earlier writing on the recidivist premium, argues that multiple offense sentencing should be based primarily on what the offenses reveal about the offender's character. Thus, a person convicted of five burglaries, thefts, or street-level drug sales should be seen as a burglar, thief, or drug dealer, and an appropriate sentence determined by comparison with sentences typically received by rapists, robbers, or others convicted of more serious crimes. This resembles the interoffense comparison approach but with a big difference. That approach begins with the offenses and then asks whether any number of them can be regarded as being as serious and deserving of punishment as a more serious crime. It is not whether robbers are worse people than thieves, but whether robberies are worse than thefts.

Lee essentializes offenders and asks, what do "thieves" or "rapists" deserve? There is no way, he writes, "for the criminal justice system to avoid commenting on the actor's bad character traits" and accordingly that the "criminal law punishes persons for their actions *only when . . . the actions display their character defects* [emphasis added]." By labeling a person a "rapist," the state is "commenting on a set of traits that the person has that has generated the wrongful act of rape." This tidily addresses lots of multiple offense scenarios. Six thefts compared with four present no problem because the core message is "He is a thief." Simultaneous convictions for a rape and a burglary are no problem since rapists' character traits are even less attractive than burglars'. Nothing worse is shown by the burglary. Punishment for the rape is enough.

There are fundamental problems and practical ones. The first is that reification of types of offenders is difficult to reconcile with justice. It categorizes people who are also fathers, husbands, conservatives, Catholics, carpenters, and tennis players on the basis of one small part of a life. Once sentencing shifts focus from culpable conduct to characterological assessment, the slope becomes slippery. At its bottom are convictions and punishments for antisocial personality or other indicators of less than stellar character.

The second is that criminal law jurisprudence in every democratic country focuses on offenses. Values of consistency, equality, and procedural fairness require this. The defendant's identity, character, and personality should not matter. Otherwise the criminal law risks becoming an instrument for the exercise of political, class, racial, economic, or religious power.

It is sometimes said that judges are powerfully influenced by their assessments of defendants' character, and that it is hypocritical and perverse to pretend otherwise. Yes, but. Human beings inevitably sometimes fail to do what they are supposed to do, and some judges no doubt take characterological assessments into account. It is a giant step, however, from the observation that judges sometimes disregard applicable legal and moral norms to the normative claim that it is right that they do so.

The third problem is the elusiveness and artificiality of the concept of character "trait" or "defect." In a drunken assault, is the defect lack of self-control, inability to control alcohol intake, poor anger management, or willingness to strike another person? For a trait to be a relevant determining consideration, presumably it has to be a static characteristic such as low intelligence, egocentrism, aggressiveness, or callousness. Large fractions, probably large majorities, of sexual and physical assaults, however, are committed while under the influence of alcohol or drugs. Causal explanations have to take account of interactions between static characteristics and substance effects. The dispositive character trait is then presumably something like willingness to use drugs or alcohol under circumstances in which there is a nontrivial chance of an assault occurring. It is not obvious how that can sensibly be related to interoffender comparisons. In any case, much crime is situational and occurs as much because of background conditions as of static or other traits of individuals. The only conception of "character trait" that appears workable, and the one Lee seems to have in mind, is a generic characterization of people convicted of robbery as "robbers." This, however, quickly collapses into a simple interoffense comparison. If that is true, the argument provides no distinctive justification for the bulk discount.

A fourth set of problems concerns implementation of Lee's model. A number of questions need answers. For one, once a person who commits multiple offenses becomes "a burglar" or "a rapist," is the number of offenses germane?

On Lee's account, an offender convicted of burglary and rape need be punished only for the rape. The implication is that punishments for rape should be the same whether one, two, or five rapes were committed. The extras presumably provide no additional information about the "rapist's" character. It is possible to riff at length about this. If—this must be the case—two or five rapes should be punished more severely than one, determining the incremental significance of each after the first raises all the problems that are raised by multiple offenses generally. Setting that aside, should the interoffense comparison for, say, multiple burglaries be made with the normal sentence for a single rape or for multiple rapes? Unless a single rape provides a license for committing others without additional penalty, the number of rapes must affect punishment. If that is true, there is no single benchmark with which multiple burglaries can be prepared.

Empirical research provides little support for reification of types of offenders based on their offenses. Four decades of longitudinal, developmental, and criminal careers research findings show that most offenders are generalists, not specialists. The essentialization of burglars, robbers, rapists, and drug dealers is almost always an empirical mistake. One can say that a particular defendant was convicted of five burglaries, but seldom accurately that "burglar" is his or her essential character, even as an offender.

Bennett's and Lee's theoretical analyses cannot justify the bulk discount. The lawyers' explanations make sense but are difficult to generalize.

III. Sentencing Multiple Offenders

A number of conclusions emerge. The first is that positive retributivism cannot be reconciled with either the recidivist premium or the bulk discount. If the recidivist premium cannot be justified, as most retributivists believe, neither can the bulk discount.

The second is that punishments more severe than can meaningfully be said to be proportionate to an offender's blameworthiness in relation to the offense of which he or she is convicted are unjust. Although it is impossible to say precisely what punishment is deserved for a specific offense, relatively uncontroversial ordinal scales of offense severity can be developed in any time and place that provide bases for saying that punishments are or are not disproportionately severe.

The third is that systems of punishment based on negative retributivism, or consequentialist models like Braithwaite and Pettit's republican theory that respect proportionate upper limits, can deal with both sides of the multiple offense paradox. Nothing, including multiple prior convictions, can justify imposition of a punishment more severe than is proportionate for the worst instance of the most serious of the current offenses. This is the logic of the interoffense comparison defense of the bulk discount and allows for imposition of somewhat more severe punishments for multiple current convictions. The typical offense is not the most serious of its kind.

The fourth is that punishment decisions must be individualized if they are to be based on offenders' blameworthiness and take account of the circumstances of their lives. This is the moral of all of the lawyers' justifications for the bulk discount. The essence of the arguments about morbid psychology, crushing sentences, interoffense comparisons, and mercy is that decisions about just punishments of individual human beings should be based on consideration of them, their life situations, and the circumstances of their offenses. That consideration can lead to mitigation of punishments but also sometimes to aggravation. Particularly culpable offenders, the drug bosses, organized crime principals, especially calculating white-collar offenders, and users of gratuitous violence and cruelty can be punished more than others convicted of otherwise comparable offenses, but not more than the proportionate upper limit for their most serious offense. All of this can be done without taking account of defiance, disrespect, disreputability, bad character, or public opinion.

The American legal system often does not allow judges to do this, especially for more serious crimes, even though most judges probably wish that they could. Laws calling for mandatory minimum sentences, requiring disproportionately long prison terms for repeat offenders, and authorizing sentences of life without parole make it impossible. Sentencing guidelines systems that give greater weight to criminal history than to current offenses and plea bargaining practices aimed at maximizing punishments make it exceedingly difficult.

PART II

Preventing Crime

6

Deterrence

THERE IS NO need to choose between punishing offenders justly and preventing crime. Zero-sum games exist, but this is not one. It is in the nature of things that convictions and punishments have preventive effects. They are such miserable experiences that many offenders are mortified, decide "never again," and stick to it. They reinforce important societal norms. Those involving confinement or restrictions on mobility incapacitate. To the extent that threats of punishment deter, they deter. To the extent that terms of imprisonment are proportionate, they deter rationally, reinforcing social norms about the relative seriousness of different crimes.

Crime cannot be eliminated. It is part of the human condition. Much is egoistic, emotional, and situational, some involving desperate people. Much is shaped by mental health problems, alcoholism, and drug dependence. Some is subcultural, the product of deep disadvantage, social isolation, and an absence of moral guidance. These things exist in all countries and at all times. They can be ameliorated by social welfare policies, but are only slightly susceptible to influence by the criminal law.

It is also part of the human condition that each society criminalizes the behaviors that worry it most; those worries change. In earlier times, apostasy, sacrilege, gambling, vagrancy, miscegenation, adultery, and same-sex intimacies were criminal. Most kinds of domestic violence and commercial fraud were not. In the twentieth century, white-collar crimes and ingestion and distribution of many psychotropic drugs were newly criminalized, as increasingly in our time are hate crimes, environmental despoliation, and cybercrime. Tobacco use, group libel, and lesser sexual indignities tremble on the verge. Emile Durkheim ([1895] 2014), the pioneering French sociologist, believed that these kinds of changes are inevitable and socially healthy. They reflect evolving ideas about right and wrong within a society and provide a mechanism for reinforcing new and emerging norms. Even a society of saints would have a criminal law and sanction wrongdoing, he said, although by secular standards the wrongs—oversleeping, shirking work, having impure thoughts, not praying when prayer is due—might to others seem venial.

Most punishment theories call for more serious crimes to be punished more severely than lesser ones. Utilitarians and other consequentialists believe that provides incentives to would-be offenders to commit less harmful wrongs. Positive retributivists believe that justice requires that more blameworthy offenders be punished more severely. Negative retributivists believe maximum punishments should be proportioned to offense severity. People concerned about moral education want punishments to be proportionate so that they reinforce important social norms and reflect prevailing ideas about right and wrong.[1]

All of those normative rationales are violated if thefts are punished more severely than robberies, drug sales than rapes, or auto thefts than child abuse. To utilitarians, that would be perverse, seemingly encouraging people to commit more serious offenses: why not, if the punishments are less severe? To retributivists it is per se unjust. To moral educators, it defies common morality. Emile Durkheim ([1893] 2014), the originator of systematic ways of thinking about the role of law in reinforcing social norms, believed that the heavy lifting, the important socialization, occurs in primary institutions such as the family, the church, the school, the neighborhood, and the workplace. Punishment, he believed, plays only a marginal back-up role, but even so the law's dramaturgical effects are important. They must reinforce, not undermine, fundamental social norms.

No one in principle opposes the proposition that punishments should be as just as human institutions can make them. Many people, however, believe that there is an inherent tension between justice and public safety, that achievement of deterrent and incapacitative goals sometimes justifies or requires that people be punished more severely than they deserve.[2] The fundamental

---

1. Proponents of restorative justice believe that no one should ever be punished more than he or she deserves but that proportionality is otherwise unimportant. They also believe, however, that agreements of offenders, victims, and others about appropriate resolutions of particular cases express and reinforce basic social norms (e.g., Braithwaite and Pettit 1990, 2001).

2. In earlier times, especially at the height of indeterminate sentencing, many people believed that disproportionately severe punishments, for example, imprisonment when a community punishment would normally be appropriate, could be justified for rehabilitative reasons. Few people since the 1970s have approved use of imprisonment solely for purposes of rehabilitation. In any case substantial empirical evidence indicates that prison treatment programs are less effective than comparable programs in the community and that all else being equal

deterrence question is whether unjustly severe punishments achieve significantly greater crime prevention effects than just ones. The robust and uncontroversial answer is "no." The fundamental incapacitation question is whether unjustly severe punishments of people predicted to be dangerous achieve significantly greater preventive effects than just ones. The answer is more complicated. Predictions of dangerousness can identify people who pose higher risks of reoffending, but reliance on them in sentencing requires acceptance of racial, gender, and socioeconomic injustices that no free society should accept. In this chapter I discuss deterrence; in the next, incapacitation.

The critical deterrence question is whether offenders may or should be punished more severely than they otherwise would be if doing so has greater deterrent effects. The negative empirical answer, a half-century of research findings demonstrate, is clear. There is little or no basis for believing that disproportionately severe punishments provide more effective deterrents than proportionate punishments do. The ethical answer is also clear. All mainstream theories of punishment agree that no one should be punished more severely than he or she deserves: retributivists never, consequentialists if little or nothing of value would be achieved.

There have been several recent authoritative surveys of deterrence research. The National Academy of Sciences Committee on Causes and Consequences of High Rates of Incarceration exhaustively examined the literatures on both deterrence and incapacitation (Travis, Western, and Redburn 2014, chaps. 1, 3, and 5). Nagin, Cullen, and Jonson's *Deterrence, Choice, and Crime* (2018) provides the most comprehensive distillation of deterrence research to date. In the following discussion, I repeatedly cite Daniel Nagin (1978, 1998, 2013, 2018), who has over four decades written a series of highly respected syntheses of the deterrence literature and, hands down, is the world's pre-eminent scholar of the subject. Five key lessons stand out:

- Harsher punishments deter violent, property, and drug crimes no more effectively than lesser ones.
- Sentences to imprisonment, all else about particular offenders being equal, do not reduce the likelihood of reoffending but appear to increase it.
- The death penalty is not a more effective deterrent to homicide than other available punishments.

---

imprisonment increases rather than reduces the likelihood of reoffending. The major research findings are discussed in this chapter.

- In economists' theories, increases in the severity of punishment should increase deterrent effects, but mandatory minimum sentences, lengthy prison terms, and laws increasing sentence severity have in practice failed to do so.
- Credible threats of immediate punishment can measurably influence behavior, but slow and cumbersome court processes make immediate punishments impossible.

The policy implications are straightforward.

- Reduce use of jail and prison sentences; shorten those that remain.
- Abolish capital punishment.
- Repeal mandatory minimum sentence and similar laws and enact no new ones.
- Reallocate public expenditures from prisons and jails to community corrections and treatment programs.

None of those policies is likely to be adopted at scale any time soon. Public officials are not willing to do so. Ideological and partisan political considerations have dominated policymaking since the 1970s. Crime rates have been declining for three decades and crime has nearly disappeared as an electoral issue, but few public officials are willing to risk accusations of softness. Despite a recent, much ballyhooed convergence of support by liberal and conservative activists and organizations for policy changes, few major changes have been made. Most target crimes by youthful, first-time, property, and minor offenders. Treating such people more thoughtfully and compassionately makes sense, but it will not significantly reduce prison populations, incarceration rates, or public expenditure. That will require fundamental changes in policies and practices affecting people convicted of violent crimes.

Policy inertia also results from understandable but mistaken conventional wisdom. Everyone knows rational people are influenced by some threats of punishment. Drivers instinctively slow down when they see a police car. Warnings about Denver boots, tow trucks with running motors, and nearby meter readers dramatically reduce proclivities for illegal parking. Those common experiences, however, involve minor misbehavior, nearly immediate discovery, and close to certain consequences. That makes them fundamentally different from violent, property, drug, and public order offenses for which apprehension is unlikely and conviction and punishment are far from certain.

Until recently, the "of course, deterrence works" mindset was often supported by research by economists,[3] but refuted by other social scientists (e.g., Nagin 1978, 2018; Doob and Webster 2003; Pratt et al. 2006).[4] The refutations include panels of the National Academy of Sciences in 1978, 1993, 2012, and 2014, in each case including leading economists and econometricians.[5] The best-informed economists now agree with the overwhelming majority of other social scientists (e.g., Donohue and Wolfers 2005; Durlauf and Nagin 2011; Chalfin and McCrary 2017; Chalfin and Tahamont 2018).

In this chapter, I explain why the lessons to be learned from recent surveys of knowledge are almost certainly correct, and why they should be taken seriously. In the first section, I summarize the burgeoning evidence on the deterrent effects of punishment. Cesare Beccaria and Jeremy Bentham, the eighteenth-century pioneers of deterrence theory, anticipated many modern conclusions, particularly that the speed and certainty of punishment are what counts and that severity is much less—if at all—important. In the second section, I discuss normative and theoretical literatures on punishment to show that almost all imply punishment systems that are irreconcilable in principle with commonly held intuitions about deterrence, but nonetheless, assuming punishment has deterrent effects, would if implemented effectively deter crime. The final section briefly outlines policy changes, premised on current knowledge about deterrent effects of punishment, that would be

---

3. Influential literature reviews by economists draw almost entirely on analyses by other economists (e.g., Lewis 1986; Ehrlich 1996; Levitt 2002; Shepherd 2004). They neither cite nor discuss the much larger deterrence literature produced by noneconomists which invariably discusses the economics literature (e.g., Pratt et al. 2006; Nagin 2013, 2018).

4. Here is a typical bottom-line conclusion. Travis Pratt and colleagues (2006, p. 379) concluded from an influential and widely cited meta-analysis that as "noted by previous narrative reviews of the deterrence literature . . . the effects of severity estimates and deterrence/sanctions composites, even when statistically significant, are too weak to be of substantive significance (consistently below -.1)."

5. In the text I describe findings of the Committee on the Causes and Consequences of High Rates of Incarceration (Travis, Western, and Redburn 2014) and quote key conclusions of the historic Panel on Research on Deterrent and Incapacitative Effects (Blumstein, Cohen, and Nagin 1978). The Panel on Deterrence and the Death Penalty concluded that there is no credible evidence that capital punishment is a more effective deterrent than other sanctions that might be imposed (Nagin and Pepper 2012). The Panel on Understanding and Controlling Violence showed that the average prison sentence per violent crime in the United States *tripled* between 1975 and 1989. "What effect has increasing the prison population had on violent crime?" the panel asked. Its answer, "Apparently very little" (Reiss and Roth 1993, p. 10).

less expensive, much less damaging, and no less effective as crime prevention measures than current American policies.

I. Empirical Knowledge

Cesare Beccaria, an Italian nobleman, in *Of Crimes and Punishments* ([1764] 2007), offered the first relatively full depiction of a deterrent approach to punishment. Decrying the arbitrariness and severity of the shaming, corporal, and capital punishments in use in his time, he proposed that punishment be made more humane, and be justified and applied on deterrent rationales. Accepting Enlightenment ideas about human autonomy, rationality, and rights, he famously described three pillars of deterrence: celerity (speed), certainty, and severity. Of these, he believed, celerity and certainty are far more important than severity. Jeremy Bentham added a fourth pillar, parsimony. By this, Bentham meant that no punishment should be more severe than its deterrent rationale could justify. Anything more, he wrote, would not influence decisions to commit crimes, and was therefore useless and gratuitously cruel. Building on the four pillars, Bentham worked out the details of a deterrence-based punishment system ([1789] 1970).

These men were no fools. They understood that law is a blunt instrument, that much crime cannot be prevented, and that ignorance, impulse, intoxication, and emotion make many crimes undeterrable. Detached reflection about costs and benefits is unlikely in any of those circumstances. Bentham recognized that the influence of threatened punishments is inherently limited, observing, for example, that for many crimes the "chance of detection [is] very small" and that "whether a given offence shall be prevented in a given degree by a given quantity of punishment, is never anything better than a chance" (pp. 170, 68). Beccaria and Bentham believed that a punishment system premised on ideas about human rationality would be incomparably better than one based on doing harm to offenders.

In the late nineteenth and early twentieth centuries, utilitarian emphases on rational calculation and deterrence were eclipsed in the United States by two other ideas. The first is that much offending is a product of offenders' disadvantaged backgrounds, defective socialization, mental and psychological problems, and inadequate educations and work skills (Rothman 1971). The second is that the only rational response to crime is to try to rehabilitate offenders to enable them to live productive, law-abiding lives (Allen 1981). In our time, almost everyone supports programs that aim to facilitate prisoners' successful re-entry into the free community (Jonson and Cullen 2015).

In the 1970s, however, as I discuss in chapter 2, rehabilitative programs fell from favor and were replaced by attempts to control crime through deterrence and incapacitation and to apportion severity of punishments to seriousness of crimes. The former objectives were pursued in mandatory minimum, career criminal, three-strikes, truth in sentencing, life without parole, and similar laws; the latter in determinate sentencing laws and sentencing guidelines in a few states, all of which also later enacted mandatory minimums and similarly severe sentencing laws that undermined their efforts to achieve consistency and proportionality.

Modern American sentencing and punishment are thus based largely on the deterrent and incapacitative premises that underlie mandatory minimums and lengthy prison terms. Deterring criminal behavior through legal threats has, however, proven much less effective than its proponents expected and to involve more complex social, situational, and psychological processes than Beccaria and Bentham foresaw.

The complexities are beginning to be unraveled. Threats of punishment cannot affect behavior unless people know they exist and what they threaten. Everyone knows that traditional property, violent, and drug crimes are unlawful and that people who commit them may be punished, but almost no one knows what punishments are authorized, or imposed, for particular crimes.[6] If people do not know what punishments particular crimes trigger, they are even less likely to know that laws or practices have changed or to be influenced by the changes. Legal threats in any case are irrelevant most of

---

6. The general public has little knowledge of authorized punishments, criminal law provisions, or punishments imposed. Mark Warr (2000, p. 22), in a classic overview, concluded: "The evidence suggests that public knowledge of statutory punishments is quite limited; most individuals simply have no idea what the punishments for crimes are." Darley, Carlsmith, and Robinson (2001, p. 181) surveyed citizens' knowledge of starkly different criminal law provisions in different states (e.g., among others, whether or not a citizen may use fatal force in self-defense without retreating, or to prevent property crimes) and found little difference: "Citizens showed no particular knowledge of the laws of their states." MacCoun et al. (2009, p. 347) compared knowledge about penalties for marijuana possession in states where it had and had not been decriminalized, and found little difference: "The percentages who believe they could be jailed for marijuana possession are quite similar in both [sets of states]. . . . The average citizen's awareness is pretty tenuous." Kleck and Barnes (2013) surveyed citizens' knowledge of sentences imposed and concluded that they greatly underestimate prison use and except for murder overestimate sentence lengths. Hough and Roberts (1999, pp. 16–17) surveyed British citizens' knowledge of punishments imposed and found that "large majorities of respondents provided estimates of current imprisonment rates which were much too low. . . . For rape, 97 per cent of adult males convicted in 1995 were sent to prison. . . . Respondents' median estimate, however, was 50 per cent." Similar differences existed concerning street robberies and burglaries.

the time for the large majority of people who have been socialized into law-abiding values.

Many things condition or nullify the effects of legal threats:

- Personal experience with the criminal justice system, or knowledge of others' personal experience, may make legal threats more vivid or less frightening, and that may influence behavior (Paternoster 2018).
- Subcultural or antisocial values associated with gang membership, peer pressures, influence of deviant role models, and living in deeply dysfunctional neighborhoods can largely nullify the effects of legal threats (Sullivan and Lugo 2018).
- Even for people who subscribe to mainstream values, and more so for people who do not, impulse, intoxication, emotion, and extreme situational pressures nullify the effects of legal threats (Loughran, Paternoster, and Piquero 2018).
- Differences between people, and their circumstances, and the situations in which they find themselves, substantially affect their likelihood of wrongdoing (Apel and DeWitt 2018; Wilcox and Cullen 2018).

Those advances in understanding are good, of course, but they merely qualify the now robust finding that deterrent effects of criminal sanctions are weaker, less predictable, and more complex than Beccaria and Bentham imagined.

A. General Deterrence

The evidence is clear. After the first exhaustive examination of empirical research on deterrence, the 1978 National Academy of Sciences Panel on Research on Deterrent and Incapacitative Effects concluded, "In summary . . . we cannot assert that the evidence warrants an affirmative conclusion regarding deterrence" (Blumstein, Cohen, and Nagin 1978, p. 7). Nearly 40 years later, the National Academy of Sciences Committee on the Causes and Consequences of High Rates of Incarceration, echoed that conclusion:

Knowledge about mandatory minimum sentences has changed remarkably little in the past 30 years. Their ostensible primary rationale is deterrence. The overwhelming weight of the evidence, however, shows that they have few if any deterrent effects. Analyses finding deterrent effects typically observe, as we do in Chapter 5, that existing knowledge is too fragmentary or that estimated effects are so small or contingent on particular circumstances as to have no practical relevance for policy making. (Travis, Western, and Redburn 2014, p. 83)

The overwhelming weight of the evidence is that increased penalties have few if any deterrent effects greater than lesser penalties would have had (Nagin 2013, 2018). Similar skepticism about deterrence has long been expressed by advisory bodies and government agencies in other Western countries.[7]

B. Celerity

Rapid disposition of cases processed through the criminal justice system is impossible to achieve. Processes are slow and cumbersome. Outcomes are often unpredictable. Hopes of deterrence through speedy court disposition are misplaced. Deterrence through police or other rapid responses may be a different matter (Lum and Nagin 2017).

Pratt and Turanovic (2018) completed the most exhaustive survey to date of research on the effects of speedy punishments on crime. Their conclusion: "The bottom line from the criminological literature is that there is no clear evidence of celerity effects in criminal justice processing" (p. 191). They observe that effects of immediate punishments are found in laboratory experiments with animals, in which negative reinforcement is immediate, and in psychology lab experiments with college students, in which negative reinforcement occurs within seconds or minutes. However, they point out, "*Implementing celerity of punishment into the criminal justice system in a meaningful way is a practical impossibility.* The criminal justice system is not built for speed" (p. 193; emphasis in original).

---

7. E.g., Canadian Sentencing Commission (1987); Home Office of England and Wales (1990); Törnudd (1993 [Finland; Ministry of Justice]); von Hirsch et al. (1999 [England and Wales Home Office]); Germany (2006); Australia (2013). The Second [Federal Government] report on the State of Interior/Domestic Security in Germany of the federal Justice and Home Affairs Ministries, concluded that "harsher and/or longer penalties did not produce less recidivism than lenient penalties did" (Germany 2006, paras. 6.4.3.2, 6.4.3.3). The Legal and Constitutional Affairs Committee of the Australian Senate observed: "Jurisdictions across Australia have relied, and continue to rely, on incarceration as a deterrent to criminal offending at great cost . . . [I]t has not been successful in addressing offending behaviour—prison is not a deterrent" (Australia 2013, para. 8.6).

C. Severity

Three questions arise concerning severity. One is whether increased severity yields measurable reductions in crime. Another is whether a credible case can be made for particular deterrent effects of any specific level of severity. The third is whether punishments, especially prison sentences, have specific deterrent effects on individuals who experience them. Putting the third question differently: Does being punished make people less likely to commit crimes in the future? The answers are "at best, possibly a little," "no," and "no."

1. *Marginal Deterrence.* There is little credible evidence that increased severity has greater deterrent effects than did previous, lesser punishments. The question is whether there are measurable reductions in crime attributable to increments of increased punishment. Daniel Nagin (2018, p. 158) concluded: "There is little evidence that increases in the length of already long prison sentences yield general deterrent effects that are sufficiently large to justify their social and economic costs."

Even that hedged conclusion overstates the evidence. Both the 2014 National Academy of Sciences report and Nagin base their conclusions on six deterrence studies that they viewed as being especially sound. Three found no deterrent effects.

Of the others, two were measures of the combined effects of celerity and certainty, not severity. Weisburd, Einat, and Kowalski (2008) conducted a randomized field experiment on strategies for inducing payment of court-ordered fines. The key finding was that a believable threat of immediate imprisonment, even for a short period, produced higher rates of payment. This is little different from the commonplace observation that drivers slow down when they see a police car. Hawken and Kleiman (2009) evaluated a Hawaiian program in which probationers who failed drug tests or violated other conditions received immediate but short periods in jail. Police cars again.

Neither of these studies is relevant to the question of whether increased punishments have general deterrent effects. Both involved convicted offenders already under supervision and believable threats of immediate imprisonment. Most assessments of marginal deterrence involve offenders in the community for whom apprehension, arrest, and conviction are highly uncertain and immediate imposition of punishment is impossible.

The last study examined deterrent effects of California's three-strikes law (Helland and Tabarrok 2007). It compared offending of people convicted of two "strikes" with that of people convicted of one strike but who had been tried but not convicted for an offense that would have been a second. Arrest rates for the one-strike group were about 20 percent lower than for the two-strikes group, which the researchers concluded showed that the harsher sentence threatened by a third-strike conviction had a deterrent effect.

There are reasons to be skeptical. California's three-strikes law mandated minimum 10-year sentences for second-strike convictions and minimum 25-year sentences for third-strike convictions. The stakes were already high for offenders with one strike. It is difficult to imagine that a 10-year minimum sentence is substantially less threatening than a 25-year one. Second, 18 of 20 earlier quantitative studies of the California law by others concluded that no deterrent effect could be shown (Tonry 2009, table 3). Of the two finding deterrent effects, one offered this hedged observation: "The approach taken in California has not been dramatically more effective at controlling crime than other states' efforts. . . . [California's law] is not considerably more effective at crime reduction than alternative methods that are narrower in scope" (Chen 2008, pp. 362, 365).

2. *Absolute Severity.* Except concerning capital punishment, surprisingly little research has been done on whether punishments of any particular severity have deterrent effects or whether modest increases, say from 1 to 2 years or 2 to 3, have marginal deterrent effects. Both Nagin and the National Academy of Sciences committee focused on severe sentences. The latter concluded, for example, "One of our most important conclusions is that the incremental deterrent effect of increases in lengthy prison sentences is modest at best" (Travis, Western, and Redburn 2014, p. 131).

That conclusion, focusing on three-strikes laws and lengthy mandatory minimums, does not explicitly address changes in sentences measured in months or a few years. To the question, thus, of whether increasing sentences from 1 to 2 years, 2 to 3, or 3 to 5, has marginal deterrent effects, the literature is silent. Given, however, the findings on marginal deterrence in relation to severe punishments and that citizens have little knowledge of sentencing laws or practices,[8] it is highly unlikely that such changes have any significant effects.

3. *Specific Deterrence.* The specific deterrence hypothesis is that offenders will learn from the experience of being punished and cease offending. At least concerning imprisonment this is unlikely. Since the first important prison reformer, John Howard, an eighteenth-century Englishman, popularized the term, prisons have been recognized to be "Schools for Crime." Inside, prisoners are exposed to deviant subcultures, are socialized into inmate subcultures,

---

8. See note 6.

establish personal relationships with active offenders, and are separated from their families, jobs, and communities. Once outside, they experience stigma, often return to damaged or broken families, and face difficulties finding work and developing satisfying lives. That many released prisoners commit new crimes should not be unexpected.

The research confirms this. Here is Nagin's summary, based in part on the most exhaustive survey of the evidence done to date (Nagin, Cullen, and Jonson 2009) and confirmed by recent research (e.g., Mears and Cochran 2018): "I have concluded that there is little evidence of a specific deterrent effect arising from the experience of imprisonment compared with experience of noncustodial sanctions such as probation. Instead, the evidence suggests that reoffending is either unaffected by imprisonment or increased" (Nagin 2018, p. 158). Several of the comprehensive surveys of the literature are less cautious and conclude that all else being equal, people sentenced to imprisonment are more likely to reoffend than people sentenced to community punishments.[9]

D. Certainty

As the fine collection and probation studies discussed above show, there is reason to believe that the threat of immediate punishment can affect behavior. Patrolling police cars and idling tow trucks show the same thing. Certainty and immediate punishment, however, are not properties of the criminal justice system and cannot reasonably be expected. Nagin's conclusions are typical:

> I conclude, as have many prior reviews of deterrence research, that evidence in support of the deterrent effect of various measures of the certainty of punishment is far more convincing and consistent than for the severity of punishment. However, the certainty of punishment is conceptually and mathematically the product of a series of conditional probabilities—the probability of apprehension given commission of a crime, the probability of prosecution given apprehension, the probability of conviction given prosecution, and the probability of sanction given conviction. The evidence in support of certainty's deterrent effect pertains almost exclusively to apprehension probability. Consequently, the conclusion that certainty not severity is the more

---

9. E.g., Cullen, Jonson, and Nagin (2011); Jolliffe and Hedderman (2015); Villettaz, Gillieron, and Killias (2015); Mears and Cochran (2018).

effective deterrent is more precisely stated as certainty of apprehension and not the severity of the legal consequence ensuing from apprehension is the more effective deterrent. (2018, p. 158)

E. Parsimony

Jeremy Bentham called the idea frugality, Norval Morris called it parsimony, and the *Model Sentencing Act* called it the least restrictive alternative: punishments should not be imposed that are more severe than is necessary to achieve their aims. To a positive retributivist such as Immanuel Kant or Andreas von Hirsch, anything more than is deserved is unjust. To a negative retributivist like Morris, anything more severe than is deserved is unjust and so is anything more than the least severe appropriate punishment unless good evidence-based reasons exist to do more. To classic utilitarians such as Bentham, anything that causes more suffering to offenders than its imposition will prevent for others is unjust. To modern consequentialists such as the drafters of the *Model Sentencing Act* and the *Model Penal Code*, anything more severe than is minimally necessary to obtain its ends is unjust.

No one to my knowledge has ever conducted empirical research on the effects, including deterrent, of parsimonious use of punishment. However, findings on certainty, severity, and celerity shed relevant light. Beccaria's and Bentham's view that certainty and celerity are what count and that severity is much less important are confirmed by modern research. The robust finding that penalty increases produce little if any measurable deterrent effects, when turned around, indicates that lesser punishments are equally effective. So does the consistent finding that, among otherwise comparable offenders, those receiving prison sentences often have higher reoffending rates that those sentenced to community-based punishments.[10]

The bottom line is that there is little reason to believe that severe punishments imposed by judges have greater deterrent effects than lesser ones or that differences among the effects of lesser punishments are consequential. Were there no economists writing about punishment, research findings on the general deterrent effects of changes in punishment laws and practices would

---

10. Frase and Roberts (2019, p. 80), survey the American and international literature, discussing the studies I cite in detail, and conclude that the robust finding is of "the same or higher recidivism rates for custody than for community sanctions."

have been boringly consistent over the past five decades: no deterrent effects can be shown or they are so small and contingent as to be neither generalizable nor policy relevant.

The mystery is why economists' findings were for so long different. The solution is confirmation bias. Many economists until recently expected to find deterrent effects and, Anthony Doob and Cheryl Webster (2003) showed, usually found them. Economists assumed that punishment increases are like price increases. Raise the prices of goods and fewer consumers will buy them; increase punishments of crimes and fewer people will commit them.

Ronald Coase (1960, pp. 4, 7), the Nobel Prize-winning founder of the law and economics movement, observed that economists "rarely shrink from applying in every context the model of rational, self-interested, human behavior that they borrow from economics proper." Concerning deterrence, he later wrote, "Punishment, for example, can be regarded as the price of crime. *An economist will not debate whether increased punishment will reduce crime; he will merely try to answer the question, by how much?*" (1978, p. 210; emphasis added). Isaac Ehrlich, an influential early writer on the economics of crime and punishment, likewise observed that the " 'market model' . . . builds on the assumption that offenders, as members of the human race, respond to incentives. . . . This has been the justification for applying economic analysis to all illegal activities, from speeding and tax evasion to murder. . . . *At least in the economic literature*, there has been little controversy concerning this approach" (Ehrlich 1996, pp. 43–44; emphasis added). Note that Ehrlich generalizes from speeding, which is deterrable, to murder, which usually is not. Many, until recently most, economists simply assumed that increased penalties will reduce crime through deterrent effects.

The reality is more complicated, Franklin Zimring explained. Prices, he said, are unambiguously expressed in money. Punishments, however, "are not monetary but are a difficult-to-measure mix of unpleasant circumstances like incarceration, social disapproval, and stigma. . . . Then, of course, threatened consequences are conditional on apprehension" (2008, p. 259). This contingent amalgam of social meaning and physical discomfort bears little resemblance to a simple cash price. In any case, the gap between economists and other social scientists in their conclusions about the limited or nonexistent deterrent effects of punishment has largely disappeared.

People who remain attached to commonsense intuitions about deterrence, however, need not be troubled. All mainstream theories of punishment emphasize the importance of proportionality, albeit for differing reasons. So long as more serious crimes are punished more severely than less serious ones, the deterrent messages that crime has consequences and more serious crimes have greater consequences will continue to be sent.

II. Normative Theory

Retributive, consequentialist, and moral educative conceptions of punishment dominate contemporary thought. All are irreconcilable with deterrent crime control strategies except to the extent that deterrent effects are incidental to imposition of punishments that can be justified in other ways. Reasonably well-developed normative theories of punishment have existed since Jeremy Bentham and Immanuel Kant offered their utilitarian and retributive accounts in the late eighteenth and early nineteenth centuries. Emile Durkheim's sociological theory of punishment, while not in itself a normative theory, emphasizes moral education and reinforcement of social norms ([1893] 2014). All three accounts, though starting from radically different premises, place primary emphasis on proportionality, apportioning the severity of punishment to the seriousness of wrongdoing.

A. Retributivism

Kant believed that moral autonomy, a capacity for moral choice, is what distinguishes human beings from other mortal creatures. People who commit crimes should be punished in relation to the degree of their moral wrongdoing. Punishing them more or less than they deserve is, in effect, to treat them as less than human, as creatures who lack moral autonomy, who lack capacity to make moral choices. Thus deserved punishments are acts of respect that validate the offender's humanity. Undeserved punishments deny the offender's humanity. In contemporary language, punishment should be based on blameworthiness and proportionate to the seriousness of the crime or crimes.

Kant believed in a "principle of equality," by which he meant that comparably culpable people should receive comparable punishments: "Only the *law of retribution (jus talionis)* . . . can . . . specify definitely the quality and quantity of punishment; all other . . . principles are fluctuating and unsuited for a sentence of pure and strict justice because extraneous considerations are mixed into them" (p. 115). Hegel was even more emphatic. Deterrence is thus an irrelevant and morally impermissible consideration unless it is merely incidental to imposition of deserved punishments.

Contemporary retributive theories are based on different premises than Kant's and Hegel's and differ in matters of detail, but they all agree that punishments more severe than is deserved are unjust. Retributive proportionality includes a vertical requirement that more blameworthy acts deserve greater punishment than lesser ones and a horizontal requirement that comparably blameworthy acts deserve comparable punishments. Insofar as laws premised on deterrent considerations punish less blameworthy offenses (e.g., street-level drug sales) more harshly than more blameworthy offenses (e.g., sexual assaults), they are unjust. Insofar as laws punish some among comparably blameworthy offenders more severely than others, they are unjust. Insofar as laws such as three-strikes and mandatory minimum sentence laws require punishments more severe than the vertical dimension of blameworthiness allows, they are unjust.

B. Consequentialism

Consequentialism encompasses a venerable set of ethical theories that are traceable to pre-Socratic Greece. By far the most influential contemporary consequentialist theory of punishment, usually contrasted with retributive theories, is a broad conception of utilitarianism that includes all preventive effects. Earlier generations referred to that broad conception as positivism. Restorative justice theories are also consequentialist, but are seldom discussed in relation to punishment generally.

Bentham's proposals, which I mostly discuss in chapter 2 but also elsewhere, are detailed and complex. Here I discuss them only in relation to proportionality. Like modern economists, he believed that human beings are rational and make decisions based on self-interest. Unlike many economists, however, he believed that proportionate punishments are a necessary part of any punishment system. He specified three overriding objectives:

> [The] first, most extensive, and most eligible object, is to prevent, in as far as it is possible, and worth while, all sorts of offences whatsoever: in other words, so to manage, that no offence whatsoever may be committed.
>
> But if a man must needs commit an offence of some kind or other, the next object is to induce him to commit an offence *less* mischievous, *rather* than one *more* mischievous: in other words, to choose always the *least* mischievous, of two offences that will either of them suit his purpose.

When a man has resolved upon a particular offence, the next object is to dispose him to do *no more* mischief than is *necessary* to his purpose: in other words, to do as little mischief as is consistent with the benefit he has in view. (1970, p. 165; emphases in original)

Once the punishment is determined, however, Bentham's insistence that it be adapted to take account of offenders' different sensibilities makes it clear that he believed that people convicted of comparable crimes should receive comparable punishments.

Thus, for Bentham, proportionality was essential not as a matter of retributive principle, but because he believed it necessary to offer incentives to offenders to commit less rather than more serious offenses and to cause the least possible harm to themselves and their victims.

C. Expressive Punishments and Moral Education

Emile Durkheim emphasized the role of punishment in expressing moral values and reinforcing basic social norms. It is the basis of "positive general prevention," the predominant punishment jurisprudence in Scandinavia, which emphasizes proportionality and certainty of punishment but not severity (Lappi-Seppälä 2011, 2020).

Every society, Durkheim wrote, has a common set of values and traditions that prescribe fundamental norms of right and wrong conduct that are essential to social cohesion. Crimes are wrongful actions that violate those norms and understandably and, rightly, are condemned. The criminal law exists to respond to those harms and thereby to reassert and reinforce the violated norms. Punishment's "function is to maintain inviolate the cohesion of society by sustaining the common consciousness in all its vigor" ([1893] 2014, p. 83).

From this norm reinforcement goal comes both the justification for punishment and, because some proscribed harms are worse than others, the requirement that punishments be proportionate:

Above all it [punishment] should be an *expiation* for the past. What proves this are the meticulous precautions we take to make the punishment fit the seriousness of the crime as exactly as possible. These precautions would be inexplicable unless we believed that the guilty person must suffer because it is he who has done the injury, and indeed must suffer in equal measure. In fact this gradation is unnecessary if punishment is only a defense mechanism. ([1893] 2014, p. 69; emphasis in original)

Durkheim was well ahead of his time in his skepticism about the instrumental effects of punishment other than through the reinforcement of norms: "It [punishment] does not serve, or serves only very incidentally, to correct the guilty person or to scare off possible imitators. From this dual viewpoint its effectiveness may rightly be questioned; in any case it is mediocre" ([1893] 2014, p. 83).

For Durkheim, as for Kant and Bentham, proportionality was what mattered. Punishments that were not scaled to the seriousness of the offenses for which they were imposed would undermine, not reinforce, fundamental social norms. To all three of them, deterrent crime control strategies that generate disproportionately severe punishments, or different punishments for comparably blameworthy offenders, are unjust and both contradict and undermine fundamental social norms.

III. Taking Account of Deterrence Research

Three main conclusions emerge from this chapter. First, there is substantial reason to be skeptical that increases in penalties, or harsher compared with milder penalties, have significant if any marginal deterrent effects. Second, however, any imaginable American sentencing system will convey the deterrent messages many peoples' intuitions tell them are necessary. All mainstream theories of punishment insist that punishments either be scaled to the seriousness of crimes or be no more severe than is proportionately deserved. Legal threats thus will exist for all crimes; the more serious the crime, the greater the threat. Third, American criminal justice systems can be made much less expensive to operate, less punitive, and less characterized by unwanted collateral damage to offenders, their families, and their communities.

A. Reduce Use of Jail and Prison Sentences; Shorten Terms

Shorter proportionate sentences would be just, acknowledge victims' losses and suffering, reinforce fundamental behavioral norms, and save taxpayers vast sums of money. Offenders spared confinement could be sentenced to community punishments that cost much less than imprisonment to administer and provide treatment and other programs that improve offenders' chances of living productive, law-abiding lives.

B. Abolish Capital Punishment

The National Academy of Sciences Panel on Deterrence and the Death Penalty concluded unequivocally that there is no credible evidence that capital punishment is a more effective deterrent to murder than other punishments that might be imposed (Nagin and Pepper 2012). The only credible argument for capital punishment is a moral one about which reasonable people deeply disagree. Debates should be couched in those terms. All other developed Western countries have abandoned use of capital punishment on moral or human rights grounds.

C. Repeal Mandatory Sentencing Laws; Enact No New Ones

Knowledge about mandatory minimum sentences has changed remarkably little in the past 200 years (Hay 1975; Tonry 2009). The overwhelming weight of the evidence is that they have few if any deterrent effects. The deterrent case for mandatory minimum, three-strikes, career criminal, and life without parole laws cannot convincingly be made. The undesirable and unjust consequences of their application cannot be avoided. There is overwhelming evidence that practitioners often evade or circumvent them, that they create stark disparities between cases in which they are circumvented and cases in which they are not, and that they often result in imposition of sentences in individual cases that everyone directly involved believes to be unjust.

D. Reallocate Public Spending

Vast sums could be saved if the American imprisonment rate were reduced by a half or two-thirds to levels that would still by far be the highest among Western countries. Forty billion dollars a year in 2008–2010 constant dollars is the most conservative, credible estimate of the annual cost of American imprisonment (Kyckelhahn 2014). Most analysts consider this a substantial underestimate. A substantial drop in the imprisonment rate would save tens of billions of dollars a year. That's not small change.

The system that will result if those changes are made will look much like the legal systems of other Western developed countries, cost much less to operate, and do less harm. Penalties will be apportioned to blameworthiness and be consistent with the intuition that incentives and disincentives matter. More serious crimes will be punished more, less serious ones less. It would be consistent with the major conclusions that a half-century's accumulation of deterrence research supports: celerity and certainty are what matters, not severity. It would also comport with parsimony, the fourth utilitarian pillar: punishments would be no more severe than they need to be to achieve valid public purposes.

7

Prediction and Incapacitation

"LOCK 'EM UP" might at first blush seem like a surefire way to prevent crime. Turns out, it's not, but that lesson needs to be relearned every generation. The contemporary scholarly literature on incapacitation focuses on use of predictions of dangerousness to prevent violent crime. Its proponents are enthusiastic, but unaware of, or oblivious to, what our predecessors knew. In the 1970s and 1980s, ambitious efforts to develop incapacitative crime control strategies ran into dead ends. Harvard University political scientist James Q. Wilson (1975), a political conservative who was the most influential criminal justice scholar of his time, proposed a system of "collective incapacitation." Every offender convicted of a particular offense would receive a fixed, often short, prison sentence. Crime rates would plummet, he surmised. Wilson's proposals and related work by others were pored over by the National Academy of Sciences Panel on Deterrent and Incapacitative Effects (Blumstein, Cohen, and Nagin 1978). Wilson himself was a member. The panel unanimously concluded that collective incapacitation was unworkable: the numbers of people to be locked up were unimaginable, the preventive effects would be meager at best, and the risks of injustice to individuals would be enormous.[1]

RAND Corporation researchers Peter Greenwood and Allan Abrahamse (1982) were the most prominent proponents of "selective incapacitation." Their proposals were based on surveys of prison and jail inmates in California, Texas, and Michigan who were asked, in confidence, to describe all the offenses they had committed. Self-reported offending rates were remarkably high: for

---

1. The report and a classic, exhaustive, essay by Jacqueline Cohen (1983) provide detailed explanations. Cohen also provides incisive discussion of the research underlying the selective incapacitation proposals discussed in the following paragraph.

high-rate offenders 31 robberies and 156 burglaries per year. Statistical models were developed that related prisoners' personal characteristics to their self-reported offending. Greenwood and Abrahamse argued that use of their model and others like it to identify and imprison high-rate offenders would prevent huge numbers of crimes: imprisonment of one high-rate robber for 10 years, for example, would prevent 310 robberies (given various assumptions that proved to be untenable). Their proposals, their research, and related work by others were examined by the National Academy of Sciences Panel on "Career Criminals" and Criminal Careers (Blumstein et al. 1986). James Q. Wilson was again a member. The panel, again unanimously, concluded that selective incapacitation is unworkable and that its assumptions are unrealistic. Greenwood and Abrahamse's model did a fine job retrospectively describing existing prisoners, but, used prospectively, was much too inaccurate and presented much too great likelihood of injustice to individuals.[2] Incapacitative crime control strategies largely disappeared from scholarly agendas for three decades until the contemporary literature on prediction of dangerousness revived them.

The 2014 report of the National Academy of Sciences Committee on the Causes and Consequences of High Rates of Incarceration revisited the subject. Its conclusions were as skeptical of incapacitation as its two predecessors' had been.[3] Incapacitation has, however, as the obverse of rehabilitation,

---

2. Franklin Zimring and Gordon Hawkins (1988, p. 429) performed the coup de grâce on selective incapacitation. The number of people held in American prisons increased by 237,000 between 1977 and mid-1986. Zimring and Hawkins showed that, using 1977 crime rates as a starting point, "crime [should have] disappeared some time ago" if each additional prisoner would have committed 187 serious crimes per year as RAND estimated.

3. There are four main reasons. First, the replacement effect. For some categories of offenders, for example, drug sellers and gang members, most or all sent to prison are quickly replaced (e.g., Kleiman 1997). Good sites for drug sales seldom remain unoccupied for long. Successors are ready, willing, and available to take the places of gang members and leaders who are taken out of circulation. Michael Smith and Walter Dickey (1999, p. 8), for example, showed that 94 drug arrests were made within a 3-month period at the corner of Ninth and Concordia in Milwaukee in the mid-1990s. "These arrests, [the police officer] pointed out, were easy to prosecute to conviction. But . . . the drug market continued to thrive at the intersection." Second, the age/crime curve. Very large percentages of young people commit offenses; rates peak in the mid-teenage years for property offenses and a year or two later for violent offenses (e.g., Farrington 1986). Most quickly desist while still teenagers. People entering adulthood have interests and stakes—intimate relationships, marriage, children, jobs, career prospects, hopes for a better life—that are too important to risk. Imprisoning most young offenders delays or obstructs natural desistance processes. Third, residual criminal careers. Most criminal careers are short. Even the most persistent offenders typically desist by their early thirties (e.g., Farrington 2003). Most people who receive long sentences are in their twenties; there is little incapacitative gain to be realized by imprisoning them for long periods. Keeping people in

remained a low-visibility component of corrections research and practice since the 1980s. Correctional managers need to classify prisoners for various purposes. It is common, for budgetary reasons, for example, to target correctional treatment programs on high-risk offenders. The rationale is that most low and moderate risk offenders will naturally desist anyway, making their participation a waste of time and money. Courts want to take account of offending risks in making bail decisions and parole boards in making release decisions. For all these reasons, corrections researchers, public agencies, and private companies have developed a plethora of risk prediction instruments.

That is where things stood when recent statistical developments and continuing policy emphasis on crime prevention revived interest in use of predictions of dangerousness in sentencing. All of the statistical, policy, and normative problems that underlay rejection of collective and selective incapacitation four decades ago are raised by predictive sentencing, but have largely been forgotten.[4]

Were the American philosopher Yogi Berra a social scientist, and alive, he would likely describe recent debates as déjà vu all over again. Except concerning technical statistical issues, almost all the major critiques offered in recent years were offered in the 1970s and 1980s. Predictions of future violence by individuals are substantially more often wrong than right. Check. Minority offenders are more often incorrectly predicted to be violent than are white offenders. Check. White offenders are more often incorrectly predicted to be nonviolent than are minority offenders. Check. Use of socioeconomic status variables is per se unjust and disproportionately affects minority offenders. Check. Use of criminal history variables exaggerates differences between minority and white offenders, and increases racial and ethnic disparities. Check. It is unjust ever to punish someone more severely than he or she deserves because of a prediction of dangerousness (or for any other reason). Check. Increasing the severity of a sentence on the basis of risk prediction "punishes" offenders in advance for crimes they would not have committed. Check. There is one new critique: judges and others using prediction instruments

---

prison beyond their mid-thirties is, incapacitatively speaking, mostly a waste of money. Fourth, criminogenic prisons. There is good evidence, discussed in chapter 6, that imprisonment does not reduce the likelihood of later offending and probably increases it (e.g., Nagin, Cullen, and Jonson 2009).

4. These issues were widely discussed (e.g., Morris 1974; Hoffman 1983, 1995; Morris and Miller 1985; von Hirsch 1985; Tonry 1987).

more often disregard low-risk predictions for poor offenders than for affluent ones (e.g., Skeem, Scurich, and Monahan 2019).

Those issues were on research and policy agendas four decades ago for several reasons.[5] Support for indeterminate sentencing and its rehabilitative aims had collapsed. Efforts were afoot to figure out what should come next. Determinate sentencing based on retributive ideas was the leading candidate: punishment should be based mostly or entirely on offenders' blameworthiness, on what they "deserved." Among politicians—much less among scholars and law reform advocates—a system based on instrumental goals of deterrence and incapacitation was an alternative, and had very different implications. Comparably blameworthy offenders could and should be treated differently if punishing one more severely than another would prevent crime more effectively.

Through the mid-1980s, neither approach entirely won out. Retributivism was more influential in some times and places, consequentialism in others. In practice, both were influential and had to be reconciled. The normative literature on prediction of dangerousness considered how that might be done. Agreement quickly emerged among most legal scholars and social scientists, and many practitioners, that the offender's blameworthiness should set an absolute upper limit on punishment's severity; some argued that consequentialist considerations were irrelevant and others that they might be relevant, but only if proportionate upper limits were respected. Conservative social scientists and many policymakers were primarily interested in crime prevention. Thence came the proposals for collective and selective incapacitation.

By the early 1980s, something close to a consensus emerged on how to reconcile retributive and consequentialist views in policy terms. The evolution of the US Parole Commission's "Salient Factor Score," used in its release guidelines, is illustrative. See Table 7.1.

1. *Violence.* The initial scoring system included a record of auto theft convictions as an aggravating factor that, if present, would delay release. This made sense if the goal was to predict any future offense, including minor ones, since low-level property offenders often accumulate lengthy records. They are especially likely to commit minor crimes. The commission

5. Sources concerning intellectual and policy developments discussed in this introductory section are well known. Chapter 2; Travis, Western, and Redburn (2014, chap. 3); and Tonry (2016b, chap. 1) provide them.

Table 7.1 US Parole Board Salient Factor Score variables

	1973 version	1976 version	1991 version
Convictions	Yes	Yes	Yes
Incarcerations	Yes	Yes	Yes
Age at first commitment	Yes	Yes	No
Age at current commitment	No	No	Yes
Recent commitment free period	No	No	Yes
Not auto theft	Yes	Yes	No
Not check fraud	No	Yes	No
No parole revoke, offense on parole	Yes	Yes	Yes
Custody status			Yes
No drug dependence	Yes	Yes	Yes
Education	Yes	No	No
Employment	Yes	Yes	No
Family status	Yes	No	No

Source: Hoffman (1976, 1983, 1995).

decided that only risks of future violence could justify lengthier prison sentences. The auto theft factor was dropped. The addition and removal of a check fraud factor illustrate the same point.

2. *Racial Disparities.* The initial system included "age at first commitment" as a factor. The commission soon recognized, however, that ages at first commitment were typically younger for blacks than for whites, partly because of racial and geographical differences in how police respond to young peoples' behavior. Stops and arrests are more likely in minority and disadvantaged areas. Use of age at first commitment meant that black offenders were held longer in prison than whites. It was dropped. The discussion below of social disadvantage illustrates the same point.

3. *Social Disadvantage.* The initial system included education, employment, and family stability as factors because weak educational and employment records and unstable residential and family circumstances are predictors of later offending. The commission gradually recognized that use of these factors meant that more privileged people would be held in prison for shorter periods than disadvantaged people, who seldom in any meaningful sense choose to be poor, badly educated, or erratically employed, or to live chaotic lives. Larger percentages of minority than white people

live deeply disadvantaged lives; the socioeconomic factors increased racial disparities. They were all dropped.

The literature on ethical and legal issues in prediction dried up after the mid-1980s, partly due to the emergence of "tough on crime" politics. Mandatory minimum sentence, three-strikes, truth in sentencing, life without parole, and similar laws shifted the crime prevention focus from decisions by judges and parole boards in individual cases to legislative prescription of extended confinement for whole categories of offenders defined only by the offenses of which they are convicted. Parole release was abandoned in a third of the states, made available if at all only to people convicted of minor crimes in the 26 states that enacted truth in sentencing laws, fundamentally compromised by mandatory minimum, three-strikes, and life without parole laws, and where it remained available was granted much less often by risk-averse parole boards.

Explanations of why normative and policy literatures on prediction of dangerousness have re-emerged are straightforward. Correctional managers have continuously since the 1980s been developing prediction instruments for use in classifying offenders for treatment and transferring them between programs. A private sector industry has long made its money by selling prediction instruments to correctional managers. In efforts to expand their markets and increase their profits, private companies in recent years began marketing them to courts for use in pretrial detention, sentencing, and probation revocation proceedings. Companies found new markets partly because of efforts to diminish mass incarceration. Starting with the re-entry movement of the late-1990s, reformers emphasized the need to reduce recidivism rates, divert low-level and low-risk offenders, and reserve imprisonment for serious and violent offenders. Legislatures increasingly direct judges to take reoffending predictions into account in making sentencing decisions. Sentencing commissions are building risk predictions into their guidelines (Hester et al. 2018; Hester 2019b).

Use of predictions of dangerousness in sentencing presents the same challenges and raises the same normative and policy issues in our time as it did four decades ago. US Attorney General Eric Holder (2014) warned the US Sentencing Commission against using dangerousness predictions, and has since repeatedly decried their use.[6] Their increased use has attracted the

---

6. Holder's critique identifies many of the problems discussed in this chapter: "By basing sentencing decisions on static factors and immutable characteristics—like the defendant's

attention of legal scholars and social scientists. The development of "big data" and machine learning approaches to prediction has attracted the interest of statisticians who have extensively debated trade-offs between technical and ethical issues.

The normative and policy issues raised in the 1970s and 1980s by collective and selective incapacitation are once again receiving attention. In this chapter, I re-examine them. Following the lead of the US Parole Commission, I focus on violent and otherwise serious crime. Reoffending is so common among chronic property, drug, prostitution, and public disorder offenders that application to them of predictive incapacitation strategies would generate palpably unjust punishments.[7] Blumstein, Farrington, and Moitra (1985) long ago showed that the probability of a subsequent arrest exceeds 90 percent for anyone who has been arrested eight or more times. Section I provides an overview of the current debates. To a large extent they consist of people talking past each other. Section II canvasses familiar objections to use of predictions of dangerousness in sentencing, including their inaccuracy; their reliance on ascribed characteristics such as age and gender;[8] their use of socioeconomic status characteristics such as education, marital status, and employment; and their reliance on criminal history indicators that are based in part on discriminatory police practices. All of these features of contemporary prediction methods systematically disadvantage poor and minority people.

Section III addresses justifications offered for predictive sentencing. One is that normative considerations related to punishment are too contested,

---

education level, socioeconomic background, or neighborhood—[risk assessments] may exacerbate unwarranted and unjust disparities that are already far too common in our criminal justice system and in our society. Criminal sentences must be based on the facts, the law, the actual crimes committed, the circumstances surrounding each individual case, and the defendant's history of criminal conduct. They should not be based on unchangeable factors that a person cannot control, or on the possibility of a future crime that has not taken place." He communicated his views to the US Sentencing Commission (letter, Jonathan J. Wroblewski, Director, Office of Policy and Legislation, US Department of Justice, to the Honorable Patti Saris, Chair, US Sentencing Commission, July 29, 2014).

7. Leading English sentencing specialists, both former members of the English Sentencing Council, argue that chronic minor offenders should normally receive reduced sentences because their offending patterns signal the presence of serious personality maladjustments (Ashworth and Wasik 2017).

8. Changes in gender self-identification are more common or more often declared in our time than in earlier times. They remain relatively rare. In the text, I use "gender" in its traditional bimodal sense. Inevitably, however, the issue will be raised in individual cases in which gender attributions matter whether individuals may or must be categorized according to birth-identified or self-identified gender.

unrealistic, or indeterminate to guide real-world decisions. Another is that racial, ethnic, age, and gender disparities should not be troubling because they reflect real behavioral differences between groups. A third is that, ho hum, predictive sentencing raises issues indistinguishable from public health quarantines and use of actuarial predictions in medicine, public health, credit scoring, and insurance. A fourth is that predictive sentencing is an essential tool for minimization of crime.

In the final section, I explore diverse ways to reconcile competing claims and aspirations. Realpolitik arguments are often made that predictions will be used one way or another, that crime is too emotional a topic for rational argument and analyses to be relevant, and that there is no point in explaining why predictive sentencing is unjust. I disagree with all those propositions. Better that officials treating other human beings unjustly be reminded again and again that that is what they are doing. They or their successors may someday decide to do better.

A critic might accuse me of being insensitive to the suffering of victims of crimes. I'm not. Prevention of foreseeable harms, however, requires trade-offs between interests and costs. There is no cost-free way to prevent bad things—including crimes, automobile accidents and fatalities, occupational injuries, environmental degradation, and slips in bathtubs—from happening. No one is prepared to forbid use of automobiles, industrial production, or bathing. Instead we try to make activities as safe as they affordably can be while acknowledging their importance.

Crime is no different. There would be little violent crime in the community if all males aged 19 to 35 were locked up. That's not going to happen. The suggestion is rhetorical, of course, but the reason it is unimaginable is important. Human beings value liberty and autonomy too much. No one wants to be a crime victim, but no one wants to be the victim of mistaken, extreme, or excessive state intrusions into their lives.

Incapacitation resulting from predictions of dangerousness diminishes the liberty and autonomy of knowable individual people, disproportionately poor and disadvantaged ones, in exchange for predicted prevention of crimes to hypothetical victims. Those predictions are much too often wrong, for two reasons. The first is technological. The state of the art is not good enough to produce violence predictions that are accurate even half of the time.

The second reason is seldom if ever discussed and is equally important. It is a fly-in-amber problem. Crime rates and patterns of past years become locked into prediction instruments used later on. If cultural attitudes, criminal opportunities, technologies, economic conditions, and law enforcement priorities change substantially, the world that prediction instruments assume exists no longer will. Probably no one would want to use 1920s data in instruments designed for use in the 2020s. Exactly the same problems arise in using data from the 2000s, or later, in instruments for the 2020s. Empirically grounded prediction instruments are necessarily based on and validated using data from earlier years. If crime rates and patterns change radically, as has happened in the past 30 years, between the time to which the data pertain and the time when instruments are used, predictions will be systematically wrong. That is what has happened.

American rates of violent crime were at all-time highs in the 1980s, but since 1991 have declined by two-thirds, almost continuously. The decline is equally evident in police data compiled in the FBI's *Uniform Crime Reports* and in survey data from the National Crime Victimization Survey. This means that data from 1990, 2000, or 2010 have little pertinence in 2020. Prediction instruments based on 1991 data would, if used in 2020, predict three times more violent incidents than would instruments based on 2018 data.[9] Two-thirds of the crimes that would have been predicted using 1991 data did not happen. In the early 1990s, many people predicted that violent crimes would continue to increase; remember the obsession with "super-predators" (DiIulio 1995)? The people imprisoned on the basis of those exaggerated predictions, and related fears, were deprived of much or all of their lives as free citizens and had any remaining years of freedom blighted. Judges in 1995 seldom consulted risk prediction instruments when deciding on sentences in individual cases. The predictions were effectively made by legislatures when they enacted mandatory minimum sentence, three-strikes, and similar laws. Because the crime decline has been nearly continuous, any prediction instrument developed in the past 30 years overpredicts.

The trade-off is thus between punishing specific people more than they deserve, on the basis of predictions that are more often than not wrong, and preventing an unknowable number of future crimes. That price, like the costs associated with banning private use of automobiles or bathtubs, is too high.

---

9. This is a back-of-an-envelope calculation, but the main point has to be true. The two-thirds drop in violence rates between 1991 and 2020 is influenced by changes in prevalence rates (the percentage of offenders in the population) or in incidence rates (the frequency of separate incidents) or, most likely, both. Both need to be modeled to create detailed estimates of the temporal lag effect. If population composition and prevalence rates remained constant, declining crime rates would signal declining incidence. If population composition and incidence rates remained constant, declining crime rates would signal falling prevalence.

Violent crimes are as much an inevitable fact of life as auto accidents and bathroom falls. They are a price we pay for personal freedom.

I. Debates

Peoples' views about use of predictions of dangerousness in sentencing sometimes appear to be irreconcilable, as two high-profile exchanges between statisticians demonstrate. Hart, Michie, and Cooke (2007) evaluated use of several well-known instruments and concluded that the "group and individual risk estimates" they produce are too imprecise to be useful. The predictions are too often wrong, they said; using them does serious unjustifiable harm to individuals who would not have been violent. Statisticians Peter Imrey and Philip Dawid (2015) responded in an article described by John Monahan (2017), America's most distinguished prediction specialist, as the leading statistical work on actuarial risk assessment. They insisted that the best-known instruments, their results, and their applications are based on sound statistical practice.

Imrey and Dawid didn't understand, or pretended not to understand, the critics' objections. Individuals are not treated unjustly, they wrote; decisions are "individualized." A judge saying that would mean that he or she took into account all available information concerning a particular crime and a particular defendant and thought carefully about what to do. What Imrey and Dawid meant was different: "Individualized risk [is] derived from an external group and projected onto the subject" (2015, p. 39). That is, the riskiness attributed to an individual is not his or her own, but the average of a group in which he or she is included for purposes of statistical analysis. They distinguished this from "latent individual risk intrinsic to the subject herself." This, though obscurely phrased, is what most people have in mind when they say that a sentencing decision is individualized.

The second exchange began when Angwin et al. (2016) analyzed Broward County, Florida data on use of COMPAS, a proprietary prediction instrument licensed by a for-profit company.[10] Their title tells their conclusion: "There's

---

10. COMPAS (Correctional Offender Management Profiling for Alternative Sanctions) is an industry leader. Its instruments are used throughout the United States. Dressel and Farid (2018) report on a stunning analysis of 462 lay peoples' predictions of dangerousness, using the Broward County, Florida, data set used by Flores, Bechtel, and Lowenkamp (2016), and find that lay peoples' predictions of reoffending were as accurate as COMPAS's. Dressel and Farid presented short descriptions of the crimes with which 1,000 defendants were charged and (only) the defendant's sex, age, and previous criminal history. COMPAS, by contrast, uses 137 variables. In order to prevent participant exhaustion, defendants were divided into 20 sets

Software Used across the Country to Predict Future Criminals. And It's Biased against Blacks." Their three key findings: blacks had higher average risk scores than whites, relatively more blacks than whites were wrongly predicted to be violent (exposing more to harsher treatment), and relatively fewer blacks than whites were wrongly predicted to be nonviolent (making fewer eligible for milder treatment). Those foreseeable racial disparities—crucial to people they affect—are what the critics meant by "bias."

Flores, Bechtel, and Lowenkamp (2016) did not deny that racial disparities exist, but insisted that the critics had not shown *statistical* bias. Blacks have higher crime rates than whites, they explained, and more often have socioeconomic and other characteristics correlated with offending: no bias, just sound statistical practice. They sidestepped the critics' objections.

Talented, passionate people were on both sides of those exchanges, but couldn't find common ground. The prediction defenders viewed the issues as primarily technical: let the chips fall where they may. The critics viewed the issues as primarily substantive: knowingly punishing more blacks than whites unduly severely is wrong.

Many fault lines permeate prediction debates. Some consider it irresponsible not to use state-of-the-art prediction methods. Others believe that punishments should be closely proportioned to offenders' blameworthiness and that it is unjust to punish some offenders more severely than others only because of predictions. Still others believe that reducing use of imprisonment depends on identifying offenders likeliest to reoffend, and locking them up, so that others need not be. Some people believe that racial, ethnic, and class disparities caused and exacerbated by prediction instruments are morally wrong and want them to end.

In writing the preceding paragraphs, I tried to avoid polemic. The facts, ma'am, just the facts, as Sergeant Joe Friday used to say. I did not mention assertions that political and ideological agendas and racial, ethnic, and class biases, conscious and implicit, underlay adoption in the United States of unprecedentedly severe crime control policies in the 1980s and early 1990s. I set those allegations aside. My interest is in the intellectual challenges posed by

---

of 50 cases. Each participant was asked for one defendant set to predict reoffending within 2 years of the defendant's most recent crime. In one round of questions, participants were not given the defendant's race. In a second round, they were (for a different set of offenders than in the first round). The participants were recruited through Amazon's Mechanical Turk, an online crowd sourcing marketplace where people are paid to perform a wide variety of tasks. The participants' predictions in both rounds were as accurate as COMPAS's. Racial differences in false positive rates were lower than in Flores et al.'s analysis.

widely different, good faith, views about prediction, and whether and how they can be reconciled.

The difficulty, as Isaiah Berlin (1959) long ago explained, is that the implications of equally valid first principles often conflict. Few would disagree that maintenance of public order and security is a good thing. Were that the only relevant consideration, it would be self-evident that efforts to diminish crime's effects on victims should be maximized.

Other no less important values, however, are at stake. If assuring that offenders be punished exactly as much as they deserve were all that mattered, predictions about future offending would be irrelevant. If only equal treatment mattered, people convicted of equally serious crimes should be punished equally severely; predictions would again be irrelevant. If avoidance of policies that cause or exacerbate racial and ethnic disparities, or that rely on factors tinged with invidious bias, was overridingly important, all existing prediction systems would be abandoned.

The values underlying all of those things matter, and they conflict. People resolve the conflicts in different ways. Some allow one goal to trump others (e.g., reducing mass incarceration by using imprisonment only for "dangerous" people: Flores, Bechtel, and Lowenkamp 2016; reducing social and racial injustice: Harcourt 2008; preventing crime: Slobogin 2019). Imrey and Dawid (2015, p. 40) observed, "If groups of individuals with high and low propensities for violence recidivism can be distinguished, and courts act upon such distinctions, recidivism will decline to the extent that groups most prone to violence are incapacitated. . . . And both society and offenders will be better served even if we cannot be sure . . . from precisely which individual offenders this betterment derives." Offenders who are imprisoned, or held longer, because they were mistakenly predicted to be violent, are unlikely to agree that they have been "better served."

Some writers acknowledge the problem but duck. When writing about punishment theory generally, American philosopher Douglas Husak (2020, p. 97) observes, "Sentencing according to the principle of proportionality is crucial if the state is to treat offenders as they deserve." However, concerning risk prediction, he adopts a "pluralist" stance and writes, "Retributivists should preserve the role of desert while weakening its strength. . . . We can preserve proportionality but allow exceptions when we have a good rationale for them. . . . If we have good reason to inflict different amounts of punishment on two offenders who have committed equally serious crimes, we should not be worried that our decision does not preserve proportionality. Admittedly, the results produced [may be] messy; sentencing, like morality more generally, is not governed by an algorithm" (Husak 2019, pp. 44–45).[11] English philosopher Matt Matravers (2019, p. 205) offers an account of punishment in which censure of blameworthy behavior and crime prevention are independent governing principles: "The results may well be counterintuitive," he writes, to punish people convicted of less serious crimes more severely than people convicted of more serious ones for incapacitative reasons, but it "is not inconsistent" so long as retributive and consequentialist goals are independent. The challenge, as Isaiah Berlin insisted, however, is in deciding what to do when the implications of the independent goals conflict.

Not everyone sidesteps. Psychologists John Monahan and Jennifer Skeem (2016) survey the literature, work through all the major problems, and propose ways to limit unwanted effects of prediction (notably by allowing them to be used only to reduce but not to increase sentence severity). Berk et al. (2018, p. 1) in one of a series of increasingly subtle analyses of trade-offs between ethical issues and predictive accuracy, observe, "Except in trivial cases, it is impossible to maximize accuracy and fairness at the same time, and impossible simultaneously to satisfy all kinds of fairness."

However, they too throw up their hands: "In the end, it will fall to stakeholders—not criminologists, not statisticians, and not computer scientists—to determine the tradeoffs. . . . These are matters of values and law, and ultimately, the political process" (p. 33). Not terribly helpful or reassuring to anyone concerned about unjust or racially disparate treatment of individuals, or to individuals serving long prison sentences premised on inaccurate predictions. The political process produced mass incarceration and three-strikes, life without parole, and similar laws.

II. Problems

Three sets of problems bedevil use of predictions of dangerousness in sentencing. The first is that they are not very accurate. When the aim is to predict serious sexual or other violence, more predictions are wrong than are right. If used to determine prison sentence lengths, many people who would not have committed serious violence will be held longer. The second set of problems concerns variables used in nearly all prediction instruments: some over which individuals have no control, such as age and gender, are fundamentally unjust and would not be permitted in other contexts; some concern

---

11. The newest and purportedly most accurate prediction devices employing big data and machine learning *are* algorithms (Berk et al. 2018; Berk 2019).

inherently personal matters such as marriage, work, and education; some relate to aspects of criminal records that are contaminated by conscious and implicit bias and discriminatory practices. The third set concerns racial and ethnic disparities; almost all variables used in prediction instruments correlate with race and ethnicity and inexorably make punishments of minority group members harsher than those of whites.

A. Accuracy

Violence is rare, even among known offenders. Making accurate predictions of rare events is inherently difficult. As a result, the technology of violence prediction is not very good. The predictions are more often inaccurate than accurate. I was astonished to learn, when reviewing the contemporary literature as background for writing this chapter, that accuracy is little better now than it was four decades ago.

Norval Morris (1974), in an influential early synthesis, concluded that predictions of future violence were wrong two-thirds of the time. The most exhaustive contemporaneous analysis by John Monahan (1981) reached the same conclusion. Predictions that people will not be violent were overwhelmingly correct, but that is trivial: if only 10 percent of a group are violent, a prediction that no one will commit a violent crime will be correct 90 percent or more of the time. Morris argued that then current knowledge did not justify imposing longer prison terms on people predicted to be violent: "'Dangerousness' must be rejected for this purpose, since it presupposes a capacity to predict future criminal behavior quite beyond our present technical ability" (1974, p. 62). Locking up three people predicted to be violent when only one will be is, he said, deeply unjust. Two would be wrongfully deprived of extended periods of liberty.

Analyses of prediction studies conventionally distinguish, as Morris did, between "true" and "false positives." True positives are predicted to reoffend, and do. False positives are predicted to reoffend, but do not. True and false negatives are defined similarly. In Morris's time, the state of the predictive art, as Table 7.2 shows using Morris's example, was that two-thirds of individuals predicted to be violent were false positives.

The technology of violence prediction is vastly more sophisticated than it was four decades ago. The early studies were based on clinical predictions by doctors, mental health specialists, judges, and correctional personnel. The contemporary literature is actuarial, and based on sophisticated statistical analyses, mathematical models, machine learning, and "big data." One might

Table 7.2 Violence predictions, true and false: an illustration

Crime Type	Prediction	Result—No Violence	Result—Violence
No violence	70	65 (true negatives)	5 (false negatives)
Violence	30	20 (false positives)	10 (true positives)
Total	100	85	15

Source: Adapted from Morris (1974, Table 1).

expect that violence predictions today are vastly more accurate than in the 1970s. They aren't.

One leading meta-analysis of the accuracy of prediction instruments concludes that further improvements are unlikely: "After almost five decades of developing risk prediction tools, the evidence increasingly suggests that the ceiling of predictive efficacy may have been reached with the available technology" (Yang, Wong, and Coid 2010, p. 759). Consistently with this caution, two major meta-analyses conclude that the most commonly used violence prediction instruments are indistinguishable in their accuracy.[12]

The most influential meta-analysis, analyzing research on the nine most commonly used instruments, concluded that positive violence predictions are on average correct 42 percent of the time (Fazel et al. 2012; Fazel 2019). Morris, recall, was troubled that only one-third of positive predictions (two of six) were correct. Forty-two percent accuracy, put differently, means that two of five positive predictions are correct. As in Morris's time, substantially more than half of people predicted to be violent will not be.

Two of the leading meta-analyses conclude that positive predictions of future violence are too inaccurate to be used in sentencing:

Because of their moderate level of predictive efficacy, they should not be used as the sole or primary means for clinical or criminal justice

---

12. Yang, Wong, and Coid (2010, p. 259): "If prediction of violence is the only criterion for the selection of a risk assessment tool, then the tools included in the present study are essentially interchangeable." Campbell, French, and Gendreau (2009, p. 253): "This analysis found little difference among the predictive validities of actuarial and structured instruments for violent reoffending." Meta-analyses of research on instruments used to predict any, as opposed to only violent, reoffending reach the same conclusion: "Overall, no one instrument stood out as producing more accurate assessments than the others, with validity varying with the indicator reported" (Desmarais, Johnson, and Singh 2016, p. 213).

decision making that is contingent on a high level of predictive accuracy, such as preventive detention. (Yang, Wong, and Coid 2010,
p. 761)

These tools are not sufficient on their own for the purposes of risk assessment. . . . The current level of evidence is not sufficiently strong for
definitive decisions on sentencing, parole, and release or discharge to
be made solely using these tools. (Fazel et al. 2012, pp. 5, 6)

Even outspoken defenders of risk prediction agree. Flores, Bechtel, and
Lowenkamp (2016), whom I discussed above concerning disagreements
about racial disparities, emphasized that "we want to make it clear that we are
not supporting or endorsing the idea of using risk assessment at sentencing"
(p. 39).

There is thus no credible scientific case to be made in favor of use in
sentencing of statistical, actuarial, or algorithmic predictions of future
violence.

B. Unjust Variables

Except for race and, though they are seldom explicitly discussed, presumably
also ethnicity, nationality, and religion, developers of prediction instruments
include as variables any offense and offender characteristics on which they
can obtain data. In other public policy settings, for example, educational,
public health, and medical research, equivalent strategies including use even
of racial and other usually verboten data makes sense. The aims are to improve public services generally, to understand and address problems affecting
subpopulations, or to diagnose and treat health problems.

Violence prediction in courts is different.[13] The aim is usually to identify
individuals for pretrial or postconviction preventive detention. Public health
and educational research and related policies seldom target individuals.
Medical decision-making does, but the aim is to prevent or minimize human

---

13. Different considerations may be pertinent concerning some uses of prediction instruments
in correctional settings. Some "culturally appropriate" treatment programs, for example, target
special needs of women or members of specific minority groups. Other treatment programs
target higher-risk offenders on the efficiency rationale that low-risk offenders will usually not
reoffend whether or not they participate. Prediction instruments are used to match offenders
to treatment programs generally, to set or vary treatment or supervision intensity, and to
measure changes relative to program goals. They are also used in institutional custody level
decisions which raises issues similar to those concerning sentencing.

suffering. Sentencing decisions are intended to cause human suffering. That is why Jeremy Bentham called all punishment, even when warranted, evil.

Suspect variables fall into three categories. Race, gender, and age ought to be off-limits because they are human characteristics for which individuals bear no causal, personal, or moral responsibility. Increased punishments for any of these reasons are inherently unjust. A host of socioeconomic characteristics including employment, education, marital status, living arrangements, and parental responsibilities are correlated with offending but are not the criminal law's business. These are matters of individual choice in a free society. Punishing people for making the "wrong" choices is also inherently unjust. Socioeconomic and other personal characteristics including many related to criminal history are highly correlated with race and ethnicity; many are shaped by invidious discrimination. Their use causes and exacerbates adverse racial and ethnic disparities.

C. Immutable Characteristics

No one would think people should be punished more severely because of their eye or hair color or adult height, characteristics over which they have no control. Gender, race, ethnicity, and age raise the same issue. So, despite their greater mutability, would religion and nationality most of the time.

1. *Age*. Individuals have no more control of their age than of their eye color. All else being equal, an offender's age should be irrelevant, except to mitigate the severity of punishments imposed on young and elderly offenders.[14] Young offenders have traditionally in all Western countries, including the United States, been punished less severely than adults and usually in specialized courts using specialized procedures and imposing less severe punishments.[15]

---

14. Many European countries have strong legal presumptions against imprisonment of the elderly (typically, 70 or older). That is why former Italian Prime Minister Silvio Berlusconi was sentenced to community service as a hospital orderly, rather than to the multiyear prison sentence he would otherwise have received following conviction for public corruption offenses. As the Madoff Ponzi scheme and Bill Cosby cases and the reluctance of most American prisons to release terminally ill and elderly prisoners demonstrate, the United States as in many penal policy matters is an outlier in its handling of the aged and infirm.

15. In western European countries, for example, the age of criminal responsibility is typically 14 or 15 years (in Belgium 18 for most offenses). In most, waiver of young offenders to adult courts is not legally possible; nor is direct prosecution in adult courts. In German courts, the vast majority of 18- and 19-year-olds convicted of serious crimes are sentenced as if they were juveniles (Tonry and Chambers 2012).

The reasons are self-evident. Most young offenders are less experienced and mature than most adults, are at developmental stages in which risk-taking, thrill-seeking, and experimentation are common, and are more malleable. Research on "age/crime curves" and desistance has long shown that many adolescents commit crimes as teenagers but most soon desist.[16] Neurological and developmental research has demonstrated details of adolescent brain development and behavioral controls that strengthen the rationale for more forgiving handling of young offenders (Monahan, Steinberg, and Piquero 2015). Even the conservative US Supreme Court is convinced. Banning mandatory life sentences without parole for juveniles, it emphasized that "children are constitutionally different from adults for purposes of sentencing" and that "mandatory penalties, by their nature, preclude a sentence from taking account of an offender's age and the wealth of characteristics and circumstances attendant to it" (*Miller v. Alabama*, 132 S. Ct. 2455, 2467 [2012]).

Youth nonetheless is widely used as a variable in prediction instruments and as an aggravating factor in sentencing. I discuss Virginia's notorious sentencing guidelines, in use for more than 25 years, because they are premised on prediction-based incapacitation. They call, all else being equal, for harsher punishments for younger offenders than for older ones. This is wrong in principle and, in light of a growing body of research showing that imprisonment is criminogenic, perverse (e.g., Mears and Cochran 2018; Frase and Roberts 2019).

The Virginia guidelines set out criteria that identify nonviolent offenders for whom prison sentences are specified but whom judges are encouraged to divert to community-based punishments. In fraud guidelines, 22 "points" are given for being aged 20 or younger (Virginia Sentencing Commission 2014).[17] Being male adds 10 more points, for a total of 32. Only offenders who receive 31 or fewer points qualify for diversion; thus no matter how minor the offense or the criminal record, no male under 21 satisfies the diversion criteria.

Virginia's remarkable treatment of young people becomes starker when compared with provisions for offenders 30 and over; they receive seven "age points." Five points are given for having one or two prior felony convictions and four points for having been incarcerated as an adult one to nine times. Put it together: a 30-year-old (7 points) male (10) with two prior felony

---

16. Farrington (1986) and Laub and Sampson (2001) are the classic sources.

17. The details are slightly different for larceny. Being male adds 9, not 10, points. The system is otherwise similar.

convictions (5) and two prior adult incarcerations (4) totals 26 points, and falls below the 31-point diversion threshold. An 18-year-old with no past criminal record does not.

There are three explanations for this strange policy. The first is ideological. Virginia's guidelines were developed at the height of the tough-on-crime period under the administration of Republican Governor George Allen, who ran for office on a "parole abolition" platform (Tonry 2016*b*). They were developed under the leadership of ultraconservative William Barr, author during his first term as US Attorney General of the 1992 tract *The Case for More Incarceration*. Second, although incapacitation had long before been repudiated as a crime control strategy by the National Academy of Sciences, Barr made it the premise for the Virginia guidelines. Third, because of the age/crime curve, age is a powerful predictor of future offending (though most offenses involve property or drugs and most young offenders soon desist).

The more general question is whether youth should be included in any prediction instrument meant to be used, or that might be used, in deciding whom to imprison or for how long. The trade-off is between predictive accuracy and punishing people more severely because they are young. If the trade-off concerned eye color, height, race, ethnicity, or religion, few people would consider it. Basic requirements of justice forbid their use, even if any of them—race and ethnicity do and religion probably does—predicts reoffending. Age is equally unjustifiable.

2. *Gender.* Gender cuts in different directions in different policy contexts. Assiduous efforts are made in education, employment, and public health to prevent or minimize adverse differential treatment of women. This is so even when actuarial rationales exist that might provide a basis for treating women less favorably. Because they typically live longer than men, women traditionally paid lower life insurance premiums but also received lower monthly pension benefits. Those practices have been attacked as unjust, increasingly successfully, despite their actuarial justifications. So have higher automobile insurance premiums paid by men.

The early American sentencing commissions undertook research on past sentencing patterns and invariably found that women typically received less severe punishments than men. No commission, however, chose to promulgate separate, less severe guidelines for women or to make being female a mitigating factor in sentencing. Gender-blind guidelines were expected to increase sentence severity for women, but everyone involved agreed that was required by respect for gender equality (e.g., Knapp 1984; Tonry 1996).

Gender blindness is a powerful idea. Treating people differently because they are male or female is wrong in the same way that treating people differently because they are of a particular race or religion is wrong. Gender blindness is sometimes set aside for sympathetic policy reasons. Examples targeting women include healthcare, childcare, maternity leaves, and flexible work schedules. Movements are afoot as a matter of equal treatment to make comparable provision for men. What distinguishes these gender-conscious policies is that they aim to do something for women, not to them. They do not aim to treat men worse but to meet gender-specific needs of women.

That has not stopped developers of prediction instruments from incorporating maleness as a factor. Nor has it stopped policymakers from using maleness, all else being equal, to increase punishment severity. The 10 points given under the Virginia fraud guidelines for being male (compared with one point for being female) is an example. Theft and drug sale guidelines in Virginia vary in detail but all treat men and women differently.

The rationale is actuarial. Across crime, time, and place, men's offending rates are higher than women's. Locking up more, otherwise comparable, men than women will predictably prevent more future offenses. Just as with eye color, height, race, ethnicity, religion, and age, however, that cannot justify punishing some equally culpable offenders more severely than others.

3. *Race and Ethnicity.* No American jurisdiction explicitly authorizes use of race or ethnicity (or religion or nationality) as criteria for making sentencing or parole release decisions. Doing so would violate long-settled constitutional equal protection doctrines (e.g., Starr 2014). Indirectly, however, race and ethnicity creep in when decisions are based in part on socioeconomic and criminal history variables. On average, blacks, Hispanics, and Native Americans compared with whites have lower incomes, weaker employment records, less extensive educations, less residential stability, and more extensive criminal records. All of those characteristics are correlated with higher offending risks. This is the major reason why prediction instruments produce higher false positive rates for blacks and higher false negative rates for whites.

There is no moral difference between making invidious decisions on the basis of race, and making decisions based on other considerations knowing they will affect members of different racial groups differently. If a law specifying 5-year prison sentences for black offenders and 2-year sentences for whites is wrong, it is equally wrong to use prediction instruments that foreseeably produce the same result. That moral equivalence is the reason why criminal law mens rea doctrine usually treats intention to cause a harm, knowledge that the harm will almost certainly result, and conscious disregard of a substantial and unjustifiable risk that it will occur as morally equivalent. Doing something knowing it will cause harm is little different from doing something intending to cause harm. Blowing up an airplane is equally wrong whether the aim is to kill the passengers or to defraud the insurer of a forged Rembrandt in the plane's hold, knowing that the passengers will die.

The legal and moral issues this argument raises are complex, but that does not weaken its force in relation to sentencing and punishment. There are other circumstances in which knowingly causing harm is justified. Criminal law defenses of self-defense, duress, and necessity provide examples. So does the Roman Catholic moral doctrine of double effect that justifies harms that are side effects of actions taken to accomplish a good result (McIntyre 2014; an example: acting to save a pregnant woman's life though a fetus will likely not survive). Other times harms occur for which the law affords no remedy. The US Supreme Court famously decided that public authorities may not operate segregated schools on purpose (de jure discrimination) but that segregated schools that are the outgrowth of residential patterns (de facto discrimination) are okay.

Criminal punishment is different from the harms involved in those other contexts. Sentences imposed by courts are state actions that are indisputably meant to cause offenders to suffer. No decent person would say that black and other minority people deserve to suffer more than do white offenders convicted of the same offense. We know, judges know, designers of instruments know that predictive sentencing causes blacks to be punished more severely than whites convicted of the same offenses.

Table 7.3, showing false positive and false negative rates calculated by Flores, Bechtel, and Lowenkamp (2016) in their reanalysis of COMPAS data, illustrates this. Half of whites predicted not to reoffend were rearrested, compared with only 28 percent of blacks predicted not to reoffend. The false negative rate for whites was nearly double that for blacks. Conversely, only 22 percent of whites who were predicted to reoffend did not, compared with

Table 7.3 Prediction error rates, any arrest within 2 years, by race: an illustration

	False Positive Rates	False Negative Rates
Whites	22%	50%
Blacks	42%	28%

Source: Flores, Bechtel, and Lowenkamp (2016, Table 3).

42 percent of blacks. The false positive rate for blacks was nearly twice that for whites. These are extraordinary differences. The result is that, because of use of prediction instruments, blacks are likely to be punished more severely, and whites less severely, than they otherwise would be.

Bernard Harcourt (2008) showed that predictive sentencing has a ratchet effect that worsens racial and socioeconomic disparities. Minority and disadvantaged defendants are treated more severely on average than others the first time they are convicted. When prediction instruments are used at sentencing, each subsequent conviction has compounding effects and further increases increments of additional severity. Racial differences in criminal history are a primary cause of racial disparities in imprisonment (Hester et al. 2018).

Correlations between offending and race are not random. Both official police data and victim survey data show that black people commit some crimes at higher rates than whites. That is not surprising. In every country, members of some socially and economically disadvantaged groups commit crimes at higher rates than the majority population (Tonry 1997). In the United States, the social and economic disadvantages that disproportionately afflict black, Native American, and Hispanic people, and are correlated with offending, are partly products of historical and ongoing discrimination and of diminished life chances at birth. Most people believe that mentally responsible minority offenders, like other offenders, should be punished as they deserve for the offenses they commit.[18] It should be at least discomfiting that the use of prediction instruments in sentencing exacerbates the effects of disadvantage and causes many minority offenders to be punished more harshly than they deserve to be, or would be if they were white.

D. Socioeconomic Characteristics

All of the early sentencing commissions rejected use of socioeconomic variables in their guidelines systems. The first principle set out in the "Statement of Purpose and Principles" of the Minnesota Sentencing Guidelines Commission (1980) provided, and still does: "Sentencing should be neutral with respect to the race, gender, social, or economic status of convicted offenders." Section 994(d) of the Sentencing Reform Act of 1984 directs the federal sentencing commission to "assure that the guidelines and policy statements are entirely

---

18. As chapter 4 explains, deeply disadvantaged offenders often deserve less severe punishments than do others.

neutral as to the race, sex, national origin, creed, and socioeconomic status of offenders."

The US Congress and Minnesota's sentencing commission rejected use of socioeconomic status characteristics in sentencing because their use is unjust. It feels platitudinous to write this, but it is unchallengeably true: No one should be punished more severely than they would otherwise be because they are rich or poor, well or meagerly educated, married or single, working or unemployed. None of that has anything to do with an individual human being's blameworthiness. Even the Virginia Sentencing Commission, not renowned for its sensitivity to moral and ethical issues, removed the socioeconomic factors—employment and marital status—initially included in its diversion guidelines (Ostrom and Kauder 2012). The US Parole Commission did the same thing decades earlier. The correlation of many socioeconomic characteristics with race makes their use doubly unjust.

There is another fundamental reason why socioeconomic characteristics should not be cause for harsher punishment. Many result from legitimate life style choices that are not the state's business. People living in free societies are entitled to decide whether to marry, to work a steady job, or to become well educated, whether or not being unmarried, lacking a stable work record, and being poorly educated are correlated with higher offending rates. Free citizens are entitled to seek university degrees, join apprenticeship programs, or live catch-as-catch-can, as many artists, musicians, writers, and street people do by various combinations of choice and necessity. Citizens are entitled to choose not to work at all and to live hand to mouth or on money from trust funds or indulgent parents.

Prediction instruments and sentencing policies include socioeconomic variables because research shows that they are correlated with offending. A cynic might say that anyone who chooses to live a vagabond life assumes the risk that he will be punished for it, so what's the problem? The problem is that free people are entitled to decide how to live their lives. Equally importantly, however, many offenders do not—in any fundamental sense—choose to be poorly housed, poorly employed or unemployed, poorly educated, or unmarried. Even if poor peoples' choices are more constrained than more privileged peoples', they are lawful choices all the same. Punishing people because of their lawful lifestyle choices raises the same ethical issues for a disadvantaged inner-city resident as it would for a privileged trust fund beneficiary.

Skeem, Scurich, and Monahan in 2019 showed that use of prediction instruments in sentencing worsens disparities affecting disadvantaged offenders even more than the preceding discussion suggests. Judges much more often disregard predictions that poor people are low-risk than they do concerning affluent people. Three hundred and forty experienced criminal court judges agreed to participate in a controlled experiment to test whether availability of risk assessments affects sentencing of disadvantaged offenders. The judges were asked to indicate what sentences they would impose on the basis of case vignettes that differed in only two respects, whether risk predictions were provided and whether the defendant was relatively poor ("a casual laborer in construction who dropped out of high school") or relatively affluent ("an Apple Store employee with a bachelor's degree in computer science"). Without the risk assessment, poor defendants were less likely than affluent defendants to be sentenced to imprisonment. With the risk assessment, that pattern reversed. Poor defendants were more likely to be imprisoned. The takeaway:

> When formal risk assessment information is omitted, relatively poor defendants are less likely to be incarcerated than their more affluent counterparts. When that information is provided—holding risk scores and classifications constant—relatively poor defendants are *more* likely to be incarcerated than their richer counterparts. (p. 5; emphasis in original)

Their hypothesis is that judges tend to respond compassionately to disadvantaged individuals when they do not have access to risk assessments but, when they do, the compassion is displaced by stereotypes about race, crime, and poverty.

Others report similar findings. University of Michigan law professor Sonja Starr found the same thing in a 2016 study in which law students "sentenced" offenders on the basis of vignettes. Without risk predictions, poor defendants received shorter sentences than affluent ones. That pattern reversed when risk predictions were provided. A third study using vignettes with and without risk predictions found that use of predictions worsened black/white disparities (Green and Chen 2019).

The US Parole Commission got it right 40 years ago. Socioeconomic variables, as a matter of simple social justice, have no place in prediction instruments. When they are used, as these studies show, they systematically exacerbate racial and class disparities in sentencing.

E. Criminal History

Criminal history, as chapter 5 explains, raises more complex normative and policy issues than is usually recognized, despite the existence of widely held intuitions that prior convictions justify harsher punishments for subsequent offenses. Although it appears self-evident to many Americans that previously convicted people should be punished more severely than they otherwise would be when they are convicted of new crimes, that is not self-evident to people in other countries. In the Scandinavian countries, for example, the general assumption is that punishments should not be increased because of prior convictions (Asp 2010; Lappi-Seppälä 2011). The reasoning is that the offender was punished as much as he or she deserved for the former offense and should now be punished as much as is deserved for the new one. Prior convictions are often taken into account as aggravating factors in other common-law countries, but usually subject to sharp limits (Baker and Ashworth 2010; Freiberg 2014).

Prior convictions have drastic aggravating effects in American sentencing. Under three-strikes, habitual offender, and career criminal laws, they make a huge difference. Under state sentencing guidelines systems, criminal history can result in prison sentences four to 15 times longer than are received by first offenders (Hester 2019a, 2019b). Any searching inquiry into ethical issues in American sentencing has to explore the rationales and justifications of those differences.

Criminal history variables are the primary drivers of risk predictions. It is difficult, however, to find a principled justification for increasing the severity of punishment because of an individual's criminal history. Even if one could be found, criminal history is entangled with racial bias and foreseeable disparate racial effects.

1. *Punishment Theories.* Retributivists believe that any punishment more severe than an offender deserves is unjust. Kant insisted on impositions of deserved punishments precisely calibrated to the seriousness of the offense. That requires strict proportionality so that equally serious crimes are punished equally severely and more and less serious crimes are punished appropriately differently. Negative retributivists, who believe the maximum deserved punishment may but need not be imposed, insist that anything harsher than the maximum is unjust and that the minimum deserved punishment should normally be imposed. Most retributive philosophers and criminal law theorists who have considered the matter conclude that there is no convincing moral

justification for treating people with prior convictions more severely than first-timers (e.g., Fletcher 1978; Lippke 2016; Alexander and Ferzan 2018).

Utilitarians and other consequentialists could in principle permit harsher punishments for recidivists, but only if the reductions in suffering attributable to crimes thereby prevented are greater than the additional suffering imposed on offenders. Utilitarianism also has a strong proportionality principle, based on a deterrence logic: punishments should be scaled to offense seriousness to encourage offenders to commit the less serious of alternative possible crimes. However, unlike retributive proportionality, utilitarian proportionality can be trumped by Bentham's parsimony principle that forbids unnecessary punishment. Bentham also forbade imposition of punishments whose aims can more effectively be achieved in other ways (Frase 2009a).

The problem in our time for consequentialist supporters of predictive sentencing is that contemporary knowledge of deterrence, incapacitation, and moral education provides no credible basis for believing that increasing punishments because of prior convictions will prevent greater aggregate suffering by victims. Chapter 6 summarizes the evidence. The National Academy of Sciences Committee on the Causes and Consequences of High Rates of Incarceration concluded in 2014 that deterrent and incapacitative effects of punishment are modest at best and that imprisonment is on balance criminogenic, making ex-prisoners more rather than less likely to reoffend. The evidence on rehabilitation is stronger. Well-designed, well-targeted, well-managed, and well-funded programs can reduce reoffending (MacKenzie 2006; Cullen 2013). Assignment to diagnostically appropriate treatment programs does not, however, require that previously convicted people receive harsher punishments.

2. *Racial Bias and Disparate Effects*. Use of criminal history factors in sentencing systematically disadvantages members of minority groups. Richard Frase (2009b), in the most comprehensive study ever published on racial disparities in a state sentencing system, found that two-thirds of racial disparities in Minnesota imprisonment were attributable to criminal history. Most of that disparity resulted from the heavy weight given to criminal history in Minnesota's guidelines system. More recent analyses have shown comparable patterns of criminal-history-based disparities in Kansas, North Carolina, and Washington (Hester 2019a, Table 7.5). Use of prediction instruments in those states (and others) will make racial disparities worse.

Some aspects of criminal history that are commonly included as variables in prediction instruments—age at first arrest or commitment, custody status, and numbers of prior arrests, convictions, and punishments—result in substantial part from explicit and implicit racial bias, and from police targeting of poor and minority neighborhoods and individuals. Black and Hispanic people are arrested at younger ages[19] and more often than whites for reasons that have as much to do with racially differentiated exercises of police discretion as with racial differences in offending behavior.

Police sometimes arrest more young black people for invidious reasons, but often would prefer to avoid arrests if they can. White and affluent young people, however, can more frequently than disadvantaged minority youngsters be returned to stable homes or referred to private treatment and mental health facilities. Schools refer more minority than white students to the police for conduct problems. Racial profiling by the police by definition mostly affects members of minority groups. Drug enforcement policies disproportionately target substances sold by minority sellers and the places where they sell them. All of these practices exaggerate the criminal records of members of minority groups.

3. *Other Criminal History Issues.* Use of criminal history variables in sentencing, or in prediction instruments, raises other issues. When the sentencing provisions of the 1962 *Model Penal Code* were being developed in the 1950s, there was vigorous debate over whether and how criminal history should be taken into account. Paul Tappan (1947), chairman of the US Parole Board and primary draftsman of the code's sentencing and corrections provisions, argued that with liberty at stake, only prior convictions should count. Arrests or prosecutions not resulting in a conviction should not. On the same logic, age at first arrest or commitment and custody status, all—along with arrests—commonly used as variables in prediction instruments, should not count. Tappan's view is the contemporary norm in other Western countries: only convictions count (Roberts and von Hirsch 2010). Here I only flag these issues. However, since predictions of dangerousness are often cited as reason to deprive "dangerous" offenders of more liberty than they otherwise would lose, they are as pertinent to the ethics of prediction as they are to sentencing.

---

19. The path-breaking Philadelphia birth cohort studies, for example, found that 48.7 percent of nonwhite offenders in the 1945 cohort had their first police contact before age 14, compared with 30.8 percent for whites. The corresponding figures for the 1958 cohort were 41 and 27 percent (Tracey, Wolfgang, and Figlio 1990, chap. 10). This is not a comparison that more recent longitudinal studies offer.

III. Rationalizations

Use of predictions of dangerousness in sentencing raises formidable normative problems. Predictions that particular people will commit violent offenses are more often wrong than right. Of five positive predictions, three will be false positives. The false positives are disproportionately black and other minority offenders. All prediction instruments incorporate variables such as youth and gender that are inherently unjust. All use socioeconomic status variables that produce systematically harsher dispositions of black, other minority, and disadvantaged offenders. All include criminal history variables that are inflated for black and other minority offenders by racially biased and disparate police practices.

The defenses of predictive sentencing are less weighty. One is that retributive punishment theories provide no meaningful bar to reliance on predictions (Husak 2019; Matravers 2019). A second is that prevention of predicted harms to victims is so overwhelmingly important that it trumps concerns about proportionality and equal treatment (Ryberg 2019, as devil's advocate). A third is that there is nothing special about subordinating individuals' to collective or organizational interests on the basis of predictions. Happens all the time: actuarial statistics are used in credit scoring and setting insurance premiums; statistical analyses underlie public health policies and medical practices; quarantines confine individuals (Imrey and Dawid 2015; Douglas 2019). A fourth is that concerns about racial and other disparities in punishment are misplaced: people who score badly on predictive variables commit disproportionate numbers of crimes and should bear disproportionate preventive burdens (Slobogin 2019).

A. Punishment Theory

If everyone agreed that punishment policies and practices should be assessed only in relation to their crime-reductive effects, the challenges for predictive sentencing would be immaterial. So far as I can tell, no one believes that concerning themselves and people they care about.[20] The Christian New

---

20. As a matter of ideology or political self-interest, American politicians often support policies such as life without parole for minors, three-strikes sentences of 25-years-to-life for minor property offenders, and decades-long prison sentences for street-level drug sellers that cannot be justified by any principled theory of punishment. In the 1970s and 1980s, conservative politicians deplored US Supreme Court decisions that strengthened defendants' procedural protections. Throughout a long life of observing the criminal law, however, my experience has been that politicians and other powerful people charged with crimes believe as

Testament and Kant's categorical imperative agree that we should want and do for others what we want done for ourselves. Everyone believes that crime seriousness matters. Probably no one disagrees that lengthy imprisonment for routine traffic or parking offenses would be unjustly severe, even if an effective deterrent, and that probation for stranger rapes would be unduly lenient, even if harsher punishment had no preventive effects.

The likeliest theoretical justification for predictive sentencing is either Bentham's deterrence-based utilitarianism or is a broad consequentialist conception of punishment that includes incapacitative and other goals, trading justice to individual offenders for greater crime prevention. Bentham's utilitarianism would not accommodate use of predictions of dangerousness in sentencing. He did not believe that prevention of crime justifies injustice to individuals. He endorsed strong criminal law defenses—including insanity, intoxication, and ignorance of law—so that only blameworthy people would be convicted. His parsimony principle forbids imposition of punishments more severe than deterrent considerations justify. As chapter 6 shows, the current state of knowledge provides no credible basis for believing that harsher punishments have significant marginal deterrent effects. The false positive problem puts the kibosh on predictive sentencing; how can a prediction that is substantially more likely than not to be wrong justify a harsher punishment? Any imaginable contemporary consequentialist punishment theory would be constrained by the same problems.

Retributive theories vary. Kant's foundational positive retributivist account leaves no role for predictions, although it may permit them to be taken into account in choosing between punishments of equal severity (e.g., Ryberg 2020). This was Andreas von Hirsch's view three decades ago (von Hirsch, Wasik, and Green 1989). In practice, however, that view could apply to only a small minority of crimes. Few minor ones would warrant imprisonment in place of a community punishment and there is no case to be made that a longer preventive prison term is punitively equivalent to a shorter one. For serious crimes, no sanction other than capital punishment has the same or greater potential incapacitative effect as imprisonment.

Kant and von Hirsch are positive retributivists who argue that offenders not only may but must be punished as much as they deserve. Although it

---

to themselves, their families, and close colleagues that justice requires the full panoply of procedural protections, compassionate consideration of personal circumstances, and observance of general principles of justice in punishment including imposition of the least severe possible sentence.

can never be self-evident in a given case precisely what punishment is required, as chapter 3 shows, that problem was solved as a practical matter long ago. Wide agreement exists on the relative seriousness of different crimes. Uncontroversial scales of relative offense seriousness can be devised for particular places and times. So can parallel scales of punishment severity (Duus-Otterström 2020). The two can then be linked. Comparably severe punishments can be specified for comparably serious crimes and proportionately different ones for diversely serious ones. There is no room for prediction; the overarching goals are to assure equal treatment by linking blameworthiness to punishment.

Negative retributivism is the alternative. John Monahan (2017) has argued that predictions can properly be used in sentencing so long as upper limits based on offense seriousness are respected and predictions are used to mitigate sentences for low-risk offenders but not to increase them for high-risk offenders. He refers to Virginia's approach that incorporates predictions into guidelines for diversion to alternative punishments of offenders otherwise bound for imprisonment.[21]

Negative retributivists, such as Norval Morris and the drafters of the *Model Penal Code—Sentencing,* argue that blameworthiness sets upper limits on severity. For every crime there is a maximum punishment that may justly be imposed. This varies with offense seriousness and thus provides proportionate upper limits. For some crimes—I used stranger rape earlier as an example—there are minimums that must ordinarily be observed. The default is always the minimum; Morris, like Bentham, urged recognition of a principle of parsimony that forbade imposition of unnecessary suffering. The minimum can be exceeded but only for good, evidence-based reasons. The false positive problem and the view of authors of leading meta-analyses that violence predictions should not be used in sentencing, however, cast serious doubt whether current knowledge provides an adequate justification ever to allow pursuit of predictive goals to trump parsimony concerns.

Morris insisted that there be good evidence-based reasons to justify harsher-than-minimum punishment. Concerning predictions of dangerousness, he was emphatic: four false positives for every two true positives was not good enough in 1974. That would cause too much undeserved suffering.

---

21. Monahan's proposal wouldn't work in Virginia, where the main sentencing guidelines are only advisory and judges may depart both downward and upward. Negative retributivist theories envision an unbreachable upper limit. The normal Virginia guideline recommendation is only that, not an upper limit.

It is unlikely that improvements in accuracy over four decades—three false positives for every two true positives—would have changed his view. The general case to be made is weaker now than in 1974. Morris wrote before much evidence had accumulated on the racial disparities inexorably produced by predictive sentencing, and without considering the implications of use of youth, gender, race-correlated socioeconomic status characteristics, and bias-contaminated criminal history variables. Morris's limiting retributivism does not provide the license prediction proponents might wish for.

Predictive sentencing is thus incompatible with mainstream retributive punishment theories. It is also incompatible with mainstream retributivist views on punishment of people with previous convictions. Nearly every retributivist philosopher who has considered the matter has concluded that the recidivist premium cannot be justified (e.g., among many more, Fletcher 1978; Ryberg 2001; Bagaric 2010; Alexander and Ferzan 2018): "Did the crime, did the time"; "Paid his or her debt to society."

If punishments may not justly be increased to take account of earlier convictions, it is difficult to imagine principled arguments for why punishments may be increased on the basis of predictions of future offending that are in turn substantially based on criminal history variables. Jesper Ryberg (2019, p. 67) intensively mines retributive theories looking for an overlooked nugget that can justify predictive sentencing. No such luck. He concluded thusly: "Although there is some appeal in pursuing justice and in preventing future crimes, you cannot completely achieve both."

B. Public Safety

Everyone is in favor of public safety, but that is not the only fundamental value involved. Sentencing also implicates proportionality, fairness, equal treatment, and parsimony. Any rational person would want these additional values to be honored if he or she or a loved one was charged with a crime. It is difficult to develop a morally persuasive explanation for why we as individuals deserve those things but other people whom we do not know or care about do not. Unless someone can develop a fully elaborated consequentialist theory of punishment that does not incorporate those values and justifies predictive sentencing, a principled case for predictive sentencing cannot be made.

This does not mean that pursuit of crime prevention and public safety need be abandoned. Systems such as those in Scandinavian countries, Germany, and the Netherlands in which punishment is based primarily on blameworthiness and which allow only modest increases for criminal history do not produce higher crimes rates than in the United States. Insofar as the operation of the criminal justice system deters wrongful behavior, systems of proportionate punishment will do so. They contribute to moral education by reinforcing basic social norms of right and wrong. Deserved terms of imprisonment and restrictive community punishments will continue to incapacitate inmates from committing new offenses in the community. Other demonstratively effective strategies of community, developmental, and situational crime prevention will, if pursued, continue to do their work. Expecting more than that from predictive sentencing is unrealistic.

C. Analogies

Two analogies are offered in justification of predictive sentencing. The first is that there is nothing special about it. Actuarial calculations affect private lives all the time (Skeem, Scurich, and Monahan 2019). There has been a "proliferation of statistical and other algorithmic prediction tools in banking, insurance, marketing, medicine, and other fields. . . . Prediction need not be highly accurate at the individual level for major collective benefit to accrue" (Imrey and Dawid 2015, pp. 25, 30).

So what's the problem? There are several. The most important is that predictive sentencing causes undeserved suffering to individuals whose punishments are increased. Most other uses of actuarial prediction affect peoples' private lives. No doubt it is frustrating to be denied a loan, an insurance policy, or an apartment lease, or be asked to pay higher rates. Those disappointments are, however, fundamentally different from receiving a prison sentence instead of a community punishment, or receiving a long sentence instead of a short one. Actuarial predictions in medicine are used not to cause suffering to patients, but to provide benefits by means of improved diagnostic capacities.

A criminal conviction is an authoritative public declaration by the state that an individual engaged in morally blameworthy behavior. Punishment is meant to communicate censure. It is also meant to cause suffering, and is inherently stigmatizing. Other uses of actuarial prediction are private and are not intended to communicate censure, cause suffering, or expose individuals to public stigma. People denied loans or insurance policies may feel disappointed, humiliated, even stigmatized, but only in private. No one else need know.

The second analogy is to public health quarantines. People carrying or exposed to contagious diseases are sometimes confined to minimize their spread. Being quarantined for having or being exposed to measles, malaria, the coronavirus, or Ebola is not meant to be stigmatizing, and seldom is. Sometimes when public fears are high, sick people are ostracized and stigmatized. That happened during the early years of the AIDS epidemic, when drug users and homosexuals were blamed for their afflictions, and during the Ebola epidemics in Liberia and elsewhere when victims were shunned. When such things happen, public health officials and decent people invariably consider it unjust and morally wrong. In any case, quarantines are seldom for lengthy periods; they end when the risk passes or reaches acceptable levels. People in quarantine are not held in prisons and usually receive sympathy and compassion. They are afforded the greatest material comfort that conditions allow, with as few limitations as possible on freedoms enjoyed by others. Preventive detention, imprisonment on the basis of risk predictions, is not like that.

Some have argued, unconvincingly, that preventive detention is morally equivalent to quarantine. Thomas Douglas (2019) tries mightily to demonstrate that they are indistinguishable, or under some circumstances could be. He assumes both sets of restrictions are morally undeserved. No one deserves to be sick or to be punished more severely than he or she deserves. He sets aside the question of "soft moral difference," whether preventive detention is typically harder to justify than quarantine, and considers only the narrower question of "hard moral difference," whether preventive detention is always in at least one respect more morally suspect than quarantine.

Douglas concludes that preventive detention is not always in at least one respect worse. He may or may not be right, but in the real world, as he acknowledges, that is not important:

> Whether preventive detention is *typically* more problematic than quarantine will depend heavily on the facts about how these two practices are typically imposed and what effects they normally have on those subject to them, on those whom they are intended to protect, and on those required to fund them. (2019, p. 70; emphasis in original)

That is, of course, correct. In the United States, conditions in prisons are incomparably worse and the intrusions into peoples' lives are measured in years, decades, and lifetimes, not the days, weeks, or months typical of quarantines.

Other arguments that quarantine offers a valid analogy to preventive detention are no more convincing. Gregg Caruso (2016) and Derek Pereboom (2014) argue that quarantine and preventive detention are indistinguishable to people who are skeptical about the existence of free will. That is because

"What we do, and the way we are, is ultimately the result of factors beyond our control and because of this we are never morally responsible for our actions in the basic desert sense—the sense that would make us truly deserving of blame or praise" (Caruso 2016, p. 26).

Caruso and Pereboom agree that, in a world without free will, neither "dangerous" offenders nor carriers of serious contagious diseases are morally responsible for the risks they pose and that both may be subjected to state controls to minimize those risks. For the state to do that, they argue, implies reciprocal state obligations to make minimal intrusions into offenders' lives and provide humane conditions and serious efforts at treatment. Given their premise of free will skepticism, those are plausible and necessary ethical propositions. They bear no resemblance to life as an American prison inmate.

Arguments about free will, hard determinism, and compatibilism are intellectually interesting and conceptually important. However, accepting the validity of Caruso's and Pereboom's analyses requires first accepting the validity of free will skepticism. That is unlikely on a widespread basis any time soon.

D. Group Differences in Offending

The argument is that prediction instruments are designed and used to predict crimes, that some predict future offending by minority and white people with comparable accuracy, and accordingly that instruments such as COMPAS are not statistically biased. It is regrettable, but black, other minority, and disadvantaged offenders disproportionately have characteristics that predict future offending. So be it:

> COMPAS is based on an actuary designed to inform the probability of recidivism across its three stated risk categories. To expect the COMPAS to do otherwise would be analogous to expecting an insurance agent to make absolute determinations of who will be involved in an accident and who won't. Actuaries just don't work that way. This error discredits their [Angwin et al. 2016] main finding that black defendants were more likely to be incorrectly identified as recidivists (false positives) while white defendants were more likely to be misclassified as non-recidivists (false negatives). (Flores, Bechtel, and Lowenkamp 2016, p. 45)

Two things about this quotation warrant mention. First, it acknowledges no reason for concern about suspect variables: COMPAS uses every variable discussed in this chapter except race, ethnicity, and religion.[22] Second, the claim that their analysis discredits Angwin et al.'s conclusions about racial distributions of false positives and false negatives is refuted by their own findings (see Table 7.3 presenting their findings on true and false positive rates for black and white offenders). What they presumably meant is that racial disparities do exist, but are not important because they result from an algorithm that is not statistically biased.

Flores, Bechtel, and Lowenkamp (2016) are interested only in maximizing the accuracy of predictions of reoffending. This is made explicit when they offer two prediction models with very different false positive and negative rates, but reject out of hand the model that identifies fewer purportedly high-risk offenders, as if any reasonable person would agree:

> The [second model's effects]—a decrease in false positive rates and an increase in false negative rates—might be preferred by some, as it limits the number of individuals that are identified as "high-risk." For others with a low tolerance for recidivism and victimization, the [first model] would be preferred. (p. 42)

Use of socioeconomic and criminal history variables that differentially affect blacks and whites does not to them, as Lady Catherine de Bourgh would put it, signify. To people concerned about racial and punitive justice, it does.

The RAND Corporation in a 2019 survey of use of algorithms in predictions observed of systems like COMPAS:

> As [John] Rawls and other egalitarian philosophers have argued, race is morally arbitrary and should not factor into the probability that one is in jail or free. By accurately reflecting base rate criminality and thereby treating black people as higher risk than white people, COMPAS perpetuates a disproportionate impact along racial lines. Indeed, a high COMPAS score even creates feedback that increases racial differences in base rate criminality. If existing base rates are unjust (because of historical factors and structural racism), it can be argued

---

22. They note that predictive accuracy was not improved when they added an interaction term between race and COMPAS into their analyses (Flores, Bechtel, and Lowenkamp 2016, p. 43). This is irrelevant, as modelers have recognized for four decades (Fisher and Kadane 1983; Berk et al. 2018). Because race and other variables covary, most or all of any race effect is carried by the other variables. They most likely found no separate race effect because it was already present in the other variables COMPAS uses.

that accurate algorithms, such as COMPAS, are complicit in and contribute to this society-wide injustice. (Osobo et al. 2019)

IV. Moving Forward

In a just and rational world, judges would take no account of predictions of dangerousness in deciding how severely individual offenders should be punished.[23] No one should be punished more severely than he or she deserves in relation to the severity of punishments justly imposed on others for the same and different offenses. Predictive sentencing to the contrary trumps considerations of justice by focusing primarily on prevention of harm to hypothetical victims.

Prevention of crime is an important policy goal, but so are proportionality, fairness, equal treatment, and parsimony. Each derives from fundamental ideas about human dignity and limits state power over individual lives (Dan-Cohen 2002; Luban 2007; Waldron 2014). Processes for responding to crimes should be publicly known, implemented in good faith, and applied even-handedly. All people, including offenders, should be treated as equals; their interests should be accorded respect and concern when decisions affecting them are made. No one should be punished more severely than can be justified by appropriate, valid, normative purposes.

Predictive sentencing is premised on contravening all those values. It is unjust because it results in harsher-than-deserved punishments. It is unfair because it bases decisions on actuarial statistics rather than on characteristics of particular offenses and individual offenders. Few defense lawyers, if any, have sufficient knowledge or resources to challenge prediction instruments used in their cases; sometimes the technical details are inaccessible because

---

23. With two obvious qualifications. The first involves pathologically violent people and others whose conditions present the kinds of unacceptable risks to themselves or others that meet legal standards for civil commitment. Dealing with such people should not be a criminal court function, and therefore is not a sentencing decision. Most criminal court judges would presumably be amenable to prosecution motions to refer such cases to the civil courts. The second qualification concerns people whose offenses or circumstances suggest that referral to particular kinds of treatment or correctional programs would be appropriate. Swedish courts use risk predictions, but only to inform decisions about treatment needs and programs (e.g., Fazal 2019).

they are "trade secrets" of private businesses.[24] Predictive sentencing denies equal treatment by punishing people convicted of the same or closely comparable offenses in radically different ways. It denies parsimony by punishing individuals in ways, as the discussion in section II makes clear, that cannot be empirically justified. No country's legal system perfectly observes those values, but many in western and northern Europe try.

Proportionality, fairness, equal treatment, and parsimony are seldom discussed—often they are ignored—by proponents of predictive sentencing. That they are fundamental moral requirements of just punishment can be seen by imagining peoples' responses were they asked, "Do you favor a criminal justice system that punishes people unjustly, unfairly, unequally, and for no good reason?" No one would say yes; some would try to evade answering by quibbling about the meaning of the terms. Judges explaining sentences never say, "I have decided to treat this person unjustly [or unequally or unfairly] because..."

Predictive sentencing can be justified neither empirically nor morally. To many people, however, especially concerning violence, it is intuitively plausible: people in prison cannot rob banks or commit domestic assaults. Proponents of predictive sentencing take comfort in expressing sympathy for hypothetical future victims and disdain for "dangerous" people, and ignore the lives that are damaged and diminished. In the United States, the case against predictive sentencing is likely to fall on deaf ears. In realpolitik terms, it is likely to continue to command support from elected politicians, many criminal justice officials, and uninformed lay people. What to do? Less bold options than abandonment would result in less injustice.

A. Constrained Predictive Sentencing

An unprincipled but more saleable option than abandonment is to establish limits on increments of additional punishment that can be imposed in the name of prevention. Richard Frase and Julian Roberts (2019) propose maximum sentence increases of no more than 100 percent of the deserved sentence as an upper limit. I once proposed 50 percent (Tonry 2016*b*).

Something more finely tuned is needed. Under Frase and Roberts's proposal, predictions could justify a 2-month sentence if the norm was 1 month,

---

24. Osobo et al. (2019, p.18) in a RAND survey of use of algorithms in prediction: "COMPAS is a proprietary tool developed by a for-profit company, and neither the defendant nor the court can examine the algorithm to understand how it weighs factors to produce a risk score."

or a 40-year sentence if the starting point was 20 years, as in the United States it often could be. Under my proposal for a 50 percent cap, a 20-year sentence could be increased to 30. The higher numbers are unjustly severe and unimaginable outside the United States. A more constrained approach might allow increments ranging from the greater of 100 percent or 1 year for less serious offenses to the lesser of 100 percent or 3 years for more serious ones.

Those proposals, however, make pretty heroic assumptions about the willingness of American policymakers to constrain judges' authority and limit sentencing severity.

B. Predictive Mitigation

This is what John Monahan (2017) proposes. It has the great defect that it will usually worsen racial and class disparities, all else being equal, because predictions of lower risk usually result from the absence of socioeconomic, criminal history, and other characteristics disproportionately associated with minority and disadvantaged offenders. The Skeem, Scurich, and Monahan (2019) and Green and Chen (2019) studies discussed a few pages back show that use of prediction instruments worsens disparities. The end result will be the diversion of more white and advantaged offenders.

Norval Morris and I (1990) long ago argued that there is something perverse about the argument that if some offenders will be treated unduly severely, concern for equal treatment requires that others also suffer unduly. Monahan's proposal might thus reduce severity for some offenders. Some people no doubt believe that's desirable, even if it exacerbates racial disparities (so Morris believed; I was doubtful). BUT—a big but—Monahan's proposal can work only if there are strong "normal" limits on sentencing severity, from which the mitigated sentence offers a reduction. Otherwise there will be nothing to stop judges and prosecutors from providing mitigated sentences to low-risk offenders and imposing aggravated sentences on high-risk offenders. This is what happens under Virginia's advisory guidelines.

C. Limiting Retributivism

A stronger version of Monahan's proposal is to allow mitigation for low-risk offenders but establish strong upper limits for all offenders based on offense seriousness. Judges could impose less-severe-than-normal punishments on low-risk offenders but not increase punishments for high-risk ones. The difficulty with this idea is that only a handful of presumptive (Minnesota,

Washington, Kansas) and mandatory (North Carolina) American guidelines systems establish meaningful upper limits.

In such places, Norval Morris's proposals might work. The presumptive normal sentence in every case would be set at the bottom of the guideline range. Low-risk offenders could receive sentences below the normal minimum, most offenders the normal minimum, and highest-risk offenders up to the maximum. This, however, could only work if guidelines systems were radically reformulated. Current approaches provide ranges for particular offenders that take account of both offense seriousness and criminal history. The limiting retributivism approach could work only if ranges were based solely on offense seriousness. Otherwise, criminal history variables used in prediction instruments would be double-counted.

D. Sanctions and Measures

Debates raged a century ago in the United States and Europe over the wisdom and justice of indeterminate sentencing (Pifferi 2016). Supporters argued that criminal behavior results primarily from environmental influences on offenders, and psychological maladjustment; a rational sentencing system would reject retributive ideas and focus on rehabilitation of the vast majority of corrigible offenders and incapacitation of the remaining few. Opponents argued that moral blameworthiness should not be abandoned as an animating idea but should instead set limits on the state's punishment powers.

American jurisdictions—every one of them by the 1930s—adopted indeterminate sentencing (Rothman 1971). European countries including those in the United Kingdom rejected it as unjust. England and Wales established a parole release system only in 1968. To deal, however, with the problem of seemingly incorrigible dangerous offenders, European countries created a distinction between sanctions, deserved punishments based on blameworthiness, and measures, crime prevention powers based on assessments of risk. In theory, measures are not punishments but extraordinary actions—essentially crisis interventions—designed to deal with special challenges. This is hypocritical, of course, since extended confinement will feel like additional punishment to any affected offender, but it has worked much as intended (cf. de Keijser 2011). Measures targeting violence prevention are rarely used (Weigend 2016), but are available for special cases. Anders Breivik, the Norwegian mass murderer of 77 people in 2011, was sentenced to 21 years' imprisonment, the longest term possible, but was also made subject to a measure. If he continues to be considered dangerous when his "sanction" expires, the measure provides authority to continue to hold him.

The sanctions and measures distinction could in theory provide a mechanism for taming predictive sentencing in the United States. All offenders would receive proportionate sanctions based on the seriousness of their crimes and respecting concerns for fairness, equal treatment, and parsimony. A tiny number, a small fraction of 1 percent on the European pattern, might also be the objects of measures predicated on their dangerousness and permitting continued confinement after expiration of their prison sentences. Predictions could be used to identify cases in which a measure might be appropriate. For such a system to be a realistic option, however, there would need to be radical transformations in American popular, political, and legal cultures. That is unlikely in any foreseeable future.

PART III

Moving Forward

8

Doing Justice Better

SOME OF THE arguments and analyses in this book are detailed and complex, but its main ideas are simple:

> Treat people charged with and convicted of crimes justly, fairly, and evenhandedly, as anyone would want done for themselves or their children.
> Take sympathetic account of the circumstances of peoples' lives.
> Punish no one more severely than he or she deserves.

Those propositions are implicit in the rule of law and its requirement that the human dignity of every person be respected. In continental Europe, the German term *Rechtsstaat* is commonly used as shorthand to refer to the ideal of a state governed by the rule of law, respectful of human dignity, and committed to treatment of all people as equals.

Were Western criminal justice systems to be ranked in terms of their compliance with the *Rechtsstaat* ideal, the United States would be last. The reasons are well known.

- In other Western countries, judges and prosecutors are career civil servants, insulated from public, political, and media influences, and ethically obligated to disregard them. Most American judges and chief prosecutors by contrast are elected or are appointed by elected politicians for partisan or ideological reasons. Consciously or not, American judges and prosecutors pay attention to public opinion, the media, and the political implications of their decisions.

- Trials are rare. Plea bargaining prosecutors, not judges, make most sentencing decisions, often on impersonal, assembly-line bases, sometimes for self-interested or political reasons. American-style plea bargaining exists nowhere else. Elsewhere, judges determine guilt and impose punishments.

- Every state has enacted mandatory minimum sentencing and other laws that tie judges' hands and give prosecutors enormous, unreviewable power. So did the federal government. Comparable laws are rare in other Western countries—in most, there are none. Where they exist, judges almost always have authority to disregard them in the interest of justice. They are seen elsewhere as inappropriate intrusions into matters of justice that should be dealt with only by independent, impartial judges.

The costs of America's dysfunctional criminal justice system are clear. The headlines include mass incarceration; the world's highest imprisonment rate; prison sentences measured in decades and lifetimes; extreme disparities, especially affecting members of racial and ethnic minority groups; and high rates of wrongful conviction. The details include assembly-line case processing; overuse of pretrial confinement, fees, fines, and imprisonment; and a general absence of respectful consideration of offenders' interests, circumstances, and needs.

The changes needed are enormous. The impediments are daunting. Constitutional amendments are required if elections of judges and prosecutors are to be eliminated and meritocratic recruitment systems, insulated from political influence, are to be established. The politics of crime control must change radically before rigid and overly severe sentencing laws are repealed on a widespread basis. Bureaucratic resistance to change—"Reform, reform, don't speak to me of reform; things are bad enough as it is," decried one Victorian administrator—exists everywhere. Judges and prosecutors, for example, believe the courts will grind to a halt if plea bargaining is eliminated, even though experience in other developed countries shows that isn't true. Correctional administrators can explain in detail why almost any significant proposed change is excruciatingly difficult or impossible to implement.

Rather than throw up my hands and declare that meaningful changes are impossible, chronic injustices are inevitable, and America's dismal *Rechtsstaat* ranking is unalterable, in the remaining pages I sketch two sets of necessary changes. Those in the first set are fundamental and structural; they are unlikely in the near term, but essential if some day sentencing and punishment in the United States are to become routinely just. Those in the second set are less fundamental and, if made, will greatly reduce the risks and extent of injustices suffered by individuals. Both kinds of changes are needed at the federal level but, partly because making constitutional changes in the federal system is incomparably more difficult than in the states and partly because state courts handle the vast majority of criminal cases, I mostly discuss the states.

Three major structural changes are needed if the United States is to improve its *Rechtsstaat* ranking. First, selection of judges and prosecutors, and their day-to-day work, must be insulated from political influence. That will require constitutional changes.

Second, mandatory minimum sentence, three-strikes, life without parole, truth in sentencing, and similar laws must be repealed. Unless and until that happens, prosecutors will control sentencing of most serious crimes, judges will remain bystanders, and manifest injustices will remain common.

Third, correctional and prosecution systems must be centralized in unified state agencies. This will require legislation. Criminal codes apply statewide and prison and parole are state functions, but prosecution and community corrections systems are balkanized. Most chief prosecutors and country sheriffs are elected and funded at local levels. This means that policies, practices, programs, and resources vary widely between counties. What happens in individual cases often depends more on where a defendant is convicted than on what he or she has done. This may be the easiest of the three major structural changes to accomplish. It has been done before. Alaska, Delaware, Rhode Island, and Vermont have long had unified state corrections systems comprising prisons, jails, probation, and parole. Connecticut and Hawaii operate unified prison and jail systems. Alaska, Connecticut, and Delaware have long had unified state prosecution systems in which, except for the state attorney general, all staff are civil servants.

Four less ambitious changes are needed. Each would do justice more effectively if prosecutors and judges were better insulated from political pressures, the harshest sentencing laws were repealed, and state prosecution and corrections systems were unified. First, every state that does not have one should establish a sentencing commission with authority to develop presumptive sentencing guidelines. This is the only policy initiative of the past 50 years that has been convincingly shown to reduce disparities, enable states to regulate the sizes of their prison systems, and allow administrators to manage their budgets and develop adequately informed strategic plans.

Second, every state should establish a meaningful system of appellate review of sentencing. This is much easier and likelier to be effective in systems with presumptive sentencing guidelines.[1] Judges sometimes make aberrant,

---

1. The only meaningful systems of appellate sentence appeal in the United States are in states, most notably Minnesota and Washington, which promulgated presumptive sentencing

idiosyncratic, or biased decisions. As a practical matter, most offenders in most states have no way to challenge their sentences when that happens. Few states have effective sentence appeal systems. By contrast, sentence appeals are available and relatively common in other Western countries. Extreme sentences are sometimes overturned by American appellate courts *sotto voce*, on the basis of purported procedural or evidentiary problems, but that is rare, arbitrary, and not a meaningful solution.

Third, every state should revise its criminal code to categorize all crimes either as misdemeanors or as being in one of five to seven felony classes, each subject to maximum authorized punishments scaled to crime seriousness.[2] This is a low-visibility, wonkish subject, but an important one. There are two major problems to be addressed. The first is that many criminal codes are crazy quilts of laws enacted one by one over a century or more, often in response to notorious crimes, which set widely diverse and inconsistent maximums. The second is that maximums are often much too long. Reasonable people can disagree about the appropriateness of a 10- or 15-year maximum for rape or robbery. No reasonable person should disagree that 10 or 15 years is much too long for a burglary, auto theft, assault, or minor drug sale. Many states authorize 20- or 30-year prison sentences for these offenses, and sometimes longer ones. In the large majority that do not have presumptive sentencing guidelines or meaningful systems of appellate sentence appeals, lengthy sentences for lesser crimes are irremediable. Felony classes subject to maximum prison sentences of 2, 3, 5, 7, 10, 13, and 15 years, for example, would prevent many gross injustices. A 10-year sentence for auto theft is impossible if the maximum is 3 years. So is a 5-year sentence for sale of marijuana or shoplifting if the maximum is 2.

---

guidelines. Judges who impose sentences other than as directed by the guidelines must explain their reasoning. When cases are appealed, appellate judges decide whether the explanations are persuasive. The late federal judge Marvin Frankel (1973) first proposed establishment of sentencing commissions and promulgation of presumptive guidelines with the expressed hope that a "common law of sentencing" would emerge from appellate review of sentencing. In Minnesota and Washington, it has.

2. This can be accomplished indirectly by promulgation of presumptive sentencing guidelines. The US Supreme Court held in *Blakely v. Washington*, 542 U.S. 296 (2004), that sentences more severe than presumptive guidelines specify may be imposed only on the basis of proof beyond a reasonable doubt of circumstances that would justify a harsher punishment. Put differently, harsher punishments may be imposed only if—in effect—the prosecutor charges and proves the defendant committed a more serious offense than the one of which he was convicted. The most severe presumptively appropriate sentences authorized by guidelines thus become the equivalent of statutory sentence maximums.

Fourth, plea bargaining should be abolished. This is not as radical a proposal as some might think. It was proposed in 1973 by the National Commission on Criminal Justice Standards and Goals, appointed by Republican President Richard M. Nixon, and chaired by Republican Delaware Governor Russell Peterson. In every legal system, including European systems without plea bargaining, the vast majority of defendants plead guilty or confess their crimes. There is no reason to doubt that would continue to happen in the United States if plea bargaining was abolished.

Sentencing would become a judicial function, as it always should have been, and two abusive but common prosecutorial practices would be avoided. The first, illustrated by *Bordenkircher v. Hayes*, 434 U.S. 357 (1978), discussed in chapter 2, is to intimidate defendants by threatening to file charges subject to lengthy mandatory sentences if the defendant refuses to plead guilty to a lesser charge. In *Bordenkircher*, the defendant refused to accept a 5-year prison sentence for embezzlement and, after the new charge was filed, received a mandatory life sentence. The second is to require defendants, as a condition of the plea bargain, to waive all appeal rights, including appeals of sentences.

These proposals are not Pollyannaish. Comparably large changes, sometimes requiring constitutional amendments and novel legislation, were made in the 1960s and 1970s when indeterminate sentencing fell from favor. And, critically, countless practitioners understand the nature and extent of current injustices and their causes, and want to do better. Most sentencing judges and many, alas fewer, prosecutors want to do justice in every case, to treat people convicted of crimes justly, fairly, and even-handedly, to take sympathetic account of the circumstances of their lives, and to punish no one more severely than he or she deserves.

Sometimes it is within the authority of court officials, prosecutors, and correctional managers to make transformative changes on their own. Some prosecutors, for example, in the 1970s and 1980s, attempted to eliminate plea bargaining in their jurisdictions and for a time succeeded. Some prosecutors today are trying to reduce the use of pretrial detention, fines, and fees. Some state and many local courts in the 1970s and 1980s attempted to reduce sentencing disparities by developing guidelines systems. Parole boards established parole guideline systems. Prison officials have much broader powers than is widely recognized. Some of the earliest home confinement programs, for example, were established by correctional managers who decided that prisoners living in their homes remained "within the custody" of the prison department.

Prevailing ways of thinking about crime and punishment are shifting. Laws and practices are beginning to change. The challenges are large and the obstacles are formidable. They can be met and overcome. Someday they will be. In the 1950s and 1960s, American human rights ideals and criminal justice reforms were models for the world. Americans played major roles in drafting the Universal Declaration of Human Rights and influenced the writing of the European Convention on Human Rights. The rule of law and respect for human dignity are indispensable parts of any system of criminal law that aspires to be just. The challenge for contemporary Americans is to make them part of ours.

References

Adriaenssen, An, Letizia Paoli, Susanne Karstedt, Jonas Visschers, Victoria A. Greenfield, and Stefaan Pleysier. 2018. "Public Perceptions of the Seriousness of Crime: Weighing the Harm and the Wrong." *European Journal of Criminology* https://doi.org/10.1177/1477370818772768.

Advisory Council of Judges, National Council on Crime and Delinquency. 1963. *Model Sentencing Act*. Hackensack, NJ: National Council on Crime and Delinquency.

Advisory Council of Judges, National Council on Crime and Delinquency. 1972. *Model Sentencing Act*, 2nd ed. Hackensack, NJ: National Council on Crime and Delinquency.

Aebi, Marcelo F., Galma Akdeniz, Gordon Barclay, Claudia Campistol, Stefano Caneppele, Beata Gruszczyńska, Stefan Harrendorf, Markku Heiskanen, Vasilika Hysi, Jorg-Martin Jehle, Anniina Jokinen, Annie Kensey, Martin Killias, Chris J. Lewis, Ernesto Savonna, Paul Smit, and Rannveig Bórisdóttir. 2014. *European Sourcebook of Crime and Criminal Justice Statistics: 2014*. 5th ed. Helsinki: Helsinki European United Nations Institute.

Alabama Civil Rights and Civil Liberties Law Review. 2011. "Rotten Social Background in the Twenty-First Century: Reconsidering the Role of Socio-Economic Deprivation in Criminal Justice." Symposium issue, vol. 2.

Albrecht, Hans-Jörg. 1994. *Strafzumessung bei schwerer Kriminalität: Eine vergleichende theoretische und empirische Studie zur Herstellung und Darstellung des Strafmaßes*. Berlin: Duncker and Humblot.

Alexander, Larry, and Kimberly Kessler Ferzan. 2018. *Reflections on Crime and Culpability: Problems and Puzzles*. New York: Cambridge University Press.

Allen, Francis A. 1959. "Legal Values and the Rehabilitative Ideal." *Journal of Criminal Law, Criminology, and Police Science* 50:226–32.

Allen, Francis A. 1981. *The Decline of the Rehabilitative Ideal*. New Haven, CT: Yale University Press.

Alschuler, Albert. 1978. "Sentencing Reform and Prosecutorial Power." *University of Pennsylvania Law Review* 126:550–77.

American Bar Foundation Survey, *see* Newman (1966), Dawson (1969), and especially Remington (1969).

American Law Institute. 1962. *Model Penal Code—Proposed Official Draft*. Philadelphia: American Law Institute.

American Law Institute. 2017. *Model Penal Code—Sentencing*. Proposed Final Draft. Philadelphia: American Law Institute.

Ancel, Marc. 1965. *Social Defence: A Modern Approach to Criminal Problems*. London: Routledge Kegan Paul.

Angwin, Julia, Jeff Larson, Surya Mattu, and Lauren Kirchner. 2016. "Machine Bias: There's Software Used across the Country to Predict Future Criminals. And It's Biased against Blacks." *ProPublica*, May 23. https://www.propublica.org/article/machine-bias-risk-assessments-in-criminal-sentencing.

Apel, J. Robert, and Samuel E. DeWitt. 2018. "Formal versus Informal Deterrence." In *Deterrence, Choice, and Crime: Contemporary Perspectives*, edited by Daniel S. Nagin, Francis T. Cullen, and Cheryl Lero Jonson. New York: Routledge.

Arnold, Thurman. 1937. *The Folklore of Capitalism*. New Haven, CT: Yale University Press.

Ashworth, Andrew J. 1983. *Sentencing and Penal Policy*. London: Weidenfeld and Nicolson.

Ashworth, Andrew J. 1988. "Criminal Attempts and the Role of Resulting Harm under the Code, and in the Common Law." *Rutgers Law Review* 19:725–72.

Ashworth, Andrew J. 1993. "Taking the Consequences." In *Action and Value in Criminal Law*, edited by Stephen Shute, John Gardner, and Jeremy Horder. Oxford: Clarendon.

Ashworth, Andrew J. 2015. *Sentencing and Criminal Justice*, 6th ed. Cambridge: Cambridge University Press.

Ashworth, Andrew J., and Julian V. Roberts. 2016. "The Evolution of Sentencing Policy and Practice in England and Wales, 2003–2015." In *Sentencing Policies and Practices in Western Countries: Comparative and Cross-national Perspectives*, edited by Michael Tonry. Chicago: University of Chicago Press.

Ashworth, Andrew J., and Martin Wasik. 2017. "Sentencing the Multiple Offender: In Search of a 'Just and Proportionate' Total Sentence." In *Sentencing Multiple Crimes*, edited by Jesper Ryberg, Julian V. Roberts, and Jan de Keijser. New York: Oxford University Press.

Asp, Petter. 2010. "Previous Convictions and Proportionate Punishment under Swedish Law." In *Previous Convictions at Sentencing: Theoretical and Applied Perspectives*, edited by Julian V. Roberts and Andrew von Hirsch. Oxford: Hart.

Asp, Petter. 2012. "The Prosecutor in Swedish Law." In *Prosecutors and Politics: A Comparative Perspective*, edited by Michael Tonry. Chicago: University of Chicago Press.

Australia, Legal and Constitutional Affairs References Committee. 2013. *Value of a Justice Reinvestment Approach to Criminal Justice in Australia*. Canberra: Senate Printing Unit, Department of the Senate, Parliament House.

Baker, Estella, and Andrew Ashworth. 2010. "The Role of Previous Convictions in England and Wales." In *Previous Convictions at Sentencing: Theoretical and Applied Perspectives*, edited by Julian V. Roberts and Andrew von Hirsch. Oxford: Hart.

Bagaric, Mirko. 2010. "Double Punishment and Punishing Character: The Unfairness of Prior Convictions." *Criminal Justice Ethics* 19:10–28.

Barr, William P. 1992. *The Case for More Incarceration*. Washington, DC: US Department of Justice, Office of Policy Development.

Bazelon, David L. 1976a. "The Morality of the Criminal Law." *Southern California Law Review* 49:385–405.

Bazelon, David L. 1976b. "The Morality of the Criminal Law: A Rejoinder to Professor Morse." *Southern California Law Review* 49:1269–74.

Bazelon, David L. 1988. *Questioning Authority*. New York: Knopf.

Beccaria, Cesare. 2007 [1764]. *On Crimes and Punishments, and Other Writings*, translated by Aaron Thomas and Jeremy Parzen. Toronto: University of Toronto Press.

Bennett, Christopher. 2010. "'More to Apologise For': Can We Find a Basis for the Recidivist Premium in a Communicative Theory of Punishment?" In *Previous Convictions at Sentencing: Theoretical and Applied Perspectives*, edited by Julian V. Roberts and Andrew von Hirsch. Oxford: Hart.

Bennett, Christopher. 2017. "Retributivism and Totality: Can Bulk Discounts for Multiple Offending Fit the Crime?" In *Sentencing Multiple Crimes*, edited by Jesper Ryberg, Julian V. Roberts, and Jan Willem de Keijser. New York: Oxford University Press.

Bentham, Jeremy. 1970 [1789]. *An Introduction to the Principles of Morals and Legislation*, edited by J. H. Burns and H. L. A. Hart. Oxford: Clarendon.

Berk, Richard. 2019. *Machine Learning Risk Assessments in Criminal Justice Settings*. New York: Springer.

Berk, Richard, Hoda Heidari, Shahin Jabbari, Michael Kearns, and Aaron Roth. 2018. "Fairness in Criminal Justice Risk Assessments: The State of the Art." *Sociological Methods and Research*. https://doi.org/10.1177/0049124118782533.

Berlin, Isaiah, 1959. *Two Concepts of Liberty*. Inaugural lecture in 1958 as Chichele Professor of Social and Political Theory at Oxford. Oxford: Oxford University Press.

Blackstone, William. 1979 [1769]. *Commentaries on the Laws of England*, vol. 4. Chicago: University of Chicago Press.

Blumstein, Alfred, Jacqueline Cohen, Susan E. Martin, and Michael Tonry, eds. 1983. *Research on Sentencing: The Search for Reform*. 2 vols. Washington, DC: National Academy Press.

Blumstein, Alfred, Jacqueline Cohen, and Daniel Nagin, eds. 1978. *Deterrence and Incapacitation: Estimating the Effects of Criminal Sanctions on Crime Rates*. Washington, DC: National Academy of Sciences.

Blumstein, Alfred, David P. Farrington, and Soumyo Moitra. 1985. "Delinquency Careers: Innocents, Desisters, and Persisters." In *Crime and Justice: An Annual*

Review of Research, vol. 6, edited by Norval Morris and Michael Tonry. Chicago: University of Chicago Press.

Blumstein, Alfred, Jacqueline Cohen, Jeffrey A. Roth, and Christy A. Visher, eds. 1986. *Criminal Careers and "Career Criminals."* Washington, DC: National Academies Press.

Bottoms, Anthony E. 1998. "Five Puzzles in von Hirsch's Theory of Punishment." In *Fundamentals of Sentencing Theory*, edited by Andrew J. Ashworth and Martin Wasik. Oxford: Oxford University Press.

Bottoms, Anthony E. 2017. "Exploring an Institutionalist and Post-desert Theoretical Approach to Multiple Offence Sentencing." In *Sentencing Multiple Crimes*, edited by Jesper Ryberg, Julian V. Roberts, and Jan de Keijser. New York: Oxford University Press.

Braithwaite, John. 2018. "Minimally Sufficient Deterrence." In *Crime and Justice: A Review of Research*, vol. 47, edited by Michael Tonry. Chicago: University of Chicago Press.

Braithwaite, John, and Philip Pettit. 1990. *Not Just Deserts: A Republican Theory of Criminal Justice.* Oxford: Clarendon.

Braithwaite, John, and Philip Pettit. 2001. "Republicanism and Restorative Justice: An Explanatory and Normative Connection." In *Restorative Justice: Philosophy to Practice*, edited by John Braithwaite and Heather Strang. Burlington, VT: Ashgate.

Breyer, Stephen. 1988. "The Federal Sentencing Guidelines and the Key Compromises upon Which They Rest." *Hofstra Law Review* 17:1–50.

Breyer, Stephen. 1999. "Federal Sentencing Guidelines Revisited." *Federal Sentencing Reporter* 11(4):180–86.

Bureau of Justice Statistics. 2011. "BJS—2009—Time Served of Releasees," file ncrp0909.csv. Washington, DC: US Department of Justice.

Burgess, Anthony. 1962. *A Clockwork Orange.* London: Heinemann.

Burgess, Anthony. 1986. "Introduction: A Clockwork Orange Resucked." *A Clockwork Orange.* New York: Norton.

Butler, Paul. 1995. "Racially Based Jury Nullification: Black Power in the Criminal Justice System." *Yale Law Journal* 105(3):677–725.

Cahalan, Margaret. 1986. *Historical Corrections Statistics in the United States, 1850–1984.* Washington, DC: US Department of Justice, Bureau of Justice Statistics.

Campbell, Mary Ann, Sheila French, and Paul Gendreau. 2009. "The Prediction of Violence in Adult Offenders: A Meta-analytic Comparison of Instruments." *Criminal Justice and Behavior* 36:567–90.

Canadian Sentencing Commission. 1987. *Sentencing Reform: A Canadian Approach.* Ottawa: Canadian Government Publishing Centre.

Caruso, Gregg D. 2016. "Free Will Skepticism and Criminal Behavior: A Public Health—Quarantine Model." *Southwest Philosophy Review* 32:25–48.

Chalfin, Aaron, and Justin McCrary. 2017. "Criminal Deterrence: A Review of the Literature." *Journal of Economic Literature* 55(1):5–48.

Chalfin, Aaron J., and Sarah Tahamont. 2018. "Economic Theory." In *Deterrence, Choice, and Crime: Contemporary Perspectives*, edited by Daniel S. Nagin, Francis T. Cullen, and Cheryl Lero Jonson. New York: Routledge.

Chau, Peter. 2012. "Duff on the Legitimacy of Punishment of Socially Deprived Offenders." *Criminal Law and Philosophy* 6:247–54.

Chen, Elsa Y. 2008. "Impacts of 'Three Strikes and You're Out' on Crime Trends in California and Throughout the United States." *Journal of Contemporary Criminal Justice* 24:345–70.

Coase, Ronald. 1960. "The Problem of Social Cost." *Journal of Law and Economics* 3:1–44.

Cohen, Jacqueline. 1983. "Incapacitation as a Strategy for Crime Control: Possibilities and Pitfalls." In *Crime and Justice: An Annual Review of Research,* vol. 5, edited by Michael Tonry and Norval Morris. Chicago: University of Chicago Press.

Cohen, Mark A. 2005. *The Costs of Crime and Justice.* London: Routledge.

Cohen, Mark A., Roland T. Rust, Sara Steen, and Simon T. Tidd. 2004. "Willingness-To-Pay for Crime Control Programs." *Criminology* 42(1):89–110.

Cook, Philip J., and Jens Ludwig. 2000. *Gun Violence: The Real Costs.* Oxford: Oxford University Press.

Corda, Alessandro. 2016. "Sentencing and Penal Policies in Italy, 1985–2015: The Tale of a Troubled Country." In *Sentencing Policies and Practices in Western Countries: Comparative and Cross-national Perspectives,* edited by Michael Tonry. Chicago: University of Chicago Press.

Cottingham, John. 1979. "Varieties of Retribution." *Philosophical Quarterly* 29(116):238–46.

Cullen, Francis. 2013. "Rehabilitation: Beyond Nothing Works." In *Crime and Justice in America: 1975–2025,* edited by Michael Tonry. Chicago: University of Chicago Press.

Cullen, Francis T., Cheryl Lero Jonson, and Daniel S. Nagin. 2011. "Prisons Do Not Reduce Recidivism." *Prison Journal* 91(3):48–65.

Dan-Cohen, Meir. 2002. *Harmful Thoughts: Essays on Law, Self, and Morality.* Princeton: Princeton University Press.

Darley, John M., Kevin M. Carlsmith, and Paul H. Robinson. 2001. "The Ex Ante Function of the Criminal Law." *Law and Society Review* 35(1):165–90.

Darley, John M., and Paul H. Robinson. 1995. *Justice, Liability, and Blame: Community Views and the Criminal Law.* Boulder: Westview.

Davis, Kenneth Culp. 1969. *Discretionary Justice: A Preliminary Inquiry.* Baton Rouge: Louisiana State University Press.

Dawson, Robert O. 1969. *Sentencing.* Boston: Little, Brown.

de Keijser, Jan W. 2011. "Never Mind the Pain, It's a Measure! Justifying Measures as Part of the Dutch Bifurcated System of Sanctions." In *Retributivism Has a Past: Has It a Future?* edited by Michael Tonry. New York: Oxford University Press.

Delgado, Richard. 1985. "'Rotten Social Background': Should the Criminal Law Recognize a Defense of Severe Environmental Deprivation?" *Law and Inequality* 3:9–90.

Delgado, Richard. 2011. "The Wretched of the Earth." *Alabama Civil Rights and Civil Liberties Law Review* 2:1–22.

Dershowitz, Alan. 1976. *Fair and Certain Punishment*. New York: Twentieth Century Fund.

Desmarais, Sarah L., Kiersten L. Johnson, and Jay P. Singh. 2016. "Performance of Risk Assessment Instruments in US Correctional Settings." *Psychological Services* 13(3):206–22.

DiIulio, John J. Jr. 1995. "The Coming of the Super-Predators." *The Weekly Standard* (November 27).

Dominguez-Rivera, Patricio, and Steven Raphael. 2015. "The Role of the Costs-of-Crime Literature in Bridging the Gap between Social Science Research and Policy Making: Potentials and Limitations." *Criminology and Public Policy* 14(4):589–632.

Donohue, John J., and Justin Wolfers. 2005. "Uses and Abuses of Empirical Evidence in the Death Penalty Debate." *Stanford Law Review* 58(3):791–845.

Doob, Anthony N., and Cheryl Marie Webster. 2003. "Sentence Severity and Crime: Accepting the Null Hypothesis." In *Crime and Justice: A Review of Research*, vol. 30, edited by Michael Tonry. Chicago: University of Chicago Press.

Doob, Anthony N., and Cheryl Marie Webster. 2016. "Weathering the Storm? Testing Longstanding Canadian Sentencing Policy in the Twenty-First Century." In *Sentencing Policies and Practices in Western Countries: Comparative and Cross-national Perspectives*, edited by Michael Tonry. Chicago: University of Chicago Press.

Douglas, Thomas. 2019. "Is Preventive Detention Morally Worse than Quarantine?" In *Predictive Sentencing: Normative and Empirical Perspectives*, edited by Jan Willem de Keijser, Julian V Roberts, and Jesper Ryberg. Oxford: Hart.

Downes, David, and Rod Morgan. 1994. "'Hostages to Fortune'? The Politics of Law and Order in Post-War Britain." In *The Oxford Handbook of Criminology*, 1st ed., edited by Mike Maguire, Rod Morgan, and Robert Reiner. Oxford: Oxford University Press.

Downes, David, and Rod Morgan. 1997. "Dumping the 'Hostages to Fortune'? The Politics of Law and Order in Post-War Britain." In *The Oxford Handbook of Criminology*, 2nd ed., edited by Mike Maguire, Rod Morgan, and Robert Reiner. Oxford: Oxford University Press.

Downes, David, and Rod Morgan. 2002. "The Skeletons in the Cupboard: The Politics of Law and Order at the Turn of the Millennium." In *The Oxford Handbook of Criminology*, 3rd ed., edited by Mike Maguire, Rod Morgan, and Robert Reiner. Oxford: Oxford University Press.

Downes, David, and Rod Morgan. 2007. "No Turning Back: The Politics of Law and Order into the Millennium." In *The Oxford Handbook of Criminology*, 4th ed., edited by Mike Maguire, Rod Morgan, and Robert Reiner. Oxford: Oxford University Press.

Downes, David, and Rod Morgan. 2012. "Overtaking on the Left? The Politics of Law and Order in the 'Big Society.'" In *The Oxford Handbook of Criminology*, 5th ed., edited by Mike Maguire, Rod Morgan, and Robert Reiner. Oxford: Oxford University Press.

Dressel, Julia, and Hany Farid. 2018. "The Accuracy, Fairness, and Limits of Predicting Recidivism." *Science Advances* 4(1):eaao5580.

Dressler, Joshua. 2005. "The Wisdom and Morality of Present-Day Criminal Sentencing." *Akron Law Review* 38:853–65.

Dressler, Joshua. 2009. "Some Very Modest Reflections on Excusing Criminal Wrongdoers." *Texas Tech Law Review* 42:671–83.

Duff, R. Antony. 1986. *Trials and Punishments*. Cambridge: Cambridge University Press.

Duff, R. Antony. 2001. *Punishment, Communication, and Community*. New York: Oxford University Press.

Durkheim, Émile. 2014 [1893]. *The Division of Labor in Society*, edited by Steven Lukes. Translation by W. D. Halls. New York: Free Press.

Durkheim, Émile. 2014 [1895]. "Rules for the Distinction of the Normal from the Pathological." In *The Rules of Sociological Method*, edited by Steven Lukes. New York: Free Press.

Durlauf, Steven N., and Daniel S. Nagin. 2011. "Imprisonment and Crime: Can Both Be Reduced?" *Criminology and Public Policy* 10(1):13–54.

Duus-Otterström, Göran. 2020. "Weighing Relative and Absolute Proportionality in Punishment." In *Of One-Eyed and Toothless Miscreants: Making the Punishment Fit the Crime?* edited by Michael Tonry. New York: Oxford University Press.

Dworkin, Ronald. 1977. *Taking Rights Seriously*. Cambridge: Harvard University Press.

Dworkin, Ronald. 1986. *Law's Empire*. Cambridge: Harvard University Press.

Ehrlich, Isaac. 1996. "Crime, Punishment, and the Market for Offenses." *Journal of Economic Perspectives* 10(1):43–67.

Enoch, David. 2008. "Luck between Morality, Law, and Justice." *Theoretical Inquiries in Law* 9:23–60.

Ewing, Benjamin. 2018. "Recent Work on Punishment and Criminogenic Disadvantage." *Law and Philosophy* 37:29–68.

Ewing, Benjamin. 2019. "Prior Convictions as Moral Opportunities." *American Journal of Criminal Law* 45(2):253–303.

Farrington, David P. 1986. "Age and Crime." In *Crime and Justice: An Annual Review of Research*, vol. 7, edited by Michael Tonry. Chicago: University of Chicago Press.

Farrington, David P. 2003. "Developmental and Life-Course Criminology: Key Theoretical and Empirical Issues." *Criminology* 41:221–55.

Farrington, David P., Lila Kazemian, and Alex R. Piquero, eds. 2018. *The Oxford Handbook of Developmental and Life-Course Criminology*. New York: Oxford University Press.

Fazel, Seena. 2019. "The Scientific Validity of Current Approaches to Violence and Criminal Risk Assessment." In *Predictive Sentencing: Normative and Empirical*

Perspectives, edited by Jan W. de Keijser, Julian V. Roberts, and Jesper Ryberg. Oxford: Hart.

Fazel, Seena, Jay P. Singh, Helen Doll, and Martin Grann. 2012. "Use of Risk Assessment Instruments to Predict Violence and Antisocial Behavior in 73 Samples Involving 24,827 People: Systematic Review and Meta-analysis." *BMJ* 345:e4692. https://doi.org/10.1136/bmj.e4692.

Feinberg, Joel. 1965. "The Expressive Function of Punishment." *The Monist* 49(3):397–423.

Feinberg, Joel. 1995. "Equal Punishment for Failed Attempts." *Arizona Law Review* 37:117–32.

Ferri, Enrico. 1921. *Relazione sul Progetto Preliminare di Codice Penale Italiano.* Rome: L'Universelle.

Fisher, Franklin M., and Joseph B. Kadane. 1983. "Empirically Based Sentencing Guidelines and Ethical Considerations." In *Research on Sentencing: The Search for Reform,* edited by Alfred Blumstein. Washington DC: National Academy Press.

Fletcher, George P. 1978. *Rethinking Criminal Law.* Boston: Little, Brown.

Flores, Anthony W., Kristen Bechtel, and Christopher T. Lowenkamp. 2016. "False Positives, False Negatives, and False Analyses: A Rejoinder to 'Machine Bias: There's Software Used across the Country to Predict Future Criminals. And It's Biased against Blacks.'" *Federal Probation* 80(2):38–46.

Frankel, Marvin E. 1972. "Lawlessness in Sentencing." *Cincinnatti Law Review* 41(1):1–54.

Frankel, Marvin E. 1973. *Criminal Sentences: Law without Order.* New York: Hill and Wang.

Frase, Richard S. 2005. "Sentencing Guidelines in Minnesota, 1978–2003." In *Crime and Justice: A Review of Research*, vol. 32, edited by Michael Tonry. Chicago: University of Chicago Press.

Frase, Richard S. 2009a. "Limiting Excessive Prison Sentencing." *University of Pennsylvania Journal of Constitutional Law* 11(1):39–72.

Frase, Richard S. 2009b. "Racial Disproportionality in Minnesota's Prisons and Jails." In *Crime and Justice: A Review of Research*, vol. 38, edited by Michael Tonry. Chicago: University of Chicago Press.

Frase, Richard S. 2017. "Principles and Procedures for Sentencing of Multiple Current Offenses." In *Sentencing Multiple Crimes,* edited by Jesper Ryberg, Julian V. Roberts, and Jan de Keijser. New York: Oxford University Press.

Frase, Richard, and Julian V. Roberts. 2019. *Paying for the Past.* New York: Oxford University Press.

Frase, Richard S., Julian V. Roberts, Rhys Hester, and Kelly Lyn Mitchell. 2015. *Criminal History Enhancement Sourcebook.* Minneapolis: University of Minnesota Law School, Robina Institute of Criminal Law and Criminal Justice.

Freiberg, Arie. 2014. *Fox and Freiberg's Sentencing: State and Federal Law in Victoria.* 3rd ed. Melbourne: Thomson Reuters.

Freiberg, Arie. 2016. "The Road Well Travelled in Australia: Ignoring the Past, Condemning the Future." In *Sentencing Policies and Practices in Western Countries: Comparative and Cross-national Perspectives*, edited by Michael Tonry. Chicago: University of Chicago Press.

Garvey, Stephen P. 2014. "Injustice, Authority, and the Criminal Law." In *The Punitive Imagination: Law, Justice, and Responsibility*, edited by Austin Sarat. Tuscaloosa: University of Alabama Press.

Germany. 2006. *Second Report on the State of Interior/Domestic Security in Germany. Periodischer Sicherheitsbericht*. Berlin: Ministries of Justice and Interior.

Gilmore, Grant. 1974. *The Death of Contract*. Columbus: Ohio State University Press.

Glueck, Sheldon. 1928. "Principles of a Rational Penal Code." *Harvard Law Review* 41(4):453–82.

Green, Stuart P. 2010. "Hard Times, Hard Time: Retributive Justice for Unjustly Disadvantaged Offenders." *University of Chicago Legal Forum* 2010:43–71.

Green, Ben, and Yiling Chen. 2019. "Disparate Interactions: An Algorithm-in-the-Loop Analysis of Fairness in Risk Assessments." In FAT* '19: Conference on Fairness, Accountability, and Transparency. January 29–31, 2019, Atlanta, GA, New York: ACM. https://doi.org/10.1145/3287560.3287563.

Greenfield, Victoria A., and Letizia Paoli. 2013. "A Framework to Assess the Harms of Crimes." *British Journal of Criminology* 53:864–85.

Greenwood, Peter W., and Allan Abrahamse. 1982. *Selective Incapacitation*. Santa Monica, CA: RAND.

Halliday, John. 2001. *See* Home Office 2001.

Hampton, Jean. 1984. "The Moral Education Theory of Punishment." *Philosophy and Public Affairs* 13(3):208–38.

Harcourt, Bernard E. 2008. *Against Prediction*. Chicago: University of Chicago Press.

Hart, H. L. A. 1959. "Prolegomenon to the Principles of Punishment." *Proceedings of the Aristotelian Society, New Series* 60:1–26.

Hart, H. L. A. 1968. *Punishment and Responsibility: Essays in the Philosophy of Law*. Oxford: Oxford University Press.

Hart, Henry M. 1958. "The Aims of the Criminal Law." *Law and Contemporary Problems* 23:401–42.

Hart, Stephen D., Christine Michie, and David J. Cooke. 2007. "Precision of Actuarial Risk Assessment Instruments. Evaluating the 'Margins of Error' of Group v. Individual Predictions of Violence." *British Journal of Psychiatry* 190:s60–s65.

Hawken, Angela, and Mark Kleiman. 2009. *Managing Drug-Involved Probationers with Swift and Certain Sanctions: Evaluating Hawaii's HOPE* (Report No. 229023). Washington, DC: Office of Justice Programs.

Hay, Douglas. 1975. "Property, Authority, and the Criminal Law." In *Albion's Fatal Tree: Crime and Society in Eighteenth Century England*, edited by Douglas Hay, Peter Linebaugh, E. P. Thompson, and Cal Winslow. New York: Pantheon.

Hayes, David J. 2016. "Penal Impact: Towards a More Intersubjective Measure of Penal Severity." *Oxford Journal of Legal Studies* 36:724–50.

Heffernan, William C., and John Kleinig, eds. 2000. *From Social Justice to Criminal Justice: Poverty and the Administration of Criminal Law*. New York: Oxford University Press.

Hegel, Georg Wilhelm Friedrich. 1991 [1821]. *Elements of the Philosophy of Right*, edited by Allen W. Wood. Translation by H. B. Nisbet. Cambridge: Cambridge University Press.

Helland, Eric, and Alexander Tabarrok. 2007. "Does Three Strikes Deter? A Nonparametric Estimation." *Journal of Human Resources* 42(2):309–30.

Hester, Rhys. 2019a. "Disproportionate Impacts on Minority Offenders." In *Paying for the Past*, edited by Richard Frase and Julian V. Roberts. New York: Oxford University Press.

Hester, Rhys. 2019b. "Risk Assessment at Sentencing: The Pennsylvania Experience." In *Predictive Sentencing: Normative and Empirical Perspectives*, edited by Jan W. de Keijser, Julian V. Roberts, and Jesper Ryberg. Oxford: Hart.

Hester, Rhys, Richard S. Frase, Julian V. Roberts, and Kelly Mitchell. 2018. "Prior Record Enhancements at Sentencing: Unsettled Justifications and Unsettling Consequences." In *Crime and Justice: A Review of Research*, vol. 47, edited by Michael Tonry. Chicago: University of Chicago Press.

Hinkkanen, Ville, and Tapio Lappi-Seppälä. 2011. "Sentencing Theory, Policy, and Research in the Nordic Countries." In *Crime and Justice in Scandinavia*, edited by Michael Tonry and Tapio Lappi-Seppälä. Chicago: University of Chicago Press.

Hoffman, Peter B. 1976. "Salient Factor Score Validation: A 1972 Release Cohort." *Journal of Criminal Justice* 6:69–76.

Hoffman, Peter B. 1983. "Screening for Risk: A Revised Salient Factor Score (SFS 81)." *Journal of Criminal Justice* 11:539–47.

Hoffman, Peter B. 1995. "Twenty Years of Operational Use of a Risk Prediction Instrument: The United States Parole Commission's Salient Factor Score." *Journal of Criminal Justice* 22:477–94.

Holder, Eric. 2014. "Attorney General Eric Holder Speaks at the National Association of Criminal Defense Lawyers 57th Annual Meeting." Washington, DC: US Department of Justice. http://www.justice.gov/opa/speech/attorney-general-eric-holder-speaks-national-association-criminal-defense-lawyers-57th.

Holmes, Oliver Wendell, Jr. 1881. *The Common Law*. Boston: Little, Brown.

Holmes, Oliver Wendell, Jr. 1899. "Law in Science and Science in Law" *Harvard Law Review* 12:443–63.

Holroyd, Jules. 2010. "Punishment and Justice." *Social Theory and Practice* 36(1):78–111.

Home Office. 1990. *Crime, Justice, and Protecting the Public*. London: Home Office.

Home Office. 2001. *Making Punishments Work: Report of a Review of the Sentencing Framework for England and Wales*. London: Home Office Communication Directorate.

Honderich, Ted. 1989. *Punishment: The Supposed Justifications*. Cambridge: Polity.

Hough, Mike, and Julian V. Roberts. 1999. "Sentencing Trends in Britain—Public Knowledge and Public Opinion." *Punishment and Society* 1:11–26.

Howard, Jeffrey. 2013. "Punishment, Socially Deprived Offenders, and Democratic Community." *Criminal Law and Philosophy* 7:121–36.

Husak, Douglas. 1987. *The Philosophy of Criminal Law*. Lanham, MD: Rowman & Littlefield.

Husak, Douglas. 1994. "Is Drunk Driving a Serious Offense?" *Philosophy and Public Affairs* 23:52–73.

Husak, Douglas. 2019. "Why Legal Philosophers (Including Retributivists) Should Be Less Resistant to Risk-Based Sentencing." In *Predictive Sentencing: Normative and Empirical Perspectives*, edited by Jan W. de Keijser, Julian V. Roberts, and Jesper Ryberg. Oxford: Hart.

Husak, Douglas. 2020. "The Metric of Punishment Severity: A Puzzle about the Principle of Proportionality." In *Of One-Eyed and Toothless Miscreants: Making the Punishment Fit the Crime?* edited by Michael Tonry. New York: Oxford University Press.

Imrey, Peter B., and A. Philip Dawid. 2015. "A Commentary on Statistical Assessment of Violence Recidivism Risk." *Statistics and Public Policy* 2(1):25–42.

James, William. 1902. *The Varieties of Religious Experience*. New York: Longmans, Green.

Jareborg, Nils. 1998. "Why Bulk Discounts in Multiple Offence Sentencing?" In *Fundamentals of Sentencing Theory*, edited by Andrew Ashworth and Martin Wasik. Oxford: Oxford University Press.

Jolliffe, Darrick, and Carol Hedderman. 2015. "Investigating the Impact of Custody on Reoffending using Propensity Score Matching." *Crime and Delinquency* 61(8):1051–77.

Jonson, Cheryl Lero, and Francis Cullen. 2015. "Prisoner Reentry Programs." In *Crime and Justice: A Review of Research*, vol. 44, edited by Michael Tonry. Chicago: University of Chicago Press.

Kadish, Mortimer R., and Sanford H. Kadish. 1971. "The Institutionalization of Conflict: Jury Acquittals." *Journal of Social Issues* 27(2):199–217.

Kadish, Sanford H. 1994. "The Criminal Law and the Luck of the Draw." *Journal of Criminal Law and Criminology* 84:679–702.

Kant, Immanuel. 2017 [1797]. *The Metaphysics of Morals*, rev. ed., edited by Lara Denis. Translation by Mary J. Gregor. Cambridge: Cambridge University Press.

Kleck, Gary, and J. C. Barnes. 2013. "Deterrence and Macro-level Perceptions of Punishment Risks: Is There a 'Collective Wisdom?'" *Crime and Delinquency* 59(7):1006–35.

Kleiman, Mark A. R. 1997. "The Problem of Replacement and the Logic of Drug Law Enforcement." *Drug Policy Analysis Bulletin* 3:8–10.

Kleinig, John. 1973. *Punishment and Desert*. New York: Springer.

Knapp, Kay. 1984. *The Impact of the Minnesota Sentencing Guidelines: Three-Year Evaluation*. St. Paul: Minnesota Sentencing Guidelines Commission.

Kolber, Adam. 2009a. "The Comparative Nature of Punishment." *Boston University Law Review* 89:1565–610.

Kolber, Adam. 2009b. "The Subjective Experience of Punishment." *Columbia Law Review* 109:182–236.

Kolber, Adam. 2020. "The Time-Frame Challenge to Retributivism." In *Of One-Eyed and Toothless Miscreants: Making the Punishment Fit the Crime?* edited by Michael Tonry. New York: Oxford University Press.

Kuhn, Thomas. 1962. *The Structure of Scientific Revolutions*. Chicago: University of Chicago Press.

Kyckelhahn, Tracey. 2014. *State Corrections Expenditures, FY 1982–2010*. Originally released 2012; revised April 30, 2014. Washington, DC: US Department of Justice, Bureau of Justice Statistics.

Lacey, Nicola, and Hanna Pickard. 2015. "The Chimera of Proportionality: Institutionalising Limits on Punishment in Contemporary Social and Political Systems." *Modern Law Review* 78(2):216–40.

Lambert, Elizabeth Winston. 2018. "A Way Out of the 'Rotten Social Background' Stalemate: Scarcity and Stephen Morse's Proposed Generic Partial Excuse." *University of Pennsylvania Journal of Law and Social Change* 21:297–338.

Lappi-Seppälä, Tapio. 2011. "Sentencing and the Punishment in Finland: The Decline of the Repressive Ideal." In *Why Punish? How Much?* edited by Michael Tonry. Oxford: Oxford University Press.

Lappi-Seppälä, Tapio. 2016. "Nordic Sentencing." In *Sentencing Policies and Practices in Western Countries: Comparative and Cross-national Perspectives*, edited by Michael Tonry. Chicago: University of Chicago Press.

Lappi-Seppälä, Tapio. 2020. "Humane Neoclassicism: Proportionality and Other Values in Nordic Sentencing." In *Of One-Eyed and Toothless Miscreants: Making the Punishment Fit the Crime?* edited by Michael Tonry. New York: Oxford University Press.

Laub, John H., and Richard J. Sampson. 2001. "Understanding Desistance from Crime." In *Crime and Justice: A Review of Research*, vol. 28, edited by Michael Tonry. Chicago: Chicago University Press.

Lee, Youngjae. 2010. "Repeat Offenders and the Question of Desert." In *Previous Convictions at Sentencing: Theoretical and Applied Perspectives*, edited by Julian V. Roberts and Andrew von Hirsch. Oxford: Hart.

Lee, Youngjae. 2017. "Multiple Offenders and the Question of Desert." In *Sentencing Multiple Crimes*, edited by Jesper Ryberg, Julian V Roberts, and Jan Willem de Keijser. New York: Oxford University Press.

Levitt, Steve. 2002. "Deterrence." In *Crime: Public Policies for Crime Control*, edited by James Q. Wilson and Joan Petersilia. Oakland, CA: Institute for Contemporary Studies.

Lewis, C.S. 1949. "The Humanitarian Theory of Punishment." *20th Century: An Australian Quarterly Review* 3(3):5–12.

Lewis, Donald E. 1986. "The General Deterrent Effect of Longer Sentences." *British Journal of Criminology* 26:47–62.

Lippke, Richard. 2011. "Retributive Sentencing. Multiple Offenses, and Bulk Discounts." In *Retributivism: Essays on Theory and Policy*, edited by Mark D. White. New York: Oxford University Press.

Lippke, Richard L. 2014. "Chronic Temptation, Reasonable Firmness and the Criminal Law." *Oxford Journal of Legal Studies* 34(1):75–96.

Lippke, Richard L. 2016. "The Ethics of Recidivist Premiums." In *The Routledge Handbook of Criminal Justice Ethics*, edited by Jonathan Jacobs and Jonathan Jackson. Abingdon, UK: Routledge.

Lippke, Richard L. 2017. "Parsimony and the Sentencing of Multiple Offenders." In *Sentencing Multiple Crimes*, edited by Jesper Ryberg, Julian V. Roberts, and Jan de Keijser. New York: Oxford University Press.

Lippke, Richard L. 2020. "Penal Severity and the Modern State." In *Of One-Eyed and Toothless Miscreants: Making the Punishment Fit the Crime?* edited by Michael Tonry. New York: Oxford University Press.

Loeffler, Charles E., Jordan Hyatt, and Greg Ridgeway. 2019. "Measuring Self-Reported Wrongful Convictions Among Prisoners." *Journal of Quantitative Criminology* 35(2): 259–86.

Loughran, Thomas A., Ray Paternoster, and Alex R. Piquero. 2018. "Individual Differences and Deterrence." In *Deterrence, Choice, and Crime: Contemporary Perspectives*, edited by Daniel S. Nagin, Francis T. Cullen, and Cheryl Lero Jonson. New York: Routledge.

Lovegrove, Austin. 1997. *The Framework of Judicial Sentencing: A Study in Legal Decision Making*. Cambridge: Cambridge University Press.

Luban, David. 2007. *Legal Ethics and Human Dignity*. Cambridge: Cambridge University Press.

Lum, Cynthis, and Daniel S. Nagin. 2017. "Reinventing American Policing." In *Reinventing American Criminal Justice*, edited by Michael Tonry. Chicago: University of Chicago Press.

Lynch, Gerard E. 2003. "Screening versus Plea Bargaining: Exactly What Are We Trading Off?" *Stanford Law Review* 55:1399–408.

Maccoun, Robert, Rosalie Liccardo, Jamie Pacula, Chriqui Katherine Harris, and Peter Reuter. 2009. "Do Citizens Know Whether Their State Has Decriminalized Marijuana? Assessing the Perceptual Component of Deterrence Theory." *Review of Law and Economics* 5(1):347–71.

MacKenzie, Doris Layton. 2006. *What Works in Corrections: Reducing the Criminal Activities of Offenders and Delinquents*. Cambridge: Cambridge University Press.

Mackie, John L. 1982. "Morality and the Retributive Emotions." *Criminal Justice Ethics* 1(3):3–10.

Markel, Dan, and Chad Flanders. 2010. "Bentham on Stilts? The Bare Relevance of Subjectivity to Retributive Justice." *California Law Review* 98:907–88.

Masur, Jonathan, John Bronsteen, and Christopher Buccafusco. 2009. "Happiness and Punishment." *University of Chicago Law Review* 76:1037–81.

Matravers, Matt. 2006. "'Who's Still Standing?' A Comment on Antony Duff's Preconditions of Criminal Liability." *Journal of Moral Philosophy* 3(3):320–30.

Matravers, Matt. 2011. "Is Twenty-first Century Punishment Post-Desert?" In *Retributivism Has a Past: Has it a Future?* edited by Michael Tonry. New York: Oxford University Press.

Matravers, Matt. 2019. "Rootless Desert and Unanchored Censure." In Penal Censure: Engagements Within and Beyond Desert Theory, edited by Antje du Bois-Pedain and Anthony E. Bottoms. London: Hart/Bloomsbury.

Matravers, Matt. 2020. "The Place of Proportionality in Penal Theory: Or Re-thinking Thinking about Punishment." In *Of One-Eyed and Toothless Miscreants: Making the Punishment Fit the Crime?* edited by Michael Tonry. New York: Oxford University Press.

May, David C., and Peter B. Wood. 2010. *Ranking Correctional Punishments: Views from Offenders, Practitioners, and the Public.* Durham, NC: Carolina Academic.

McCloskey, H. J. 1965. "A Non-utilitarian Approach to Punishment." *Inquiry: An Interdisciplinary Journal of Philosophy* 8(1–4):249–63.

McDonald, Douglas. 1986. *Punishment without Walls.* New Brunswick, NJ: Rutgers University Press.

McIntyre, Alison. 2014. "Doctrine of Double Effect." In *The Stanford Encyclopedia of Philosophy*, edited by Edward N. Zalta. Stanford, CA: Center for the Study of Language and Information, Stanford University. https://plato.stanford.edu/archives/win2014/entries/double-effect /.

Mears, Daniel P., and Joshua C. Cochran. 2018. "Progressively Tougher Sanctioning and Recidivism: Assessing the Effects of Different Types of Sanctions." *Journal of Research in Crime and Delinquency* 55:194–241.

Menninger, Karl. 1968. *The Crime of Punishment.* New York: Viking.

Michael, Jerome, and Mortimer Adler. 1933. *Crime, Law, and Social Science.* New York: Harcourt Brace.

Michael, Jerome, and Herbert Wechsler. 1937. "A Rationale of the Law of Homicide." *Columbia Law Review* 37:701–61 (Part I), 1261–335 (Part II).

Michael, Jerome, and Herbert Wechsler. 1940. *Criminal Law and Its Administration; Cases, Statutes, and Commentaries.* Chicago: Foundation Press.

Mill, John Stuart. 1997 [1869]. *The Subjection of Women.* New York: Dover.

Minnesota Sentencing Guidelines Commission. 1980. *Report to the Legislature, 1 January 1980.* St. Paul: Minnesota Sentencing Guidelines Commission.

Model Penal Code, see American Law Institute 1962, 2017.

Model Sentencing Act, see Advisory Council of Judges, National Council on Crime and Delinquency 1963, 1972.

Moffitt, Terrie E. 1993. "Adolescence-Limited and Life-Course-Persistent Antisocial Behavior: A Developmental Taxonomy." *Psychological Review* 100(4): 674–701.

Monahan, John. 1981. *The Clinical Prediction of Violent Behavior.* Washington, DC: National Institute of Mental Health.

Monahan, John. 2017. "Risk Assessment in Sentencing." In *Reforming Criminal Justice: Punishment, Incarceration, and Release,* edited by Erik Luna. Phoenix: Arizona State University Press (for Academy for Justice).

Monahan, John, and Jennifer L. Skeem. 2016. "Risk Assessment in Criminal Sentencing." *Annual Review of Clinical Psychology* 12:489–513.

Monahan, Kathryn, Laurence Steinberg, and Alan R. Piquero. 2015. "Juvenile Justice Policy and Practice: A Developmental Perspective." In *Crime and Justice: A Review of Research,* vol. 44, edited by Michael Tonry. Chicago: University of Chicago Press.

Moore, Michael S. 1993. "Justifying Retributivism." *Israeli Law Review* 27:15–36.

Morgan, Rod, and David J. Smith. 2017. "Delivering More with Less: Austerity and the Politics of Law and Order." In *The Oxford Handbook of Criminology,* 6th ed., edited by Alison Liebling, Shadd Maruna, and Lesley McAra. Oxford: Oxford University Press.

Morris, Herbert. 1966. "Persons and Punishment." *Monist* 52:475–501.

Morris, Herbert. 1981. "A Paternalist Theory of Punishment." *American Philosophical Quarterly* 18(4):263–71.

Morris, Norval. 1953. "Sentencing Convicted Criminals." *Australian Law Review* 27:186–208.

Morris, Norval. 1968. "Psychiatry and the Dangerous Criminal." *Southern California Law Review* 41:516–547.

Morris, Norval. 1974. *The Future of Imprisonment.* Chicago: University of Chicago Press.

Morris, Norval, and Marc Miller. 1985. "Predictions of Dangerousness." In *Crime and Justice: An Annual Review of Research,* vol. 6, edited by Michael Tonry and Norval Morris. Chicago: University of Chicago Press.

Morris, Norval, and Michael Tonry. 1990. *Between Prison and Probation: Intermediate Punishments in a Rational Sentencing System.* New York: Oxford University Press.

Morse, Stephen J. 1976. "The Twilight of Welfare Criminology: A Reply to Judge Bazelon." *Southern California Law Review* 49:1247–1268.

Morse, Stephen J. 2000. "Deprivation and Desert." In *From Social Justice to Criminal Justice: Poverty and the Administration of Criminal Law,* edited by William C. Heffernan and John Kleinig. New York: Oxford University Press.

Morse, Stephen J. 2003. "Diminished Rationality, Diminished Responsibility." *Ohio State Journal of Criminal Law* 1(1):289–308.

Murphy, Jeffrie. 1973. "Marxism and Retribution." *Philosophy and Public Affairs* 2:217–43.

Murphy, Jeffrie. 1988. "Mercy and Legal Justice." In *Forgiveness and Mercy,* by Jeffrie Murphy and Jean Hampton. New York: Cambridge University Press.

Musto, David. 1973. *The American Disease: The Origins of Narcotic Control.* New York: Oxford University Press. (3rd ed. published 1999, Yale University Press).

Nagel, Thomas. 1979. *Mortal Questions.* Cambridge: Cambridge University Press.

Nagin, Daniel S. 1978. "General Deterrence: A Review of the Empirical Evidence." In *Deterrence and Incapacitation*, edited by Alfred Blumstein, Jacqueline Cohen, and Daniel S. Nagin. Washington, DC: National Academy Press.

Nagin, Daniel S. 1998. "Deterrence and Incapacitation." In *The Handbook of Crime and Punishment*, edited by Michael Tonry. New York: Oxford University Press.

Nagin, Daniel S. 2013. "Deterrence in the Twenty-First Century." In *Crime and Justice in America: 1975–2025*, edited by Michael Tonry. Chicago: University of Chicago Press.

Nagin, Daniel S. 2018. "Certainty versus Severity of Deterrence." In *Deterrence, Choice, and Crime: Contemporary Perspectives*, edited by Daniel S. Nagin, Francis T. Cullen, and Cheryl Lero Jonson. New York: Routledge.

Nagin, Daniel S., Francis Cullen, and Cheryl Lero Jonson. 2009. "Imprisonment and Re-Offending." In *Crime and Justice: A Review of Research*, vol. 38, edited by Michael Tonry. Chicago: University of Chicago Press.

Nagin, Daniel S., Francis Cullen, and Cheryl Lero Jonson, eds. 2018. *Deterrence, Choice, and Crime: Contemporary Perspectives.* New York: Routledge.

Nagin, Daniel S., and John V. Pepper, eds. 2012. *Deterrence and the Death Penalty.* Washington, DC: National Academies Press.

National Academy of Sciences Committee on Community Supervision and Desistance from Crime, *see* Petersilia and Rosenfeld 2008.

National Academy of Sciences Committee on the Causes and Consequences of High Rates of Incarceration, *see* Travis, Western, and Redburn 2014.

National Academy of Sciences Panel on "Career Criminals" and Criminal Careers, *see* Blumstein et al. 1986.

National Academy of Sciences Panel on Deterrence and the Death Penalty, *see* Nagin and Pepper 2012.

National Academy of Sciences Panel on Research on Deterrent and Incapacitative Effects, *see* Blumstein, Cohen, and Nagin 1978.

National Academy of Sciences Panel on Understanding and Controlling Violence, *see* Reiss and Roth 1993.

National Advisory Commission on Criminal Justice Standards and Goals. 1973. *A National Strategy to Reduce Crime.* Washington, DC: US Government Printing Office.

National Commission on Reform of Federal Criminal Laws. 1971. *Report: Proposed Federal Code.* Washington, DC: US Government Printing Office.

Newman, Donald. 1966. *Conviction.* Boston: Little, Brown.

Nozick, Robert. 1977. *Anarchy, State, and Utopia.* New York: Basic Books.

Nozick, Robert. 1981. *Philosophical Explanations.* Cambridge, MA: Harvard University Press.

Osoba, Osonde A., Benjamin Boudreaux, Jessica Saunders, J. Luke Irwin, Pam A. Mueller, Samantha Cherney. 2019. *Algorithmic Equity—A Framework for Social Applications*. Santa Monica, CA: RAND.

Ostrom, Brian J., and Neal B. Kauder. 2012. "The Evolution of Offender Risk Assessment in Virginia." *Federal Sentencing Reporter* 25(3):161–67.

Parent, Dale G. 1988. *Structuring Criminal Sentences: The Evolution of Minnesota's Sentencing Guidelines*. New York: LEXIS.

Paternoster, Ray. 2018. "Perceptual Deterrence Theory." In *Deterrence, Choice, and Crime: Contemporary Perspectives,* edited by Daniel S. Nagin, Francis T. Cullen, and Cheryl Lero Jonson. New York: Routledge.

Pelikan, Jaroslav. 1985. *Jesus through the Centuries: His Place in the History of Culture*. New Haven: Yale University Press.

Pereboom, Derk. 2014. *Free Will, Agency, and Meaning in Life*. Oxford: Oxford University Press.

Petersilia, Joan. 1999. "Parole and Prisoner Reentry in the United States." In *Prisons*, edited by Michael Tonry and Joan Petersilia. Chicago: University of Chicago Press.

Petersilia, Joan, and Richard Rosenfeld, eds. 2008. *Parole, Desistance from Crime, and Community Integration*. Committee on Community Supervision and Desistance from Crime. Washington, DC: National Academies Press.

Petersilia, Joan, and Susan Turner. 1993. "Intensive Probation and Parole." In *Crime and Justice: A Review of Research,* vol. 17, edited by Michael Tonry. Chicago: University of Chicago Press.

Pifferi, Michele. 2012. "Individualization of Punishment and the Rule of Law: Reshaping Legality in the United States and Europe between the 19th and the 20th Century." *American Journal of Legal History* 52:325–76.

Pifferi, Michele. 2016. *Reinventing Punishment: A Comparative History of Criminology and Penology in the 19th and 20th Century*. Oxford: Oxford University Press.

Pincoffs, Edmund. 1966. *The Rationale of Legal Punishment*. Atlantic Highlands, NJ: Humanities Press.

Pinker, Steven. 2008. "The Stupidity of Dignity." *New Republic,* May 28, 2008. https://newrepublic.com/article/64674/the-stupidity-dignity.

Piquero, Alan R., David P. Farrington, and Alfred Blumstein. 2003. "The Criminal Career Paradigm." In *Crime and Justice: A Review of Research,* vol. 30, edited by Michael Tonry. Chicago: University of Chicago Press.

Plutarch. 1957. "Whether Land or Sea Animals Are Cleverer." In *Moralia*, vol. 12, translation by Harold Cherniss. Cambridge: Harvard University Press.

Pound, Roscoe. 1910. "Law in Books and Law in Action." *American Law Review* 44:12–36.

Pratt, Travis C., Francis T. Cullen, Kristie R. Blevins, Leah H. Daigle, and Tamara D. Madensen. 2006. "The Empirical Status of Deterrence Theory: A Meta-analysis." In *Taking Stock: The Status of Criminological Theory*, edited by Francis T. Cullen, John Paul Wright, and Kristie R. Blevins. New Brunswick, NJ: Transaction.

Pratt, Travis C., and Jillian Turanovic. 2018. "Celerity and Deterrence." In *Deterrence, Choice, and Crime: Contemporary Perspectives*, edited by Daniel S. Nagin, Francis T. Cullen, and Cheryl Lero Jonson. New York: Routledge.

President's Commission on Law Enforcement and Administration of Justice. 1967. *The Challenge of Crime in a Free Society*. Washington, DC: US Government Printing Office.

Quinton, Anthony M. 1969. "On Punishment." In *The Philosophy of Punishment*, edited by H. B. Acton. London: St Martin's Press.

Rawls, John. 1955. "Two Concepts of Rules." *Philosophical Review* 64(1):3–32.

Rawls, John. 1971. *A Theory of Justice*. Cambridge: Harvard University Press.

Reaves, Brian A. 2013. *Felony Defendants in Large Urban Counties, 2009—Statistical Tables*. Washington, DC: US Department of Justice, Bureau of Justice Statistics.

Reiss, Albert J., and Jeffrey A. Roth, eds. 1993. *Understanding and Preventing Violence*. Vol. 1. Washington, DC: National Academy.

Reitz, Kevin. 2010. "The Illusion of Proportionality: Desert and Repeat Offenders." In *Previous Convictions at Sentencing: Theoretical and Applied Perspectives*, edited by Julian V. Roberts and Andrew von Hirsch. Oxford: Hart.

Remington, Frank. 1969. "Introduction." In *Sentencing*, by Robert O. Dawson. Boston: Little, Brown.

Reuter, Peter, Robert J. MacCoun, and Patrick Murphy. 1990. *Money from Crime: The Economics of Drug Dealing in Washington, DC*. Santa Monica, CA: RAND, Drug Policy Research Center.

Roberts, Julian V. 1997. "The Role of Criminal Record in the Sentencing Process." In *Crime and Justice: A Review of Research*, volume 22, edited by Michael Tonry. Chicago: University of Chicago Press.

Roberts, Julian V. 2008. *Punishing Persistent Offenders: Exploring Community and Offender Perspectives*. Oxford: Oxford University Press.

Roberts, Julian V., and Jan de Keijser. 2014. "Democratising Punishment: Sentencing, Community Views and Values." *Punishment and Society* 16:474–98.

Roberts, Julian V., and J. Pina-Sanchez. 2014. "Previous Convictions at Sentencing: Exploring Empirical Trends in the Crown Court." *Criminal Law Review* 8:575–88.

Roberts, Julian V., and Andrew von Hirsch. 2010. *Previous Convictions at Sentencing: Theoretical and Applied Perspectives*. Oxford: Hart.

Robinson, Paul H. 1987. "Hybrid Principles for the Distribution of Criminal Sanctions." *Northwestern Law Review* 82:19–42.

Robinson, Paul H. 2013. *Intuitions of Justice and the Utility of Desert*. New York: Oxford University Press.

Robinson, Paul H. 2017. "Democratizing Criminal Law: Feasibility, Utility, and the Challenge of Social Change." *Northwestern University Law Review* 111:1565–595.

Robinson, Paul H., and John E. Darley. 2007. "Intuitions of Justice: Implications for Criminal Law and Justice Policy." *Southern California Law Review* 81:1–67.

Ross, W. D. 1930. *The Right and the Good*. Oxford: Oxford University Press.

Rothman, David. 1971. *The Discovery of the Asylum: Social Order and Disorder in the New Republic*. Boston: Little, Brown.

Royko, Mike. 1981. "Evil Hearts and Minds." *Chicago Sun-Times* (Oct. 1), p. 2.

Ryberg, Jesper. 2001. "Recidivism, Multiple Offending, and Legal Justice." *Danish Yearbook of Philosophy* 36(1):69–94.

Ryberg, Jesper. 2004. *Proportionate Punishment: A Critical Investigation*. Dordrecht/ New York: Kluwer Academic.

Ryberg, Jesper. 2017. "Retributivism, Multiple Offending, and Overall Proportionality." In *Sentencing Multiple Crimes,* edited by Jesper Ryberg, Julian V. Roberts, and Jan de Keijser. New York: Oxford University Press.

Ryberg, Jesper. 2019. "Risk and Retribution: On the Possibility of Reconciling Considerations of Dangerousness and Desert." In *Predictive Sentencing: Normative and Empirical Perspectives*, edited by Jan W. de Keijser, Julian V. Roberts, and Jesper Ryberg. Oxford: Hart.

Ryberg, Jesper. 2020. "Proportionality and the Seriousness of Crimes." In *Of One-Eyed and Toothless Miscreants: Making the Punishment Fit the Crime?* edited by Michael Tonry. New York: Oxford University Press.

Sebba, Leslie. 1978. "Some Explorations in the Scaling of Penalties." *Journal of Research on Crime and Delinquency* 15:247–65.

Sellin, Thorsten, and Marvin E. Wolfgang. 1964. *The Measurement of Delinquency*. New York: Wiley.

Shepherd, Joanna. 2004. "Testimony." In *Terrorist Penalties Enhancement Act of 2003: Hearing on H.R. 2934 before the Subcommittee on Crime, Terrorism, and Homeland Security of the House Committee on the Judiciary*, 108th Congress. https://www.govinfo. gov/content/pkg/CHRG-108hhrg93224/pdf/CHRG-108hhrg93224.pdf.

Singer, Richard G. 1979. *Just Deserts: Sentencing Based on Equality and Desert*. Lexington, MA: Ballinger.

Skeem, Jennifer, Nicholas Scurich, and John Monahan. 2019. "Impact of Risk Assessment on Judges' Fairness in Sentencing Relatively Poor Defendants." University of Virginia School of Law Public Law and Legal Theory Paper Series 2019-02. https://ssrn.com/abstract=3316266.

Slobogin, Christopher. 2019. "A Defence of Modern Risk-Based Sentencing." In *Predictive Sentencing: Normative and Empirical Perspectives,* edited by Jan Willem de Keijser, Julian V. Roberts, and Jesper Ryberg. Oxford: Hart.

Smith, Michael E., and Walter J. Dickey. 1999. *Reforming Sentencing and Corrections for Just Punishment and Public Safety*. Washington, DC: US Department of Justice, National Institute of Justice.

Starr, Sonja. 2014. "Evidence-Based Sentencing and the Scientific Rationalization of Discrimination." *Stanford Law Review* 66:803–72.

Starr, Sonja. 2016. "The Odds of Justice: Actuarial Risk Prediction and the Criminal Justice System." *Chance* 29(1):49–51.

Steiker, Carol S. 2014. "'To See Justice in a Grain of Sand': Dignity and Indignity in American Criminal Justice." In *The Punitive Imagination—Law, Justice, and Responsibility*, edited by Austin Sarat. Tuscaloosa: University of Alabama Press.

Stith, Kate, and Steve Y. Koh. 1993. "The Politics of Sentencing Reform: The Legislative History of the Federal Sentencing Guidelines." *Wake Forest Law Review* 28:223–90.

Stuntz, William J. 2011. *The Collapse of American Criminal Justice*. Cambridge: Harvard University Press.

Sullivan, Christopher J., and Melissa Lugo. 2018. "Criminological Theory and Deterrence." In *Deterrence, Choice, and Crime: Contemporary Perspectives*, edited by Daniel S. Nagin, Francis T. Cullen, and Cheryl Lero Jonson. New York: Routledge.

Tadros, Victor. 2011. *The Ends of Harm: The Moral Foundations of Criminal Law*. Oxford: Oxford University Press.

Tappan, Paul. 1947. "Who Is the Criminal?" *American Sociological Review* 12(1):96–102.

Tonry, Michael. 1987. "Prediction and Classification: Legal and Ethical Issues." In *Prediction and Classification*, edited by Don M. Gottfredson and Michael Tonry. Chicago: University of Chicago Press.

Tonry, Michael. 1996. *Sentencing Matters*. New York: Oxford University Press.

Tonry, Michael. 1997. "Ethnicity, Crime, and Immigration." In *Ethnicity, Crime, and Immigration: Comparative and Cross-National Perspectives*, edited by Michael Tonry. Chicago: University of Chicago Press.

Tonry, Michael. 2004. *Thinking about Crime: Sense and Sensibility in American Penal Culture*. New York: Oxford University Press.

Tonry, Michael. 2009. "The Mostly Unintended Effects of Mandatory Penalties: Two Centuries of Consistent Findings." In *Crime and Justice: A Review of Research*, vol. 38, edited by Michael Tonry. Chicago: University of Chicago Press.

Tonry, Michael. 2012. "Prosecutors and Politics in Comparative Perspective." In *Prosecutors and Politics: A Comparative Perspective*, edited by Michael Tonry. Chicago: University of Chicago Press.

Tonry, Michael. 2016a. "Differences in National Sentencing Systems, and the Differences They Make." In *Sentencing Policies and Practices in Western Countries: Comparative and Cross-national Perspectives*, edited by Michael Tonry. Chicago: University of Chicago Press.

Tonry, Michael. 2016b. *Sentencing Fragments*. New York: Oxford University Press.

Tonry, Michael, and Colleen Chambers. 2012. "Juvenile Justice Cross-nationally Considered." In *The Oxford Handbook of Juvenile Crime and Juvenile Justice*, edited by Barry C. Feld and Donna M. Bishop. New York: Oxford University Press.

Törnudd, Patrik. 1993. *Fifteen Years of Declining Prisoner Rates*. Research Communication no. 8. Helsinki: National Research Institute of Legal Policy.

Tracey, Paul E., Marvin E. Wolfgang, and Robert M. Figlio. 1990. *Delinquency Careers in Two Birth Cohorts*. New York: Plenum.

Travis, Jeremy, Bruce Western, and Steve Redburn, eds. 2014. *The Growth of Incarceration in the United States: Exploring Causes and Consequences*. Report of the National Academy of Sciences Committee on the Causes and Consequences of High Rates of Incarceration. Washington, DC: National Academies Press.

US Parole Commission, *see* Hoffman 1976, 1983, and 1995.

US Government Accountability Office. 2017. *Costs of Crime. Experts Report Challenges Estimating Costs and Suggest Improvements to Better Inform Policy*. Washington, DC: US Government Accountability Office.

Van Zyl Smit, Dirk, and Sonja Snacken. 2009. *Principles of European Prison Law and Policy: Penology and Human Rights*. Oxford: Oxford University Press.

Vibla, Natalia. 2017. "Toward a Theoretical and Practical Model for Multiple-Offense Sentencing." In *Sentencing Multiple Crimes*, edited by Jesper Ryberg, Julian V Roberts, and Jan Willem de Keijser. New York: Oxford University Press.

Villettaz, Patrice, Gwladys Gillieron, and Martin Killias. 2015. *The Effects on Re-Offending of Custodial vs. Non-Custodial Sanctions: An Updated Systematic Review of the State of Knowledge*. Oslo: Campbell Collaboration.

Virginia Criminal Sentencing Commission. 2014. *Manual*, 17th ed. Richmond: Virginia Criminal Sentencing Commission.

von Hirsch, Andreas [Andrew]. 1976. *Doing Justice: The Choice of Punishments*. New York: Hill and Wang.

von Hirsch, Andreas [Andrew]. 1981. "Desert and Previous Convictions in Sentencing." *Minnesota Law Review* 65:591–634.

von Hirsch, Andreas [Andrew]. 1985. *Past or Future Crimes: Deservedness and Dangerousness in Sentencing Criminals*. New Brunswick, NJ: Rutgers University Press.

von Hirsch, Andreas [Andrew]. 1993. *Censure and Sanctions*. Oxford: Oxford University Press.

von Hirsch, Andreas [Andrew]. 2010. "Proportionality and the Progressive Loss of Mitigation: Some Further Reflections." *Previous Convictions at Sentencing: Theoretical and Applied Perspectives*, edited by Julian Roberts and Andrew von Hirsch. Oxford: Hart.

von Hirsch, Andreas [Andrew]. 2011. "Reflections on Punishment Futures: The Desert-Model Debate and the Importance of the Criminal Law Context." In *Retributivism Has a Past: Has It a Future?* edited by Michael Tonry. Oxford: Oxford University Press.

von Hirsch, Andreas [Andrew]. 2017. *Deserved Criminal Sentences: An Overview*. Oxford: Hart.

von Hirsch, Andreas [Andrew], Anthony E. Bottoms, Elizabeth Burney, and Per-Olof H. Wikström. 1999. *Criminal Deterrence and Sentence Severity: An Analysis of Recent Research*. Oxford: Hart.

von Hirsch, Andreas [Andrew], and Nils Jareborg. 1991. "Gauging Criminal Harm: A Living-Standard Analysis." *Oxford Journal of Legal Studies* 11(1):1–38.

von Hirsch, Andreas [Andrew], Martin Wasik, and Judith Greene. 1989. "Punishments in the Community and the Principles of Desert." *Rutgers Law Review* 20:595–618.

Waldron, Jeremy. 2008. "Lucky in Your Judge." *Theoretical Inquiries in Law* 9:185–216.

Waldron, Jeremy. 2014. *What Do the Philosophers Have Against Dignity?* Public Law and Legal Theory Research Series. Working Paper 14-59. New York: NYU Law School.

Walker, Nigel. 1969. *Sentencing in a Rational Society*. London: Allen Lane.

Walker, Nigel. 1991. *Why Punish?* Oxford: Oxford University Press.

Walker, Nigel. 1999. *Aggravation, Mitigation and Mercy in English Criminal Justice*. London: Blackstone.

Warr, Mark. 2000. "Public Perceptions of and Reactions to Crime." In *Criminology—A Contemporary Handbook*, edited by Joseph F. Sheley. Belmont, MA: Wadsworth.

Wechsler, Herbert. 1961. "Sentencing, Correction, and the Model Penal Code." *University of Pennsylvania Law Review* 109(4):465–93.

Weigend, Thomas. 2016. "No News is Good News: Criminal Sentencing in Germany since 2000." In *Sentencing Policies and Practices in Western Countries: Comparative and Cross-national Perspectives,* edited by Michael Tonry. Chicago: University of Chicago Press.

Weisburd, David, Tomer Einat, and Matt Kowalski. 2008. "The Miracle of the Cells: An Experimental Study of Interventions to Increase Payment of Court-Ordered Financial Obligations." *Criminology and Public Policy* 7(1):9–36.

Whitman, James. 2004. "The Two Western Cultures of Privacy: Dignity versus Liberty." *Yale Law Journal* 113:1151–221.

Whitman, James. 2016. "Presumption of Innocence or Presumption of Mercy? Weighing Two Western Modes of Justice." *Texas Law Review* 94:933–93.

Wikström, Per-Olof, and Rolf Loeber. 2000. "Do Disadvantaged Neighborhoods Cause Well-Adjusted Children to Become Adolescent Delinquents? A Study of Male Juvenile Serious Offending, Individual Risk and Protective Factors, and Neighborhood Context." *Criminology* 38:1109.

Wilcox, Pamela, and Francis T. Cullen. 2018. "Community Members and Groups." In *Deterrence, Choice, and Crime: Contemporary Perspectives*, edited by Daniel S. Nagin, Francis T. Cullen, and Cheryl Lero Jonson. New York: Routledge.

Williams, Bernard. 1981. *Moral Luck: Philosophical Papers 1973–1980*. Cambridge: Cambridge University Press.

Wilson, James Q. 1975. *Thinking about Crime*. New York: Basic Books.

Wolf, Susan. 2001. "The Moral of Moral Luck." *Philosophic Exchange* 31(1):5–23.

Wollstonecraft, Mary. 2009 [1792]. *A Vindication of the Rights of Women*. Oxford: Oxford University Press.

Wootton, Barbara. 1959. *Social Science and Social Pathology*. London: Allen Unwin.

Wootton, Barbara. 1963. *Crime and the Criminal Law*. London: Stevens.

Yang Min, Stephen C. Wong, and Jeremy Coid. 2010. "The Efficacy of Violence Prediction: A Meta-analytic Comparison of Nine Risk Assessment Tools." *Psychology Bulletin* 136(5):740–67.

Zimring, Franklin E. 2008. "Criminology and Its Discontents." *Criminology* 46(2):255–66.

Zimring, Franklin E., and Gordon Hawkins. 1988. "The New Mathematics of Imprisonment." *Crime and Delinquency* 34:425–36.

Index

For the benefit of digital users, indexed terms that span two pages (e.g., 52–53) may, on occasion, appear on only one of those pages.

Tables are indicated by *t* following the page number.

abortion, 20
Abrahamse, Allan, 147–48
absolute severity, 137
accuracy, prediction
  dangerousness, for sentencing, 151*t*, 160–62
  future violence, 149–50
  instruments, 149–50, 151*t*, 156–59, 160–62
"actual harm done," 51–52, 60
actuarial prediction analogy, 178
Adler, Mortimer, *Crime, Law, and Social Science*, 45
adolescence-limited offenders, 81–82
affirmative defenses, 31n12, 87, 88, 96
affirmative offenses, 79, 88
age, predictive sentencing, 163–65
  elderly, 163n14, 163
  youth, 163–65
"Age and Crime" (Farrington), 82
age/crime curves, 82, 148–49n3, 164
Aggravation, Mitigation, and Mercy (Walker), 118
Albion's Fatal Tree (Hay), 90

Alexander, Larry, 51n6, 97–98, 120
Allen, Francis, 43n1, 45–46
Alschuler, Albert, 3
amends, making, bulk discounts, 120–21
American Disease: The Origins of Narcotic Control, The (Musto), 79, 80
American Law Institute, *Model Penal Code. See Model Penal Code*
analogies, predictive sentencing, 178–80
  actuarial predictions, as commonplace, 178
  public health quarantines, 178–80
Ancel, Marc, 24–25
Angwin, Julia, 156–57, 180–81
antisocial behavior, 134
  antecedents and causes, 81–82
  reoffending, 111
antisocial personality, 47n3, 121–22
apologies, recidivist premium, 108–9
Arnold, Thurman, 34
Ashworth, Andrew, 59–60, 101n7
  Sentencing and Criminal Justice, 114–15
attempts punishment, *vs.* completed offenses, 59n13, 59–60
Azzopardi v. R., 117

bad character, recidivist premium, 110–12
Barnes, J. C., 133n6
Barr, William, *The Case for More Incarceration,* 165
Bazelon, David, 77, 85
  Durham v. United States, 85
  social adversity defense, 76, 82, 84, 86
  social adversity defense, as consequentialist, 79
  social adversity defense, Morse on, 87–88
  social adversity defense, Morse on, Tonry's response, 87–89
  Tonry's support, 92
Beccaria, Cesare, 54
  certainty and celerity, 139
  On Crimes and Punishments, 23–24, 132
  deterrence theory, 131–32, 133, 134
Bechtel, Kristen, 156–57n10, 157, 158, 162, 167–68, 167t, 180–81, 181n22
Bennett, Christopher, 108, 120
Bentham, Jeremy, 6–7, 8, 22, 25, 54. *See also* utilitarianism
  certainty and celerity, 139
  deterrence theory, 131–32, 133, 134, 141, 142–43
  dignity, human, 36
  frugality, 139
  incapacitation, 24, 25n9
  Introduction to the Principles of Morals and Legislation, An, 67n20
  parsimony, 172
  punishments and offenders' sensibilities, 31, 36, 67
  punishments as evil, 162–63
  recidivist premium, 105
  rehabilitation, 24, 25n9
  sensibility, 67n20
Berk, Richard, 159
Berlin, Isaiah, 20, 33, 97
  equally valid first principles, conflicting implications, 158
  "Two Concepts of Liberty," 46–47

Berra, Yogi, 149–50
Bion of Borysthenes, 40, 61
Blackstone, William, *Commentaries on the Laws of England,* 25n9
Blakeley v. Washington, 192n2
blameworthiness, 32, 51, 96n3, 120
  1930s U.S., 185–86
  assessments, 30–31
  assessments, dispositional stage, 96n2
  assessments, judges', 30
  definition, 51
  just punishment, 33–34, 39, 40, 41
  meaning, author's, 51–52
  morbid psychology, 115–16
  multiple convictions, 97, 101–2, 104, 118, 123, 124
  Rawls and Pincoff, 46
  retributivism, 20, 23, 26, 32, 47, 109–10, 141, 142
  retributivism, determinate sentencing, 150
  retributivism, negative, 27
  retributivism, positive, 9
  sanctions, Europe, 60–61
  sentencing, length, 118, 145–46
  sentencing, proportionality, 6, 21, 51, 157, 175–76
  sentencing, Scandinavia, 177–78
  sentencing, *vs.* prior offending, 102
  sentencing severity, upper limits, 176
  Walker, Nigel, 67n21, 67
Blumstein, Alfred, 153
  National Academy of Sciences Panel on "Career Criminals" and Criminal Careers, 147–48
  National Academy of Sciences Panel on Deterrent and Incapacitative Effects, 131n5, 134, 147
Bordenkircher v. Hayes, 19–20, 62–63, 193
Braithwaite, John, 41
  republican theory, 27n11, 123–24
Breyer, Justice Stephen, 70

Bugmy v The Queen, 93
bulk discounts
  multiple offense paradox, 29–30
  multiple offenses, theory, 95, 113–23
bulk discounts, lawyers' explanations,
    114–20, 123
  crushing sentences, 114, 116–17
  interoffense comparisons, 114,
    117–18, 118n19
  mercy and compassion, 114,
    118–19, 119n20
  morbid psychology, 114–16
bulk discounts, philosophers' efforts, 120
  character, 121–23
  making amends, 120–21
Burgess, Anthony, *Clockwork
    Orange,* 45–46

California
  three-strikes law, 1, 4, 136–37
  Uniform Determinate
    Sentencing Law, 3
Campbell, May Ann, 161n12
capital punishment
  abolish, 130, 145
  Beccaria, Cesare, 132
  Panel on Deterrence and the Death
    Penalty, 131n5
  Woodson v. North Carolina, 35–36
cardinal desert, 28
career criminal, 100, 103, 123, 147–48
  residual, 116–17, 148–49n3
Carlsmith, Kevin M., 133n6
Caruso, Greg, 179–80
Case for More Incarceration, The
    (Barr), 165
Categorical imperative, Kant's,
    104–5, 174–75
celerity, deterrence, 135
censure, 23, 26, 27–28
  communication of, 64–65, 178
  crime prevention and, 158–59

deterrence and, 39
  moral, 20n6
  retributivism, 64–65
certainty of punishment, on
  deterrence, 138–39
Challenge of Crime in a Free Society, The
  (Katzenbach), 17–18
character, bulk discounts, 121–23
Chen, Yiling, 184
child protection, 20
children
  life without parole, 1, 2, 164
  mandatory life sentences, 164
Clockwork Orange (Burgess), 45–46
Coase, Ronald, 140
cocaine sentences, 4, 16n3
Cohen, Jacqueline, 147n1
  National Academy of Sciences Panel
    on Deterrent and Incapacitative
    Effects, 131n5, 134, 147
Cohen, Mark, 56
Coid, Jeremy, 161n12, 161–62
collective incapacitation, 147
Commentaries on the Laws of England
    (Blackstone), 25n9
Committee on Community Supervision
    and Desistance from Crime, 9
Common Law, The (Holmes), 73–74
community punishments, 65–66, 70–71,
    144, 175
  as default, 8
  vs. imprisonment, severity, 64, 65–66
  public safety, 177–78
  reoffending, 138
  substitution for imprisonment,
    65–66, 70
COMPAS, 180–82, 181n22, 183n24
compassion, 118–19, 130
  juries and judges, 75, 115, 170
  sympathy and, 73
compassion, bulk discounts, 114,
    118–19, 119n20

confirmation bias, 140

consequentialism, 15, 17n4, 18, 25n9, 25.
   See also utilitarianism
   1970s and earlier, 79
   deterrence, 15, 17n4, 23–24, 25n9, 25,
      33, 142–43
   incapacitation, 15
   moral education, 15
   punishment, 172
   restorative justice, 25n10, 25, 142
   social disadvantage defense, 79
   unrestrained, 33

convictions, wrongful, 2, 89, 190
   consequences, 2, 3, 9, 89
   negative stereotyping, 88 (*see also*
      negative stereotyping)

Cooke, David, 156

costs of crime
   criminal justice system, 190
   proportionality, 51n6, 55–57, 56n9, 57*t*

crime. *See also specific topics*
   disadvantage and, 80–84, 83*t*
   as human condition, 127
   linking punishments and, 68
   recategorization, 193

Crime, Justice, and Protecting the Public
   (Home Office), 111–12

Crime, Law, and Social Science
   (Adler), 45

Crime (Sentences) Act 1997, 103–4

Crime and Justice (Roberts), 103

crime rates
   current declining, 4, 130, 155n9, 155
   violent, all-time highs, 155

crime seriousness, proportionality, 54–
   62, 57*t*, 128
   conflicting realities, 58–59
   missing metric, 54–58, 57*t*
   moral luck, 59–62
   offense seriousness ranking, 58

criminal careers, 100, 103, 123, 147–48
   generalist offenders, 123, 147–48

residual, 116–17, 148–49n3

criminal history
   other issues, 173
   predictions of dangerousness for
      sentencing, 171–73
   punishment theories, 171–72
   racial bias and disparate effects, 172–73

criminalization, 106, 127–28, 133n6

Criminal Justice Act 1991 (England and
   Wales), 103–4

Criminal Justice Act 2003 (England and
   Wales), 47–48, 103–4

criminal justice policy,
   politicized, 19, 75

criminal law. *See also specific laws
      and topics*
   necessity, 127–28

Criminal Sentencing: Law without Order
   (Frankel), 18

crushing punishments (sentences), 30, 38,
   41, 100–1, 120, 121, 124
   bulk discounts, 114, 116–17

Cullen, Francis, *Deterrence, Choice, and
   Crime*, 129

Dan-Cohen, Meir, 35

dangerous offender, 100, 103–4
   chronic, 116–17
   faulty predictions, 173
   incorrigible, Europe, 185–86
   pathological, 9–10

Darley, John, 49, 117, 133n6

Davis, Kenneth Culp, 45–46

Dawid, Philip, 156, 158

Death of Contract, The (Gilmore), 79

decades-long sentences, 49–50n5, 70, 79,
   100, 174–75n20, 179, 190

deep disadvantage, 73–94. *See also*
   disadvantage, deep

defenses
   affirmative, 31n12, 87, 88, 96
   insanity, 92, 96, 115, 119, 175

insanity, deep disadvantage, 85–86,
87–88, 112
self-defense, 30–31, 31n12
social adversity (*see* social adversity
defense [Bazelon])
de Keijser, Jan, 61n15, 98–99n5, 111n15
Delgado, Richard, 85, 88
"Rotten Social Background," 76n2
"The Wretched of the Earth," 80–81
Dershowitz, Alan, 18
Desmarais, Sarah, 161n12
determinate sentencing, 3, 150
1970s upsurge, 78–79
retributivism, 150
Uniform Determinate
Sentencing Law, 3
deterrence, 127–46
American criminal code, 38–39
Beccaria, Cesare, 131–32, 133, 134
Bentham, Jeremy, 131–32, 133, 134,
141, 142–43
capital punishment, 145
consequentialism, 15
criminalization, 127–28
effectiveness, economists and
economic theories, 111–40, 131n3
effectiveness, lack, 130
empirical knowledge, 132–41
empirical knowledge, certainty, 138–39
empirical knowledge, general
deterrence, 134–35, 135n7
empirical knowledge,
parsimony, 139–41
empirical knowledge, severity, 136–38
importance, 127
jail use and prison sentence reduction;
term shortening, 144
justice *vs.* public safety, 128–29
mandatory sentencing law repeal; no
new ones, 145
moral education, punishments and,
128n1, 128

normative theory, 141–44
normative theory,
consequentialism, 142–43
normative theory, expressive
punishments and moral
education, 143–44
normative theory,
retributivism, 141–42
public spending reallocation, 145–46
punishment as legal threat,
ineffectiveness, 127, 130, 132,
133n6, 133–34
rehabilitation, 132–33
research, policy implications and
inertia, 130
research, surveys and lessons,
129–30, 131
research, taking account, 144–46
severe punishment as, 129
socioeconomics, 132
utilitarianism, 15, 17n4, 23–24,
25n9, 25, 33
Deterrence, Choice, and Crime (Nagin,
Cullen, & Jonson), 129
developmental trajectories, 81–82
Dickey, Walter, 148–49n3
dignity, human, 15–42
Bentham, Jeremy, 22, 25, 36, 54
Bordenkircher v. Hayes, 19–20, 20n6
consequentialism, 17n4, 18
constitutional jurisprudence, 34–35
Dan-Cohen, Meir, 35
definition and terminology, 34
dismissal, 21–51
equal treatment, 15–16, 16n2, 18, 21,
22–23, 27, 34, 35–38, 40, 41, 42 (*see
also* equal treatment)
fairness, 18, 21, 22–23, 34, 36–38, 40,
42 (*see also* fairness)
German Constitutional Court, 38
Hegel, George Wilhelm Friedrich, 23
indeterminate sentencing, 16–17

dignity, human (*Cont.*)
  individual rights (1970s), 18
  judge discretion, 19–20
  judges, election and limited power, 16
  jurisprudence, lack of widely
    agreed, 19, 35
  just punishment, 21, 33–42 (*see also* just
    punishment)
  Kant, Immanuel, 22, 23, 36
  mandatory minimum sentences,
    processing on, 19
  Model Penal Code, 17–18
  parsimony, 22–23, 34, 36–38, 40, 41,
    42 (*see also* parsimony)
  politicized criminal justice
    policy, 19, 75
  proportionality, 15, 16n3, 19, 21, 22–23,
    26, 27, 33–34, 36–37, 40, 42, 46, 71
    (*see also* proportionality)
  punishment, normative frameworks,
    U.S. *vs.* Europe, 15
  rehabilitation support, past, 16–17
  retributivism, 17n4, 18–19, 22, 23 (*see
    also* retributivism)
  retributivism, limited reach, 23–32 (*see
    also* retributivism, limited reach)
  retributivism, theories, 20
  sentence review, meaningful, 16n3,
    16–17, 19–20
  utilitarianism, 22, 23–24, 25 (*see also*
    utilitarianism)
  Waldron, Jeremy, 35
  Woodson v. North Carolina, 35–36
dignity principle, 35
disadvantage, deep, 73–94
  crime, 80–84, 83*t*
  excuse, 85–92
  history and overview, 78–80
  social adversity, in mitigation, 92–94
  unjust world, 87–88, 91–92
disadvantage, social
  crime and, 80–84, 83*t*

excuse and, 85–92
  Salient Factor Score, 151–52
disparate effects, 172–73
Doing Justice (Von Hirsch), 51,
  76–77, 78–79
doing justice better, 189–94
  political insulation, 6, 15–16, 189,
    190, 191
  racial justice, 190
  Rechtsstaat, 189, 190–91
dominion, 41
Doob, Anthony, 98–99n5, 140
Douglas, Thomas, 179
Downes, David, *Oxford Handbook of
  Criminology,* 103–4
Dressel, Julia, 156–57n10
Dressler, Joshua, 91, 92
Duff, Antony
  linking crimes and punishments, 68
  *Punishment, Communication, and
    Community,* 90n6, 90
  punishment as moral
    communication, 27–28
  retributive punishment,
    communicative properties, 44–45
  Trials and Punishments, 76–77, 90
Durham v. United States, 85
Durkheim, Emile, on punishment, 10
  expressive punishment, 143–44
  instrumental effects, 143–44
  justification, 143
  sociological theory, 127–28, 141
Duus-Otterström, Göran, 48–49
Dworkin, Ronald, 15–16, 35–36
  "equal concern and respect," 16n2
  Law's Empire, 89n5, 89, 110
  "rights as trumps," 37

economics and economic theories,
  deterrence, 111–40, 131n3
Ehrlich, Isaac, 140
Einat, Tomer, 136

elderly imprisonment, 163n14, 163

empirical desert, 111n15

Enoch, David, 51n6

equal treatment, 15–16, 16n2, 18,
 22–23, 27

  justice as, 6, 21

  just punishment, 34, 35–38, 40, 41, 42

  negative retributivism, 7–8

  predictive sentencing, 182–83

  proportionality, 46, 48, 50, 53

  vs. treatment as equal, 67n18

ethnicity. *See also* racial bias; racial
 disparities

  disparities, 190

  predictive sentencing, 163,
 166–68, 167t

European Convention on Human
 Rights, 194

Ewing, Benjamin, 101n7, 107n14, 107

excuse, disadvantage and, 85–92

expediency principle, 96n3, 96–97

expressive punishments,
 deterrence, 143–44

fairness, 18, 21, 22–23

  justice as, 6, 21

  just punishment, 34, 36–38, 40, 42

  negative retributivism, 7–8

  predictive sentencing, 182–83

false negatives, prediction instruments,
 167–68, 167t

false positives, prediction instruments,
 151t, 160, 167–68, 167t

Farid, Hany, 156–57n10

Farrington, David, 153

  "Age and Crime," 82

Fazel, Seena, 161

Feinberg, Joel, 18–19, 26

  punishment, linking crimes to, 35–36

  punishment, retributive,
 communicative properties, 44–45

felony murder, 59n13

Ferri, Enrico, 24–25, 96

Ferzan, Kimberly Kessler, 51n6,
 97–98, 120

Flanders, Chad, 26

Fletcher, George, 101

Flores, Anthony, 156–57n10, 157, 158, 162,
 167–68, 167t, 180–81, 181n22

Frankel, Marvin

  *Criminal Sentencing: Law without
 Order,* 18

  sentencing commissions and
 presumptive guidelines, 191–92n1

Frase, Richard, 64, 70, 139n10,
 172, 183–84

French, Sheila, 161n12

future. *See* moving forward

Future of Imprisonment, The (Morris),
 71, 103

Garvey, Stephen, 90n7

gender

  predictive sentencing, 163, 165–66

  self-identification, changes, 153n8

Gendreau, Paul, 161n12

Gilmore, Grant, *The Death of
 Contract,* 79

Glueck, Sheldon, 16–17

  "Principles of a Rational Penal Code,"
 24–25 (*see also* positivism)

Green, Ben, 184

Green, Stuart, 91–92

Greene, Judith, 65–66

Greenwood, Peter, 147–48

group differences, offending and
 predictive sentencing, 180–82

habitual offender, 100, 171. *See also*
 multiple convictions

  Kentucky Habitual Crime Act, 20n6

  lengthy/life sentences, 103–4

Halliday, John, 103–4

Hampton, Jean, 26, 44–45

Harcourt, Bernard, 165
hard treatment, 27–28, 38–39, 49,
    62, 64–65
Harmelin v. Michigan, 16n3
Hart, H. L. A., 25, 69
    insanity offense, 60n14
    proportionality, 44
    Punishment and Responsibility,
      27, 96n3
Hart, Henry, 31n13, 39
Hart, Stephen, 156
Hawken, Angela, 136
Hawkins, Gordon, 148n2
Hay, Douglas, *Albion's Fatal Tree,* 90
Hayes v. Cowan, 20n6
Heffernan, William C., *From Social
    Justice to Criminal Justice: Poverty
    and the Administration of Criminal
    Law,* 76
Hegel, George Wilhelm Friedrich, 2, 6–
    7, 23. *See also* positive retributivism;
    retributivism
    deterrence, 141–42
    positive retributivism, 27, 54
    proportionality, 44, 50, 53–54
    recidivist premium, 104–5
Hester, Rhys, 29
Holder, Eric, 152–53n6, 152–53
Holmes, Oliver Wendell, Jr., *The
    Common Law,* 73–74
Honderich, Ted, *Punishment: The
    Supposed Justifications,* 76–77
Hough, Mike, 133n6
Howard, John, 137–38
human dignity, 15–42. *See also*
    dignity, human
"The Humanitarian Theory of
    Punishment" (Lewis), 45
Husak, Douglas, 44–45, 47, 158–59

immutable characteristics, dangerousness
    predictions for sentencing, 163–68

implicit bias, 39, 159–60
imprisonment. *See also* prisons
    cost, U.S., 145
    declining, 4
    elderly, 163n14, 163
    rate, 190
Imrey, Peter, 156, 158
incapacitation, 132–33. *See also* prediction
    and incapacitation
    American criminal code, 38–39
    Bentham, Jeremy, 24, 25n9
    collective, 147
    consequentialism, 15
    positivism (Ferri), 17n4, 25
    selective, 147–48, 148n2
    skepticism, 148–49n3, 148–49
indeterminate sentencing, 61n15, 102n8
    adoption, 185–86
    Bentham, Jeremy, 24
    causes of crime, social and
      psychological, 75
    consequentialists and collapse of
      support (1970s), 18n5, 18–19, 43n1,
      102, 150
    Criminal Justice Act 2003,
      47–48, 103–4
    debates, 185
    easing (1970s), 3
    Glueck, Sheldon, 24–25
    Hart, Henry and retributivists, 39
    human dignity, 16–17
    Model Penal Code, 2, 7, 17–18, 106
    Model Penal Code, as least restrictive
      alternative, 8
    multiple convictions, 106n12, 106
    past, 16–17
    positivism, 102n8
    premise, 75
    unconstrained discretion, dangers, and
      abuses, 33, 45–46, 78–79
    U.S. adoption (1930s), 185–86
    utilitarianism, 102n8, 102

innocent person, punishing
  Hart, H. L. A., 60–61
  human rights, 37–38
  morally innocent and legally
    guilt, 31n12
  plea bargaining, 2
  predictions of dangerousness, 43
  retributivism, 37–38
  utilitarianism, 33, 37, 60–61
  wrongful convictions (*see* wrongful
    convictions)
insanity defense, 115, 119
  acquittals, jury, 92
  Bentham, Jeremy, 96, 175
  deep disadvantage, 85–86, 87–88, 112
insanity offense rationale, 60n14
insulation, political, 6, 15–16, 189, 190, 191
intent. *See also* mens rea analyses
  to commit grievous bodily harm, 59n13
interchangeability, of
    punishments, 65–66
interoffense comparisons, bulk discounts,
    114, 117–18, 118n19
*Introduction to the Principles of
  Morals and Legislation, An*
  (Bentham), 67n20

Jacobellis v. Ohio, 55
James, William, *Varieties of Religious
  Experience, The,* 40
Jarborg, Nils
  crushing sentences, 116
  living standards metric, 56–58
  standard harms, 57–58
Jesus Through the Centuries (Pelikan), 79
Johnson, Kiersten, 161n12
Jonson, Cheryl Lero, *Deterrence, Choice,
  and Crime,* 129
judges
  blameworthiness assessments, 30
  case-by-case decisions, 103
  compassion, 75, 115, 170

election and limited power, 16
just punishment, 33
political insulation, 15–16, 189, 190, 191
power, pre-retributivist revival, 75
sentencing discretion, individual
  case, 19–20
jurisprudence. *See also specific topics*
  comprehensive, just punishment, 21,
    39–40, 42
  comprehensive, multiple offense
    paradox, 40
  constitutional, 34–35
  punishment, 19
  widely agreed, lack, 19, 35
jus talionis, 23, 27, 53, 104–5, 141
just deserts, 18, 51
  in unjust society, 41
just punishment, 33–42, 128–29
  anchoring points, penalty
    scales, 41–42
  Berlin, Isaiah, 33
  competing normative claims, 33–34
  comprehensive jurisprudence, 21,
    39–40, 42
  dignity, human, 34–38, 39
  dominion, 41
  judges, retributive and consequentialist
    directives, 33
  just deserts, unjust society, 41
  Matravers, Matt, 31n13, 37, 38–39
  Model Penal Code, Herbert
    Hart on, 39
  normative claims, competing, 33–34
  ordinally deserved
    punishments, 41–42
  parsimony, 34, 36–38, 40, 41, 42
  pluralism, 33
  polar approaches, choosing between, 33
  recidivist premium, 41 (*see also*
    recidivist premium)
  retributive or consequentialist
    reasoning *vs.* other values, 37–38

just punishment (*Cont.*)
  serious *vs.* lesser crimes,
    disproportionate
    punishments, 38–39
  system, 5–6

Kagan, Elena, *Miller v. Alabama,* 73
Kant, Immanuel, 2, 6–7, 22, 23. *See also*
    positive retributivism; retributivism
  categorical imperative, 104–5, 174–75
  deterrence, 141–42
  dignity, human, 36
  "good will," 52n7
  jus talionis, 23, 27, 53, 104–5, 141
  moral autonomy, 141
  positive retributivism, 27, 53n8, 53–54
  principle of equality, 141
  proportionality, 44, 50, 51, 52–53,
    53n8, 54
  punishment, 171–72
  punishment, parsimony, 139
  punishments, upper-class sensibilities,
    31n13, 31, 67
  recidivist premium, 104–5
Katzenbach, Nicholas, *The Challenge of*
    Crime in a Free Society, 17–18
Kentucky Habitual Crime Act, 20n6
Kleck, Gary, 133n6
Kleiman, Mark, 136
Kleinig, John, 18–19, 44–45
  From Social Justice to Criminal Justice:
    Poverty and the Administration of
    Criminal Law, 76
Koch brothers, 4
Koh, Steve Y., 93–94
Kolber, Adam, 31, 66–67
Kowalski, Matt, 136
Kuhn, Thomas, 42

Lacey, Nicola, 48, 49, 69
Lambert, Elizabeth, 90–91
Lappi-Seppälä, Tapio, 47–48

"Law in Books and Law in Action"
    (Pound), 75
Law of Retribution, 23, 27, 53, 104–5, 141
Law's Empire (Dworkin), 89n5, 89, 110
Lee, Youngjae, 106–8, 121
legality principle, 96n3
legitimacy, criminal law, 105, 109,
    110–11, 111n15
Lewis, C. S., 2, 118–19
  "The Humanitarian Theory of
    Punishment," 45
life-course persistent offenders, 81–82
life without parole, 78–79, 100, 124,
    133, 145
  children and teenagers, 1, 2, 164
  crimes, 4
  judge sentencing subordination, 16
  politician support, American,
    174–75n20
  politicized criminal justice, 19
  repeal, 191
  retributivism, 2
  as unconstitutional, Germany,
    lebenslange Freiheitsstrafe, 73
  as unconstitutional, *Miller v.*
    Alabama, 73
Lippke, Richard, 29–30, 41, 91–92
living standards metric, 56–58
Loeber, Rolf, 82–84, 83*t*
Loeffler, Charles, 2
Lowenkamp, Christopher, 156–57n10,
    157, 158, 162, 167–68, 167*t*,
    180–81, 181n22
Luban, David, 39, 40
luck, moral, 59–62
Lynch, Gerard, 62–63

Maccoun, Robert, 133n6
making amends, bulk discounts, 120–21
mandatory minimum sentences, 2, 4, 10–
    11, 19, 47–48, 190
  Canada, 47–48

processing, 19
repeal, 130, 191
marginal deterrence, 136–37
Markel, Dan, 26
"Marxism and Retribution"
    (Murphy), 76
mass incarceration, 190
    media reports, 190
    mistake, 2
    National Academy of Sciences
        Committee on the Causes and
        Consequences of High Rates of
        Incarceration (Travis, Western, and
        Redburn), 8–9, 71, 129, 131n5, 134–
        35, 148–49, 172
    political process, 159
    reducing, 158
Matravers, Matt, 31n13, 37, 38–39
    "actual harm done," 51–52, 60
    blameworthiness and crime
        prevention, 158–59
    "The Place of Proportionality in Penal
        Theory," 48–49, 70
    "Rootless Desert and Unanchored
        Censure," 51–52
May, David, *Ranking Correctional
    Punishments,* 64
McCloskey, H. J., 60
McDonald, Douglas, 66
measures, 185–86
    vs. sanctions, 60–61, 61n15
    subjective, suffering, 67
    use, 60–61, 61n15
Mencken, H. L., 89
Menninger, Karl, 24–25
mens rea analyses, 58–59, 79, 115
    deeply disadvantaged, 88
    eliminating, at trial, 96n2
    English criminal law, 30–31
    moral equivalence, 166–67
    multiple convictions and morbid
        psychology, 115

mercy and compassion, bulk discounts,
    114, 118–19, 119n20
"Mercy and Legal Justice" (Murphy), 118
Michael, Jerome, 16–17, 45
    "A Rationale of the Law of
        Homicide," 17n4
Michie, Christine, 156
Mill, John Stuart, *The Subjection of
    Women,* 48–49
Miller v. Alabama, 73, 82, 164
mitigation, 77–78, 84, 85, 86–87, 90–92
    predictive, 184
    progressive loss of, recidivist
        premium, 112–13
    social adversity, 54–68
M'Naghten's Case, 85
Model Penal Code, 2–3, 7, 17–18
    Bentham, Jeremy, 24
    Bentham, Jeremy, incapacitation,
        24, 25n9
    consequentialism, 25
    criminal history, 173
    Hart's refutation, 31n13, 39
    parole release, earliest possible, 17, 78, 119
    parole release, imprisonment and, 119
    purposes clause, 102n8
    recklessness, 51
    rehabilitation, 17–18
    retributivism, limiting, 27
    social adversity defense, 86–87
Model Penal Code, on sentencing
    attempts *vs.* completed offenses, 59–60
    consecutive sentences, 116
    indeterminate, 2, 7, 17–18, 106
    indeterminate, as least restrictive
        alternative, 8
    multiple current convictions,
        105n11, 106
    purpose, 78
Model Sentencing Act, 8
    least restrictive alternative punishment,
        119, 139

Moffitt, Terrie E., 81–82

Moitra, Soumyo, 153

Monahan, John, 156, 159, 169–70, 184
  predictions of future violence, 160
  predictive mitigation, 184
  retributivism, limiting, 184–85

Moore, Michael, 26, 27, 44–45

moral autonomy, 141

moral communication, punishment
  as, 27–28

moral desert, 67n20

moral education
  consequentialism, 15
  punishment and deterrence, 128n1,
    128, 143–44

Morales v. Schmidt, 65

moral luck, 59n13, 59–62

morbid psychology
  bulk discounts, 114–16
  multiple convictions, 115

Morgan, Rod, *Oxford Handbook of
  Criminology*, 103–4

Morris, Herbert, 18–19, 26, 51
  proportionality, 43n1, 44–45
  proportionality, retributivism and, 51
  punishment, as moral
    communication, 27–28
  punishment, community, 70–71
  punishment, interchangeability, 65–66
  punishment, maximum, 69
  punishment, retributive,
    communicative properties, 44–45
  share intuitions, 27

Morris, Norval, 18, 25, 27
  Future of Imprisonment, The, 71, 103
  predictions of future violence,
    160, 161t
  predictive mitigation, 184
  punishment severity, 102
  retributivism, limiting, 71, 185
  social disadvantage, 85–86

Morse, Stephen, 79, 85, 87–88

moving forward, 182–86
  doing justice better, 189–94
  mitigation, predictive, 184
  retributivism, limiting, 184–85
  sanctions and measures, 185–86
  sentencing, constrained
    predictive, 183–84

multiple convictions, 95–124
  bulk discounts, 95, 113–23 (*see also* bulk
    discounts)
  conceptual problems, 95
  crushing punishments, 30, 38, 41, 100–
    1, 114, 116–17, 120, 121, 124
  example, 96
  expediency principle, 96n3, 96–97
  mean prison sentence, criminal history
    on, by state, 100, 100t, 101–2
  mixed theories, 96
  multiple offenses, theory, 101–23 (*see
    also* multiple offenses, theory)
  negative retributivism, 96
  past and present, 84n4, 98–101, 98t,
    99t, 100t
  positive retributivism, 96
  prior convictions and arrest, most
    serious felony, 2009, 98–100, 99t
  recidivist premiums, 95, 101n7, 102–13
    (*see also* recidivist premium)
  sentencing, 123–24
  theoretical writing, 95
  totality principle, 100–1, 113–14

multiple offense paradox, 28–30, 33
  bulk discounts, 29–30 (*see also* bulk
    discounts)
  comprehensive jurisprudence, 40
  recidivist premium, 29 (*see also*
    recidivist premium)

multiple offenses, theory, 101–23
  bulk discounts, 95, 113–23 (*see also* bulk
    discounts)
  recidivist premiums, 95, 101n7, 102–13
    (*see also* recidivist premium)

sentencing, blameworthiness *vs.* prior offending, 102

Murphy, Jeffrie, 18–19, 26
"Marxism and Retribution," 76
mercy, authority, 119n20
"Mercy and Legal Justice," 118
proportionality, 44–45

Musto, David J., *The American Disease: The Origins of Narcotic Control,* 79, 80

Nagel, Thomas
on Kant's "good will," 51n6
moral luck, 59–60

Nagin, Daniel, 129–30
certainty of punishment, on deterrence, 138–39
Deterrence, Choice, and Crime, 129
National Academy of Sciences Panel on Deterrent and Incapacitative Effects, 131n5, 134, 147
punishment and deterrence, 136, 137, 138

National Academy of Sciences Panel on "Career Criminals" and Criminal Careers (Blumstein et al.), 147–48

National Academy of Sciences Panel on Deterrent and Incapacitative Effects (Blumstein, Cohen, & Nagin), 131n5, 134, 147

National Academy of Sciences Panel on Research on Deterrence and the Death Penalty, 131n5

National Academy of Sciences Panel on Understanding and Controlling Violence, 131n5

National Academy of Sciences Committee on the Causes and Consequences of High Rates of Incarceration (Travis, Western, and Redburn), 8–9, 71, 105n11, 129, 131n5, 134–35, 148–49, 172

National Advisory Commission on Criminal Justice Standards and Goals, 193

negative retributivism, 7, 8, 26, 27, 33
multiple convictions, 96
punishment, 171–72

negative stereotyping, 39, 106
racial, minorities and disadvantaged, 88, 170
wrongful convictions, 88

Nozick, Robert, *Philosophical Explanations,* 42

offender, dangerous. *See* dangerous offender

offending. *See also specific topics*
group differences and predictive sentencing, 180–82
trajectories, 81–84, 83t

offense definitions *vs.* victims' and offenders' experiences, 58–59

On Crimes and Punishments (Beccaria), 23–24, 132

ordinal desert, 28

Osoba, Osonde, 183n24

Oxford Handbook of Criminology (Downes and Morgan), 103–4

Parent, Dale, 70

parole boards
offending risks, 148–49
power, pre-retributivist revival, 75
release dates, setting, 106n12
Salient Factor Score, 150–52, 151t
sentencing, individualized, 2, 16–17, 39, 75, 78

parole release
abandoned, 152
laws limiting, Australia, 47–48
life without (*see* life without parole)
Model Penal Code, earliest possible, 17, 78, 119
Model Penal Code, imprisonment and, 119

parsimony
  Benthamite, 22–23
  deterrence, 139–41
  justice as, 6, 21
  just punishment, 34, 36–38, 40, 41, 42
  negative retributivism, 7–8
  predictive sentencing, 182–83
  proportionality, 46, 71
Pelikan, Jasoslav, *Jesus Through the Centuries,* 79
Pereboom, Derek, 179–80
perverse incentives, 115–16
Petersilia, Joan, 64
Pettit, Philip, 41
  republican theory, 27n11, 123–24
Philadelphia birth cohort studies, 173n19
Philosophical Explanations (Nozick), 42
philosophy and policy, punishment, 1–11.
    See also specific topics
  cocaine sentences, 4, 16n3
  crime rate fall (1991+), 4
  determinate sentencing, 3
  deterrence, incapacitation, and tough laws (1980s-1996), 3–4
  Durkheim, Emile, 10
  fairness, justice as, 6
  imprisonment rate decline (2007+), 4
  indeterminate sentencing, easing (1970s), 3
  justice as equal treatment, 6
  just punishment system, 5–6
  life without parole, 2, 4, 19
  mandatory minimum sentence law, 2, 4, 10–11, 19
  mass imprisonment, 2
  Model Penal Code, 2–3, 7
  parsimony, justice as, 6
  plea bargaining, extortionate, 2
  property crime sentencing, 1
  proportionality, 4
  proportionality, justice as, 6
  public opinions, attitudes, and beliefs, 6

rebutting presumptions, 8–10
redistributive and parsimonious, 10
retributivism, 2, 3, 5, 6–7 (*see also* retributivism)
retributivism, negative, 7, 8
retributivism, positive, 7
sentencing laws, unjust, 2
shared understanding, lack, 1
three-strikes laws, 1, 2, 4, 19
truth in sentencing, 2
utilitarianism, 6–7
Pickard, Hanna, 48, 49, 69
Pifferi, Michele, 23, 61n15, 185
Pina-Sanchez, Jose, 100–1
Pincoffs, Edmund, *Rationale of Legal Punishment,* 46
"The Place of Proportionality in Penal Theory" (Matravers), 48–49, 70
plea bargaining. *See also* prosecutors
  abolish, 193
  deeply disadvantaged and social adversity defense, 87
  eliminate, 193
  extortionate, 2
  innocent persons, 2
  as practical impediment, 32
  prosecution by, 189–90
political insulation, 6, 15–16, 189, 190, 191
politicized criminal justice policy, 19, 75, 190
positive retributivism, 7, 26–27, 33, 96
positivism, 23, 24–25
  Ferri, Enrico, 24–25
  Glueck, Sheldon, 24–25
  incapacitation, 17n4, 25
  indeterminate sentencing, 102n8
Pound, Roscoe, "Law in Books and Law in Action," 75
Pratt, Travis, 131n4, 135
prediction and incapacitation, 147–60.
    See also incapacitation
  constrained predictive sentencing, 183–84

dangerousness, 154
debates, 156–59
National Academy of Sciences
    Committee on the Causes and
    Consequences of High Rates of
    Incarceration, 148–49n3, 148–49
normative and policy issues, 152–53
prediction problems, 159–73 (*see also*
    prediction problems)
predictive mitigation, 184
proportionality, fairness, equal
    treatment, and parsimony, 182–83
rationalizations, 174–82
rationalizations, analogies, 178–80
rationalizations, offending group
    differences, 180–82
rationalizations, public safety, 177–78
rationalizations, punishment
    theory, 174–77
retributivism, limiting, 184–85
Salient Factor Score, parole board,
    150–52, 151t
sanctions and measures, 185–86
unjust, 182–83
prediction instruments, 152
algorithms, 158–59, 159n11
as challenging, difficulty, 182–83
COMPAS, 156–57n10, 156–57
debates and inaccuracies, 156–59
false negatives, 167–68, 167t
false positives, 151t, 160, 167–68, 167t
first principles and values,
    conflicting, 158
inaccuracies, 151t, 160–62
inaccuracies, future violence, 149–50
literature, ethical and legal issues
    (1980s+), 152
private sector, 148–49, 152
Salient Factor Score, 150–52, 151t
prediction problems, 159–73
accuracy, 151t, 160–62
age, 163–65
criminal history, 171–73

data, old, 154–55
gender, 163, 165–66
immutable characteristics, 163–68
race and ethnicity, 163, 166–68, 167t
socioeconomic characteristics, 168–70
unjust variables, 162–63
predictive mitigation, 184
predictive sentencing, 147–60. *See also*
    prediction and incapacitation
premeditation, recidivist
    premium, 110–12
presumptive guidelines, 10–11
sentences more severe than, 192n2, 192
sentencing commissions,
    191–92n1, 191
prevention, crime, 182. *See also*
    deterrence; *specific topics*
blameworthiness, 158–59
censure, 158–59
trade-offs, interests *vs.* costs, 154
"Principles of a Rational Penal Code"
    (Glueck), 24–25
prior convictions. *See also* multiple
    offenses
    prediction and incapacitation, 171
    recidivist premium, increase
        culpability, 102
    recidivist premium, irrelevant, 102
prisons. *See also imprisonment*
    cost, U.S., 145
    criminogenic, 148–49n3
    population, 4, 148n2
    reoffending, 128–29n2, 137–38, 139
    as schools for crime, 137–38
property crime sentencing, 1
proportionality, 22–23, 43–72. *See also*
    specific topics
    abstract *vs.* comparative
        principles, 49n4
    "actual harm done," 51–52, 60
    blameworthiness, 51
    costs of crime, 55–57, 56n9, 57t
    crime seriousness, 54–62, 57t, 128

proportionality (*Cont.*)
　crime seriousness, conflicting
　　realities, 58–59
　crime seriousness, missing metric,
　　54–58, 57t
　crime seriousness, moral luck, 59–62
　definition, 43
　"degrees of guilt," 51
　disproportionally severe punishments
　　as rehabilitation, 128–29n2, 128–29
　disquiet, 47–50
　epiphenomenon, 43–44
　equal treatment, 46, 48, 50, 53
　fundamental questions, 54–68
　Germany and southern Europe, 15
　Hamelin v. Michigan and Eighth
　　Amendment, 16n3
　Hegel, 53–54
　historical literature, 43n1, 43
　innocent person punishment, 60–61
　justice as, 6, 21, 44
　just punishment, 33–34, 36–37, 40, 42
　Kant, 44, 50, 51, 52–53, 53n8, 54
　linking crimes and punishments, 68
　negative retributivism, 7–8, 44
　non-retributivism, 44
　origins, 50–54
　policymakers *vs.* practitioners applying
　　law on, 19–20
　positive retributivism, 44
　predictive sentencing, 182–83
　punishment, 144
　punishment, severity, 62–68
　recent developments, 47–48
　retributivism, 44, 51
　retributivism, theories and theorists, 4,
　　19, 26, 43–46
　rough equivalence, 68–72
　rough equivalence: maximum
　　punishment, 69–70
　rough equivalence: retributivism
　　varieties, 71–72

　rough equivalence: theory, 70–71
　Rummel v. Estelle, 16n3
　sanctions *vs.* measures, 60–61, 61n15
　Scandinavia *vs.* U.S. states,
　　49–50n5, 49
　serendipitous harm, 61–62
　shared intuitions, 27
　theorists and theories, 44–47
　tort law, 52
　utilitarianism, 68–69
"Proportionality and the Seriousness of
　Crimes" (Ryberg), 48–49, 62
prosecutors, 189–90
　charges, dismissal, 89
　charges, filing control, 4
　discretionary decisions, 37–38
　discretionary decisions, court review,
　　19–20, 190
　expediency principle countries, 96n3
　legality principle countries, 96n3
　mandatory sentencing law,
　　nullification, 89
　plea bargaining, 2, 87 (*see also* plea
　　bargaining)
　political insulation, 15–16, 189, 190, 191
　positive efforts, 193
　power, 19, 62–63, 190
　racial disparities, 80
　Rechtsstaat ideal, 189–90
　selection and election of, 16, 190, 191
　sentencing, harsh, 79
　sentencing, of recidivists, 104
　sentencing control, 16, 191
　sympathy for offenders, lack of, 75–76
　victim, favoring, 58–59
prosocial behavior, antecedents and
　causes, 81–82
protective factors, 81, 82. *See also*
　specific types
psychology, morbid
　bulk discounts, 114–16
　multiple convictions, 115

public health quarantine analogy, 178–80
public preferences, recidivist
    premium, 109–11
public safety
  justice vs, 128–29
  prediction and
    incapacitation, 177–78
public spending, reallocation, 130
Punishing Persistent Offenders:
    Exploring Community and Offender
    Perspectives (Roberts), 104, 111
punishment. *See also* sentencing;
    specific topics
  attempted crime *vs.* completed
    offenses, 59n13, 59–60
  certainty, on deterrence, 138–39
  community (*see* community
    punishments)
  crime severity, 128
  effects, individual, 31–32
  influences, 15–16
  innocent persons, 60–61
  interchangeability, 65–66
  jurisprudence, 19
  metric, 62–68
  moral education and deterrence, 128n1,
    128, 143–44
  morality and moral communication,
    27–28, 73–74
  normative frameworks, 15
  public knowledge, 133n6
  review, 16n3, 16–17, 19–20
  serendipitous harm, 61–62
  sociological theory, 127–28, 141
  speedy, on crime, 135
  theories, 23–28 (*see also* deterrence;
    positivism; retributivism;
    utilitarianism; *specific theories*)
  theories, prediction and
    incapacitation, 174–77
  threat ineffectiveness, 127, 130, 132,
    133n6, 133–34

Punishment, Communication, and
    Community (Duff), 90n6, 90
punishment, proportionality, 144
  linking crimes and, 68
  maximum punishment, 69–70
punishment, severity, 62–68
  as continuum, 118n19
  crime severity and, 128
  crushing, 30, 38, 41, 100–1, 114, 116–17,
    120, 121, 124
  disproportionate, as rehabilitation,
    128–29n2, 128–29
  maximum, 69–70
  metric, 62–65
  metric, interchangeability of
    punishments, 65–66
  metric, subjective measures of
    suffering, 67
  Morris, Norval, 102
  proportionality, 62–68
  Robinson, Paul, 102
  von Hirsch, Andreas, 102
Punishment and Responsibility (Hart),
    27, 96n3
punishment severity, on deterrence,
    129, 136–38
  absolute severity, 137
  marginal deterrence, 136–37
  specific deterrence, 137–38
Punishment: The Supposed Justifications
    (Honderich), 76–77

Quinton, Anthony, 60–61

racial bias, 3, 36–37, 39, 156–57,
    158, 171
  criminal history and prediction, 172
  disparate effects, 172–73
  legitimacy, 110–11
  predictive sentencing, 163,
    166–68, 167t
  sentencing reform, 3

racial disparities
  imprisonment, 151
  negative stereotyping, 88, 170
  prosecutors, 80
  Salient Factor Score, 151
Ranking Correctional Punishments (May
  and Wood), 64
Rationale of Legal Punishment, The
  (Pincoffs), 46
"A Rationale of the Law of Homicide"
  (Michael and Wechsler), 17n4
Rawls, John, 25, 181
  "Two Theories of Rules," 46
recidivist premium, 95, 101n7, 102–13
  apologies and implied promises, 108–9
  bad character and
    premeditation, 110–12
  classical views, 104–5
  contemporary defenses, 105–6
  first offenders receive discounts, 102–3
  human dignity, 29, 41
  judges decide case by case, 103
  just punishment, 41
  mitigation, progressive loss, 112–13
  multiple offense paradox, 29
  prior convictions, 102
  public preferences, 109–11
  reoffending, as culpable
    omission, 107–8
  reoffending, as inattention to moral
    instruction, 106–7
  as unjust, 101n7
recklessness, *Model Penal Code,* 51
Redburn, Steve, National Academy of
  Sciences Committee on the Causes
  and Consequences of High Rates of
  Incarceration, 8–9, 71, 105n11, 129,
  131n5, 134–35, 148–49, 172
rehabilitation, 132–33
  American criminal code, 38–39
  Bentham, Jeremy, 24, 25n9
  deterrence, 132–33

  disproportionally severe punishments,
    128–29n2, 128–29
  Model Penal Code, 17–18
  support, past, 16–17
Reitz, Kevin, 95n1
reoffending, 29, 128–29n2, 137–38, 139.
  See also recidivist
  antisocial behavior, 111
  community punishments, 138
  culpable omission, 107–8
  inattention to moral
    instruction, 106–7
replacement effect, 148–49n3
republican theory, 25n10, 27n11, 123–24
residual criminal careers, 116–17,
  148–49n3
restorative justice, 19, 25, 128n1
  consequentialism, 25n10, 25, 142
  republican theory, 25n10
retributivism, 2, 5, 6–7, 17n4, 18–19, 22,
  23, 26–28
  applications, real world, 32
  blameworthiness, 26, 30–31, 32
  censure and hard treatment, 27–28
  descriptions and taxonomies, 23n8
  determinate sentencing, 150
  deterrence, 141–42
  justification question, 26
  limiting, 27, 71, 184–85
  mixed theories, 27
  negative (*see* negative retributivism)
  ordinal and cardinal desert, 28
  positive (*see* positive retributivism)
  proportionality, 44
  punishment theories, 171–72
  theories and theorists, 5, 6–7, 9,
    20, 22, 23, 26–28 (*see also* Hegel,
    George Wilhelm Friedrich; Kant,
    Immanuel)
  varieties, proportionality, 71–72
retributivism, limited reach, 23–32
  conceptual impediments, 28–32

practical impediments, 32
punishment theories, 23–28 (*see
    also* positivism; retributivism;
    utilitarianism)
"Retributivism, Multiple Offending,
    and Overall Proportionality"
    (Ryberg), 97–98
Right on Crime, 4
risk factors, 81, 82. *See also specific types
    and measures*
Roberts, Julian
    bad character and
        premeditation, 111–12
    bulk discounts and recidivist premium,
        30, 95n1
    constrained predictive
        sentencing, 183–84
    crushing offense analysis, 117
    empirical desert, 111n15
    imprisonment for crimes, public
        estimates, 133n6
    interoffense comparisons, 117
    multiple convictions, 98–99n5,
        100–1, 103
    proportionality, 49
    *Punishing Persistent Offenders:
        Exploring Community and Offender
        Perspectives,* 104, 111
    recidivism rates, custody *vs.*
        community sanctions, 139n10
    recidivist premium, 109
    reoffending and antisocial tendencies,
        111n15, 111–39
    "The Role of Criminal Record in the
        Sentencing Process," 103
Robinson, Paul, 27, 49, 133n6
    interchangeability of punishments, 65–66
    punishment severity, 102
"The Role of Criminal Record in the
    Sentencing Process" (Roberts), 103
"Rootless Desert and Unanchored
    Censure" (Matravers), 51–52

Ross, W. D., 67n20
"Rotten Social Background"
    (Delgado), 76n2
Rotten Social Background in
    the Twenty-First Century:
    Reconsidering the Role of Socio-
    Economic Deprivation in Criminal
    Justice, 76
Royko, Mike, 74
Rummel v. Estelle, 16n3
R. v. Gladue, 93
R. v M, 116, 117
Ryberg, Jesper
    criminal history, 177
    offense severity as continuum, 118n19
    "Proportionality and the Seriousness
        of Crimes," 48–49, 62, 97
    "Retributivism, Multiple Offending,
        and Overall Proportionality," 97–98
    scope insensitivity and supporting
        intuition, 120

Salient Factor Score, 150–52, 151*t*
sanctions, 185–86
    vs. measures, 60–61, 61n15
scope insensitivity, 120
Scurich, Nicholas, 169–70, 184
selective incapacitation, 147–48, 148n2
self-defense, 30–31, 31n12
sensibilities
    Bentham, Jeremy, 31, 36, 67n20, 67
    Kant on, 31n13, 31, 67
sentencing. *See also* punishment;
    specific topics
    appellate review, meaningful,
        191–92n1, 191–92
    decades-long sentences, 1, 16, 19,
        49–50n5, 70, 79, 100, 174–75n20,
        179, 190
    decisions, 152–53
    deterrence research, term
        shortening, 144

sentencing (*Cont.*)
  multiple offenders, 123–24
  prediction of dangerousness, 152–53
  predictive, 147–60 (*see also* prediction
    and incapacitation)
  predictive, constrained, 183–84
  prosecutor control, 191 (*see also* plea
    bargaining; prosecutors)
  review, meaningful, 16n3, 16–17, 19–20
Sentencing and Criminal Justice
    (Ashworth), 114–15
sentencing commissions
  criminal history, 103
  offense seriousness ranking, 58
  risk predictions, guidelines,
    152–53n6, 152–53
  sentence lengths, 70
sentencing commissions, state
  establishing, with presumptive
    guidelines, 191–92n1, 191
  punishment units, 66
  socioeconomic variables, 168–69
  Virginia, youth guidelines, 164
sentencing commissions, U.S.
  objective durations of
    confinement, 63
  property losses, 55
sentencing laws and guidelines
  crushing punishments, 30, 38, 41, 100–
    1, 114, 116–17, 120, 121, 124
  federal, 63, 72
  numerical, 72
  restrictiveness, 75–76
  unjust, 2
Sentencing Reform Act (1984), 168–69
serendipitous harm, 61–62
seriousness, crime, proportionality, 54–
    62, 57t, 128
  conflicting realities, 58–59
  missing metric, 54–58, 57t
  moral luck, 59–62
  offense seriousness ranking, 58

severity, punishment. *See* punishment
    severity
Singer, Richard, 101
Singh, Jay, 161n12
Skeem, Jennifer, 159, 169–70, 184
Smith, Michael, 148–49n3
social adversity defense (Bazelon), 76,
    82, 84, 86
  as consequentialist, 79
  Morris, Norval, 85–86
  Morse, Stephen, 87–88
  Morse, Stephen, Tonry's
    response, 87–89
social disadvantage. *See*
    disadvantage, social
social injustice, 75
Social Justice to Criminal Justice: Poverty
    and the Administration of Criminal
    Law (Heffernan and Kleinig)
    From, 76
socioeconomics. *See also*
    disadvantage, deep
  crime and punishment, 73–74
  moral choices, 74–75
  predictions of dangerousness,
    sentencing, 168–70
sociological theory of punishment,
    127–28, 141
Soros, George, 4
specific deterrence hypothesis, 137–38
standard harms, 57–58
Starr, Sonja, 170
"Statement of Purpose and Principles,"
    Minnesota Sentencing Guidelines
    Commission, 168–69
statistical bias, 157
Steiker, Carol, 21, 34
step effects, 118n19
stereotyping, negative, 39, 106
  racial, minorities and disadvantaged,
    88, 170
  wrongful convictions, 88

Stith, Kate, 93–94
Stuntz, William, 2
Subjection of Women, The (Mill), 48–49
suffering, subjective measures, 67
super-predators, 155
Sweatt v. Painter, 110

Tappan, Paul, 173
teenagers
  age as predictive, 163–65
  life without parole, 1, 2, 164
  mandatory life sentences, 164
temptation structures, chronic, 91–92
Thinking about Crime (Tonry), 79, 80
three-strikes laws, 2, 19, 47–48, 103
  California, 1, 4, 136–37
  deterrent effects, 136–37
  politician support, American,
    174–75n20
  repeal, 191
Tonry, Michael
  community punishments, 70–71
  interchangeability of
    punishments, 65–66
  predictive mitigation, 184
  race and offending, 168
  Thinking about Crime, 79, 80
totality principle, 100–1, 113–14
trajectories
  developmental, 81–82
  offending, 81–84, 83*t*
transferred malice doctrine, 59n13
Travis, Jeremy, National Academy of
  Sciences Committee on the Causes
  and Consequences of High Rates of
  Incarceration, 8–9, 71, 105n11, 129,
  131n5, 134–35, 148–49, 172
Trials and Punishments (Duff),
  76–77, 90
truth in sentencing, 2
  repeal, 2, 16, 133, 152, 191
Turanovic, Jillian, 135

"Two Concepts of Liberty"
  (Berlin), 46–47
"Two Theories of Rules" (Rawls), 46

unified state correctional and
  prosecution systems, 191
Uniform Determinate Sentencing Law, 3
United States v. Alexander, 85
Universal Declaration of Human
  Rights, 194
unjust world, 87–88, 91–92
utilitarianism, 6–7, 25n9, 25. *See also*
  consequentialism
  deterrence, 15, 17n4, 23–24,
    25n9, 25, 33
  indeterminate sentencing, 102n8, 102
  proportionality, 68–69
  punishment, 172
  theories and theorists, 6–7, 8, 22,
    23–24, 25 (*see also* Beccaria, Cesare;
    Bentham, Jeremy)

variables. *See also specific types*
  socioeconomic, sentencing
    and, 168–69
  unjust, predictions of dangerousness
    for sentencing, 162–63
Varieties of Religious Experience, The
  (James), 40
Vindication of the Rights of Women, A
  (Wollstonecraft), 48–49
violence, 162n13, 162–63
  pathologically violent
    offenders, 182n23
  Salient Factor Score, 150–51
von Hirsch, Andreas, 18, 26, 27
  Doing Justice, 51, 76–77, 78–79
  living standards metric, 56–58
  measures, 61n15
  ordinal and cardinal desert, 28
  progressive loss of mitigation, 112–13
  proportionality, 44–45

von Hirsch, Andreas (*Cont.*)
 punishment, community, 65–66
 punishment, interchangeability, 65–66
 punishment, maximum, 69
 punishment, moral
  communication, 27–28
 punishment, parsimony, 139
 punishment, severity, 102
 standard harms, 57–58

Waldron, Jeremy, 21, 35, 51n6
Walker, Nigel, 43n1, 64, 67n21
 *Aggravation, Mitigation, and
  Mercy,* 118
 Why Punish?, 67
Warr, Mark, 133n6
Wasik, Martin, 101n7
Wasik, Paul, 65–66
Webster, Cheryl, 140
Wechsler, Herbert, 16–17
 "A Rationale of the Law of
  Homicide," 17n4
 Model Penal Code, 3, 17–18
Weisburd, David, 136
Western, Bruce, National Academy of
 Sciences Committee on the Causes
 and Consequences of High Rates of

 Incarceration, 8–9, 71, 105n11, 129,
  131n5, 134–35, 148–49, 172
Whitman, James, 38
Why Punish? (Walker), 64, 67n21
Wikström, Per-Olof H., 82–84, 83t
Williams, Bernard, 59–60
Wilson, James Q., 147–48
Wollstonecraft, Mary, *A Vindication of
 the Rights of Women,* 48–49
Wong, Stephen, 161n12, 161–62
Wood, Peter, *Ranking Correctional
 Punishments,* 64
Woodson v. North Carolina, 35–36
Wootton, Baroness Barbara,
 24–25, 96n3
Wordsworth, William, 82
"The Wretched of the Earth"
 (Delgado), 80–81
wrongful convictions, 2, 89, 190
 consequences, 2, 3, 9, 89
 negative stereotyping, 88
wrongfulness, of crime, 26, 44–45, 51,
 58–59, 108, 143

Yang, Min, 161n12, 161–62

Zimring, Franklin, 140, 148n2